Our fighting sisters

MANCHEStER
1824

Manchester University Press

Our fighting sisters

Nation, memory and gender in Algeria, 1954–2012

Natalya Vince

Manchester University Press

Published by Manchester University Press
Altrincham Street, Manchester M1 7JA
www.manchesteruniversitypress.co.uk

British Library Cataloguing-in-Publication Data
A catalogue record for this book is available from the British Library

Library of Congress Cataloging-in-Publication Data applied for

ISBN   978 0 7190 9107 0 hardback

First published 2015

The publisher has no responsibility for the persistence or accuracy of URLs for any external or third-party internet websites referred to in this book, and does not guarantee that any content on such websites is, or will remain, accurate or appropriate.

Typeset in Sabon by
Servis Filmsetting Ltd, Stockport, Cheshire
Printed in Great Britain by
Lightning Source

Dedication

*For my mum Mary, Rebh, Zina and
my daughter Léïla – who are all fighting sisters*

Contents

List of maps and figures

Acknowledgements

The process of researching and writing this book has been long, and would not have been possible without the support of a great number of people, including historical actors, archivists, fellow academics, friends and family members. First and foremost, I would like to express my sincere thanks and gratitude to the women who accepted to be interviewed for this book for their time, patience and generosity. I would also like to thank Badia Benbelkacem, Mourad Bouchouchi, Slimane Chikh, Zineb Derbal, Malika El Korso, Malika Ouzegane, Ryme Seferdjeli and Ouerdia Yermeche for helping me make contact with women veterans in Algeria. Invaluable feedback and intellectual inspiration for this project were provided at its various stages by Tony Chafer, Martin Evans, Emmanuel Godin, Julian Jackson, Catherine Merridale, Gilbert Meynier, James McDougall, Ed Naylor and Malika Rahal, as well as the anonymous Manchester University Press reviewers, amongst many others. I would also like to thank the publishing team at Manchester University Press for their patience and efficiency. The writing up of a significant part this book was enabled by an Arts and Humanities Research Council Early Career Fellowship. The support of the University of Portsmouth's Centre for European and International Studies Research (CEISR) and the Faculty of Humanities and Social Sciences (FHSS) in funding conference attendance, research trips and teaching relief is also gratefully acknowledged.

Finally, I would especially like to thank both my families, in the UK and Algeria, and in particular Walid Benkhaled, who has been involved in this project from the very first time he found me a copy of *Barberousse, mes soeurs* to the final editing of the conclusion, and who has been a constant source of support, constructive criticism, ideas and inspiration.

Abbreviations

ADPDF   Association de Défense et Promotion des Droits des
        Femmes (Association for the Defence and Promotion
        of Women's Rights) Created in 1989 to raise
        awareness of, and campaign to improve, the position
        of women in Algerian law. The war veteran Akila
        Ouared is president.
ALN   Armée de Libération Nationale (National Liberation
        Army) Armed wing of the FLN, created in 1954.
        Dissolved in 1962.
ANP   Armée Nationale Populaire (National People's
        Army) Algerian army, a state institution created
        in 1962.
AUMA   Association des 'Ulama Musulmans Algériens
        (Association of Algerian Muslim 'Ulama) Religious
        and cultural organisation, founded in 1931. Part of a
        reformist trend across North Africa and the Middle
        East seeking to 'purify' Muslim societies of ante-
        Islamic practices and construct a collective identity
        distinct from that of the colonial power. The 'ulama
        allied with the FLN in 1956. Unable to formally
        reconstitute after 1962, its former members and their
        ideological descendants nevertheless maintained
        influence in independent Algeria.
CCE   Comité de Coordination et d'Exécution
        (Co-ordinating and Executing Committee) Executive
        organ of the FLN, created by the Soummam
        Congress in 1956. Replaced in 1958 by the GPRA.

CDL Combattants de la Libération (Combatants of
Liberation) Armed network composed of members of
the PCA committed to armed struggle to end colonial
rule. Allied with the FLN in 1956, dissolved in 1962.

CNRA Conseil National de la Révolution Algérienne
(National Council of the Algerian Revolution)
Created at the Soummam Congress in 1956 as a
parliament representing the different geographical
regions of the FLN–ALN.

CRUA Comité Révolutionnaire pour l'Unité et l'Action
(Revolutionary Committee for Unity and Action)
Created in March 1954 by members of the MTLD's
OS to try and reconcile divergent tendencies within
the MTLD and generate support for armed struggle.
In autumn 1954, the CRUA adopted the name FLN
and carried out the 1 November attacks.

EMG Etat Major Général (General Staff) Created by the
CNRA at the end of 1959. A centralised structure
with control of the ALN, under the command of
Boumediene. Based on the Algerian frontiers, in
Ghardimaou in Tunisia and Oujda in Morocco.

ENA Etoile Nord Africaine (North African Star)
Nationalist party created by Messali Hadj in
1926 amongst the Algerian migrant community in
metropolitan France. Initially, the ENA had close
ties with the French Communist Party. Banned in
1929, it was reconstituted in 1933 as the Glorieuse
Etoile Nord Africaine (Glorious North African Star).
Banned again in 1937, it reformed as the PPA.

FF–FLN Fédération de France du FLN (FLN Federation
of France) The FLN wartime organisation in
metropolitan France, created in 1955.

FFS Front des Forces Socialistes (Front of Socialist Forces)
Created in 1963 by the former FLN leader Hocine Aït
Ahmed in opposition to the Ben Bella–EMG seizure
of power in summer 1962. The FFS briefly led an
armed rebellion in autumn 1963, which was crushed
within a year. It officially re-emerged as a political
party advocating democracy and cultural pluralism
after 1989 and the introduction of multipartyism.

FIS   Front Islamique du Salut (Islamic Salvation Front)
               Islamist party created in 1989 following the
               introduction of multipartyism. After the FIS won the
               first round of legislative elections in 1991, the army
               cancelled the electoral process. Dissolved in March
               1992, the FIS dispersed into rival armed branches
               which in the 1990s sought to overthrow the state.
FLN   Front de Libération Nationale (National Liberation
               Front) Front created in 1954, bringing together
               various political tendencies with the aim of achieving
               Algerian independence through political and armed
               struggle. After 1962, FLN designates the party of
               the single-party state. Following the introduction of
               political pluralism in 1989, it remains the dominant
               political party in Algeria.
FSN   Fonds de Solidarité Nationale (National Solidarity
               Fund) Campaign launched in 1963 to encourage
               Algerian citizens to donate their jewellery to the state
               in order to replenish meagre gold reserves.
GPRA   Gouvernement Provisoire de la République
               Algérienne (Provisional Government of the
               Algerian Republic) Executive organ of the FLN
               created in 1958 to replace the CCE, with the aim
               of strengthening Algeria's international negotiating
               position. Based in Cairo. Replaced in summer 1962
               by Ben Bella's Political Bureau.
HCE   Haut Comité d'Etat (High State Council, HCE)
               Executive body 1992–94, established after the
               Algerian army interrupted the electoral process to
               prevent an Islamist victory at the polls. Presided
               over by Mohamed Boudiaf until his assassination in
               June 1992, and then Ali Kafi. The HCE appointed
               Liamine Zéroual head of state in 1994 and was
               subsequently dissolved.
JFLN   Jeunesse du Front de Libération Nationale (Youth
               National Liberation Front) Youth wing of the FLN,
               created in summer 1962.
MNA   Mouvement National Algérien (Algerian National
               Movement) Rival nationalist movement to the FLN
               1954–62, led by Messali Hadj.

MTLD   Mouvement pour le Triomphe des Libertés Démocratiques (Movement for the Triumph of Democratic Liberties) The postwar reincarnation of the PPA which existed 1946–54, presided over by Messali Hadj. Created primarily to participate in elections in colonial Algeria on a platform of independence through all political means.

OAS   Organisation Armée Secrète (Secret Army Organisation) Right-wing paramilitary group, created in 1961 and composed of hardliner European settlers and renegade French army generals who refused to accept the end of colonial rule in Algeria. Perpetrated a series of attacks in France and Algeria in an attempt to hinder the peace process.

ONM   Organisation Nationale des Moudjahidine (National Organisation of Mujahidin) The main association representing the interests of former *mujahidin* in independent Algeria.

OS   Organisation Spéciale (Special Organisation) Clandestine wing of the MTLD, advocating revolutionary insurrection. Its members would go on to create the CRUA, which would give birth to the FLN.

PAGS   Parti de l'Avant-Garde Socialiste (Avant-Garde Socialist Party) Clandestine successor to the PCA, created in 1966. Legalised in 1989, it imploded in 1992.

PCA   Parti Communiste Algérien (Algerian Communist Party) Created in 1936, its members came from both the European and Muslim communities of colonial Algeria. It came to be broadly split into two tendencies: assimilationist (advocating greater equality through greater assimilation) and pro-independence. Many of its members in favour of the latter joined the FLN–ALN. Following independence, the PCA was banned in late 1962.

PPA   Parti du Peuple Algérien (Algerian People's Party)
             Successor nationalist party to the ENA, created by
             Messali Hadj in Algeria in 1937. Banned in 1939,
             it subsisted as a clandestine organisation in Algeria
             during the Second World War. In 1946, it was
             replaced by the MTLD.
SAS   Sections Administratives Specialisées (Specialised
             Administrative Sections) Civil administration bodies
             run by members of the French army, established
             across Algeria 1955–56.
SMA   Scouts Musulmans Algériens (Algerian Muslim
             Scouts, SMA) Established in Algeria in the interwar
             period, the Muslim Scouts movement played a
             key role in the spread of nationalist ideas amongst
             youth.
UDMA   Union Démocratique du Manifeste Algérien
             (Democratic Union of the Algerian Manifesto)
             Reformist organisation which existed 1946–56,
             created by Ferhat Abbas. Its leaders joined FLN in
             1956.
UFA (PCA)   Union des Femmes d'Algérie (Union of Women of
             Algeria) Women's branch of the PCA in the colonial
             period, disbanded around 1955.
UFMA   Union des Femmes Musulmanes d'Algérie (Union of
             Muslim Women of Algeria) Women's branch of the
             MTLD, 1947–54.
UGEMA   Union Générale des Etudiants Musulmans
             Algériens (Union of Muslim Algerian Students)
             Created in 1955 in Paris as a pro-independence
             movement distinct from the wider French student
             movement. Dissolved by the French authorities in
             1958, it clandestinely reconstituted as the student
             section of the FF–FLN. At its 1963 congress in
             Algiers it became the UNEA.
UGMVOC   Union Générale des Mères, Veuves et Orphelins de
             Chouhada (Union of Mothers, Widows and Orphans
             of Shuhada) Organisation to represent the interests
             of widows and orphans of the war dead in the post-
             independence period.

UGTA	Union Générale des Travailleurs Algériens (National Union of Algerian Workers) Created in 1956 by the FLN to organise Algerian workers to support the independence struggle and the FLN, today the main trade union in Algeria.
UNEA	Union Nationale des Etudiants Algériens (National Union of Algerian Students) Student mass organisation, 1963 to present.
UNFA	Union Nationale des Femmes Algériennes (National Union of Algerian Women) Women's mass organisation, 1963 to present.
ZAA	Zone Autonome d'Alger (Algiers Autonomous Zone) FLN–ALN structure created following the Soummam Congress in 1956 to organise armed activity and support networks in Algiers. Notably, it led the 1956–7 urban bombing campaign often referred to as the 'Battle of Algiers'.

Glossary of commonly used terms

Transliterations from standard and classical Arabic follow the style guidelines of the *International Journal of Middle East Studies*, but without diacritical marks. Transliterations from Algerian dialectical Arabic adopt spellings in common usage. The proper names of many of the individuals and places quoted in this book have differing transliterations. For clarity's sake, this book uses the spelling either preferred by the interviewee or most common in the English- and French-language literature.

autogestion [French]: the occupation and collective management of nationalised land and factories

derja [Arabic (dialectical)]: dialectical Arabic

douar [term used in French, of Arabic origin]: village

fellagas [term used in French, of Arabic origin]: pejorative term for rural guerrillas

fida'i (m. sing.), *fida'iyya* (f. sing.), *fida'iyn* (pl.), *fida'iyat* (f. pl.) [Arabic]: urban bomber(s)

fusha [Arabic]: classical Arabic

harki [term used in French, of Arabic origin]: a category of Muslim auxiliaries in the French army

hayk [Arabic]: a loose white cloth covering the body and head with a triangle of material covering the nose and mouth

maquis [French]: the rural guerrilla movement

maquisard (m. sing.), *maquisarde* (f. sing.) [French]: member of the rural guerrilla movement *mujahid* (m. sing.), *mujahida* (f. sing.), *mujahidin* (pl.), *mujahidat* (f. pl.) [Arabic]: resistance fighter(s)/ holy warrior(s)

pieds noirs [French]: European settlers in colonial Algeria

pieds rouges [French]: term coined to describe the international revolutionaries and left-wing sympathisers who flocked to Algeria after independence seeking to create the next socialist utopia

shahid (m. sing.), *shahida* (f. sing.), *shuhada* (pl.), *shahidat* (f. pl.) [Arabic]: martyr(s)/ war dead

'ulama: doctors of religion in a broad sense, but often used to refer to the Association des 'Ulama Musulmans Algériens, which emerged in the 1930s, and their ideological descendants

wilaya (sing.), *wilayat* (pl.) [Arabic]: administrative region, or during the War of Independence a military zone of the ALN

Map 1 Map of Algeria

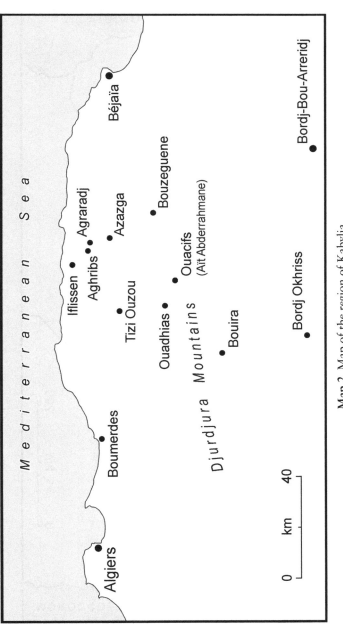

Map 2 Map of the region of Kabylia

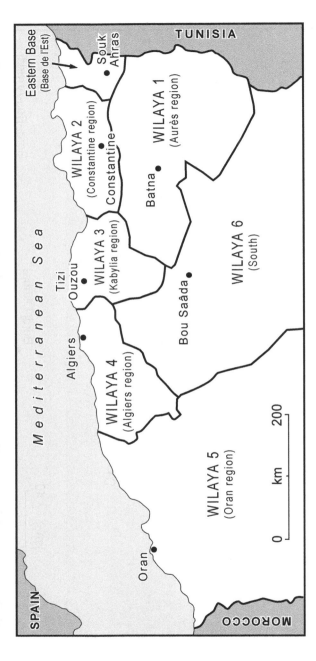

Map 3 Map of the FLN–ALN *wilayat* during the War of Independence

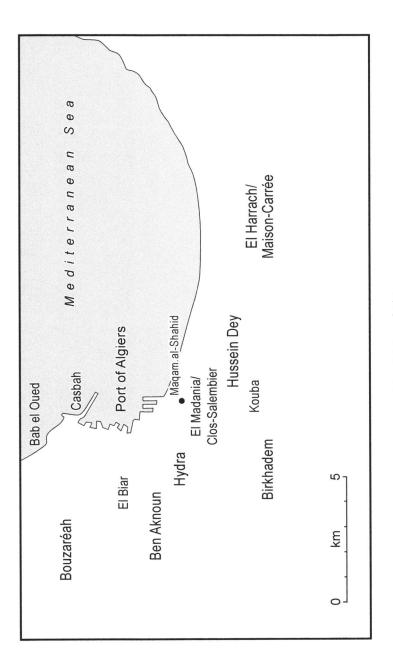

Map 4 Map of Algiers

Introduction

Hassiba Ben Bouali was nineteen years old when, on 8 October 1957, French troops dynamited her hideout in the Algiers Casbah. She died immediately, alongside Ali Ammar, otherwise known as Ali La Pointe, Mahmoud Bouhamidi and twelve-year-old Yacef Omar. They were all activists in the Algerian Front de Libération Nationale (National Liberation Front, FLN), which since 1954 had been waging an armed struggle to bring to an end more than a century of French rule. In the days following the 8 October explosion, the colonial press hailed the death of a group of dangerous criminals, whose urban bombing campaign in the previous months had terrorised the European population of Algiers. The *Journal d'Alger* triumphantly headlined 'Ali La Pointe and Hassiba Ben Bouali discovered blown to pieces by the blast'.[1] The FLN mourned the passing of men, a woman and a child whom it considered courageous freedom fighters. In 1960, a children's home run by the FLN in Morocco for girls displaced by the ongoing war was given 'the name of a young Algerian heroine, Hassiba Ben Bouali'.[2] In 1974, twelve years after Algerian independence in 1962 and seventeen years after Hassiba Ben Bouali's death, *El Moudjahid*, the official newspaper of the FLN single-party state, published a homage to the teenager entitled 'Hassiba Ben Bouali: a woman, an activist, an example'.[3]

Today, Rue Hassiba Ben Bouali is a major boulevard in Algiers. It is one of many street-sign tombstones in a city filled with the names of the war dead, an explicit attempt by the post-independence state to inscribe an officially sanctioned collective memory into public space. On 'Hassiba', as this commercial hub is colloquially called, lanes of heavy traffic crawl past lingerie shops run by bearded men, Made-in-China tea sets spill out of crockery outlets on to the pavement, young men lean on walls killing time and boys sell single cigarettes, chewing gum and peanuts from fold-out tables. If the men, women and children buying or selling on or simply trying to make their way along Rue Hassiba Ben Bouali were to look upwards, they would see Maqam al-Shahid, the Monument to the Martyr, composed of three concrete palms reaching more than ninety metres into the sky in remembrance of those who died to liberate Algeria. At the base of the monument, three statues are said to represent the different facets of *al-thawra* – 'the revolution', as the War of Independence is called in Algeria.[4] They are all figures of armed men.

Opposite Maqam al-Shahid is Mathaf al-Jaysh, the Museum of the Army, which provides a celebratory account of Algeria's most powerful institution. In the hushed space of the first floor, cabinet number twenty-three displays the child-size checked top of 'little Omar', the neatly folded white shirt of Ali la Pointe and the short-sleeved cream T-shirt of Hassiba Ben Bouali, alongside a watch and a pair of glasses with a cracked left lens. What on first glance look alarmingly like dried bloodstains on Hassiba Ben Bouali's top on closer inspection are revealed to be browning traces of the sticky tape of long-gone labels. Paintings, busts, miniature models and photographs of the FLN's 1957 urban guerrilla campaign and its participants surround the cabinet. A number of these artefacts are taken from, although not always credited to, the Italian director Gillo Pontecorvo's 1966 film *The Battle of Algiers*. Co-produced by Yacef Saadi, the former head of the FLN's Algiers network, one of the most famous scenes in the film depicts the death of Hassiba Ben Bouali and her brothers-in-arms after their refusal to surrender to the French army.

Hassiba Ben Bouali's T-shirt, however, is not the star attraction in the museum. On the ground floor, groups of schoolchildren and young army recruits on organised visits excitedly gather round the shiny black and chrome Citroën DS of Algeria's second president – and wartime colonel – Houari Boumediene. Boumediene's choice of transportation is loaded with historical significance. It was the car of statesmen, whose speed and robustness is credited with saving the life of Charles de Gaulle in August 1962, during an assassination attempt perpetrated by members of the Organisation Armée Secrète (Secret Army Organisation, OAS). This right-wing paramilitary group, composed of hardliner European settlers and renegade French army generals, were enraged that the French president had ceded Algerian independence in July of that year. For the young

Algerian museum-goers, however, the value of the vehicle as a status symbol appears to lie in its material worth rather than the political references which it may or may not evoke. Ignoring the official ban on photography in the museum, youths adopt proprietorial poses next to the car and capture the moment with shots taken on their mobile phones.

Monuments, museums and street signs: these are tried-and-tested techniques of nation-building for states across the world since the nineteenth century. By making a certain version of the past ever present, the historical and contemporary legitimacy of rulers and political systems is reinforced. By creating a set of collectively recognisable symbols, the nation can imagine itself as one.[5] Since 1962 in Algeria, the top-down state message has insisted that independence was wrenched from the colonial oppressor by a united, courageous and pious Algerian people, who had led an unwavering campaign of armed and cultural resistance to colonial rule and settler expropriation since the invasion of Algiers in 1830. In this glorified national history, the key slogans are 'one sole hero, the people' and 'by the people, for the people'. Such a revolution was fought, it is claimed, to ensure liberty, social and economic justice and the recovery of a cultural identity based on Islam and the Arabic language.

Yet the Algerian state has failed to enforce a monopoly on the language of the past. The same vocabulary of bravery, self-sacrifice and patriotism has also been used to formulate critiques of the post-independence state. The memoirs of a number of veterans disillusioned with the failure of democracy in Algeria after 1962 refer to the revolution 'betrayed' or 'confiscated'.[6] Radical Islamist movements which emerged in Algeria from the 1980s onwards have also seized upon the idea of the values of the anti-colonial struggle 'betrayed'. Amassing electoral strength after the introduction of multipartyism in 1989, Islamists accused the Algerian state of neo-colonial mimicry and dismissed leaders with so much invested in perpetuating the image of a heroic struggle as being *hizb fransa*, 'the party of France'.[7] In a very different vein, Algerian feminists marching in 1992 against the Front Islamique du Salut (Islamic Salvation Front, FIS) and the looming spectre of a theocratic state carried placards bearing slogans such as 'Hassiba Ben Bouali, if you could see our Algeria' and 'Hassiba Ben Bouali, we will not betray you'[8] – an appeal to the 'memory' of Hassiba Ben Bouali, recast as a forerunner of women's rights campaigners.

In the battleground of the past, insisting on who is absent is as important as debating the merits of who is remembered. Alongside alternative nationalist movements to that of the FLN, or indeed FLN intellectuals and politicians pushed into the shadows of more powerful army generals, women who participated in the War of Independence – and notably women who, unlike Hassiba Ben Bouali, survived the conflict – are considered to be a forgotten group by those who challenge the state's self-satisfied narrative. The recurrent theme in the literature on Algerian female combatants, a burgeoning field since the 1990s, is the idea that the war was a brief parenthesis of new roles and status for women, brutally closed in 1962 by a patriarchal nationalist movement which removed them from the historical narrative, apart from as fetishised symbols, and denied them any real role in the post-colonial project. Djamila Amrane writes that '[E]ach woman [was put] back to square one'.[9] Women were 'effaced, forgotten' according to Malika El Korso.[10] For Khaoula Taleb Ibrahimi, 'all these exceptional women were ordered to return to their homes, to their tasks of mother, wife, sister and daughter'.[11] Monique Gadant argues that the FLN's wartime discourse on women's liberation not only was devoid of meaning but has been used to 'muzzle, since independence, all demands by women', whilst providing a convenient 'response to the West and its implicit accusation that Muslims mistreat their women'.[12] Marnia Lazreg critiques the view of Algerian women as having being duped by men 'for its derogatory connotations that deprive women of will and agency', but suggests that women who participated in the war almost forgot themselves:

> Women failed to score a revolution of their own by missing the opportunity of being the cultural conscience of Algeria through using their own historical circumstances as a metaphor for the impoverishment of Algerian culture, and a model for its renaissance in a new form. Instead, they waited for men's political failures to reveal to them their implicit complicity before they awoke to a feminist discourse that had already been scripted elsewhere.[13]

Such a vision of the post-independence order is not exceptional to Algeria. As Cynthia Enloe argues, 'nationalism typically has sprung from masculinised memory, masculinised humiliation and masculinised hope'.[14] Algeria is nevertheless often depicted in the literature on gender and nationalism as the classic example of a nationalist movement 'turning' on its female supporters.[15]

Fifty years after independence, Algeria seems to provide a neat case in point of the processes which Katharine Hodgkin and Susannah Radstone describe in *Memory, History, Nation*: 'Contests over the meaning of the past are also contests over the meaning of the present and over ways of taking the past forward'.[16] Yet understanding how the language and frames of reference of the War of Independence are used in Algeria as a battleground for competing visions of the present is not straightforward. Using the war as a key to understanding post-1962 Algeria has masked the lack of historical research focused on the past half-century. With a few notable exceptions, such as James McDougall's path-breaking *History and Culture of Nationalism in Algeria*, there is very little history written about post-independence Algeria.[17] This in turn has dulled our sensitivity to shifts in the nature, political usage, relative importance and reception of the memory of the war at different points in the past fifty years. Powerful memorial discourses distort our view of history, shoe-horning it into a series of confrontations between binary opposites at dramatic moments, and at the same time we cannot deconstruct these memorial frameworks because we cannot historicise them.

This can be illustrated through the different images of Hassiba Ben Bouali and women at war presented thus far. These representations fall into two broad categories: on the one hand, glorification by the wartime nationalist movement, perpetuated by the post-independence single-party state; on the other hand, oppositional appropriation and academic recovery of lost voices. The first category has its origins in 1954–62, the second in the 1990s. Within and beyond Algeria, the independence struggle, one of the bloodiest wars of decolonisation of the twentieth century, has proved an inexhaustible subject for historical enquiry since 1962. The interest in the memory of the war dates from the 1990s, when memory studies began to flourish as a field, and the politics of remembrance, recognition and repentance made their way into legislation, courtrooms and public apologies in countries around the world. Significantly, this international historiographical and political movement coincided with the period in which Algeria experienced its biggest crisis since independence. In December 1991, the FIS won the first round of legislative elections. In January 1992, the Algerian army interrupted the electoral process. A decade-long armed struggle between the army and Islamist guerrillas for control of state and society ensued, during which an estimated two hundred thousand Algerians were killed.[18] The almost exclusive focus on the War of Independence (or the colonial period preceding it) followed by the focus on the memory of the anti-colonial conflict seen through the civil violence[19] of the 1990s has resulted in the 'squashing down' of contemporary Algerian history. That is to say, reducing the recent past to two juxtaposed periods – 1954–62 and the 1990s – at once distinct and inextricably intertwined. This has a number of consequences. Firstly, it risks contributing to the caricature of Algeria as locked in an eternal, pathological cycle of violence: a popular and academic stereotype rightly denounced by James McDougall, amongst others, as essentialising and unhelpful as an analytical framework.[20] Secondly, such an approach encourages us to see Algerian history since independence through the perspective of its relationship to France, rather than also locating Algeria in other contexts, be they African, Middle Eastern or Third Worldist.[21]

Thirdly, the focus on the war, the memory of the war and the civil violence of the 1990s privileges reading the post-1962 nation-state through a prism of trauma and repressed memory. This has produced some fascinating works. Not least amongst these is Benjamin Stora's seminal *La Gangrène et l'oubli* (Gangrene and forgetting, 1991), in which the author argues that the unhealed wounds of the past are responsible for many of the contemporary social and political fractures in France and Algeria, as well as being a major obstacle to normalising Franco-Algerian relations.[22] Yet at the same time, borrowing from a discipline that by its nature is interested in the psyche of the individual and applying psychological and emotional mechanisms of remembrance and forgetting to the collective group has led to a bypassing of an evidence-based approach. Maurice Halbwachs's *Les Cadres sociaux de la mémoire* (first published in French in 1925, translated as *On Collective Memory*) remains enduringly influential for establishing that individual memory cannot be separated from the social context in which that memory takes shape. However, as Wulf Kansteiner argues, this does not mean that individuals' memories constitute the collective memory, nor that collective memory functions in the same way as individual memory: 'Nations *can* [his emphasis] repress with psychological impunity'.[23] Moreover, as Susannah Radstone underlines in her critique of trauma theory, 'even when (and if) memory travels, it is only ever *instantiated* [her emphasis] locally, in a specific place and at a particular time'.[24] The significance of an 'event' or 'past' to individuals and societies at needs to be substantiated, rather than assumed. No less a figure than Eric Hobsbawm, whose work has been so influential in shaping how we study the role of narratives of the past in nation-building, reminds us that the 'view from below, i.e. the nation as seen [...] by the ordinary persons [...] is exceedingly difficult to discover'.[25]

Fourthly, and from a gendered perspective, 'squashing down' Algerian history perpetuates a vision of women's rights, roles and status as on a downward trajectory since 1962. Malika El Korso presents this downward trajectory in the following terms: 'As a graph, the combat led by Algerian women would give us a rising curve before 1954, a plateau between 1954 and 1962, followed by a descending line'.[26] To the outside observer, the contrast seems even more dramatic. We leave in July 1962 with images of female urban bombers challenging the colonial and gendered order – a vision anchored in public consciousness in no small measure thanks to the film *The Battle of Algiers*. We come back during the 1990s civil violence, and the photographer Hocine Zaourar's gut-wrenching and award-winning photograph of a bereaved mother crying inconsolably in the wake of the 1997 Bentalha massacre, when more than two hundred villagers were killed by armed guerrillas. From inspiring Third Worldist revolutionaries, pan-Arab movements and left-wing sympathisers the world over with its fighting sisters in the early 1960s, by the early 1990s, at the height of the First Intifada, Palestinian women were using the Algerian example as a cautionary tale. Sherna Berger Gluck describes Palestinian women activists repeatedly vowing '"We will not be another Algeria"', considering post-independence Algeria as an example of women's interests being 'subverted to political processes'.[27]

Yet these are political discourses and not historical frames of analysis. The judgement of failure has largely overshadowed the study of the events of the past fifty years. As Lila Abu-Lughod argues in her volume on Egypt and Iran, post-colonial projects with women as their object should not be seen as part of a trajectory moving from patriarchy to liberation (or vice versa) but instead placed 'squarely within the messy situations of state building, anti-colonial nationalism, changing social orders, and the emergence of new classes'.[28] And the history of Algeria's post-1962 'messy situation' is only beginning to be written.

This book is about female war veterans and their relationship to the post-colonial state and narratives of the nation, in a context where they are widely considered to have been excluded from both. Based on interviews with women who participated in the War of Independence 1954–62 and who remained in Algeria after independence was achieved, it investigates these women's postwar lives and how and why they remember their wartime roles. Challenging the view of the post-1962 period as one in which female veterans were depoliticised, this book examines the intersections between interviewees' lived experiences and competing discourses about Algerian women which were produced both during and after the war. It explores the political, social and economic reasons which explain why women engage with, appropriate, reject or ignore these discourses about them.[29] Throughout, it reflects upon the shifting importance which interviewees attach to gender as a frame for understanding their lives and position in society at different points over the past half-century.[30]

The oral history interviews in this book were carried out with twenty-seven women who participated in the War of Independence, twenty-six of whom still lived in Algeria at the time of the interview. These were all nationalist women on the side of the FLN during the war, although the wide variety of political sympathies which this front could encompass, and how their definition of and relationship to 'the FLN' shifted both during and after independence, is central to this study. The women interviewed are from different socio-economic, educational and geographical backgrounds, but can broadly be divided into two main groups: a smaller group of rural women from villages in the region of Kabylia who provided logistical support for the FLN's rural guerrillas, and a larger group of urban women who were either engaged in the FLN's Algiers bomb network or joined rural guerrilla units, usually as nurses.[31]

This book is not a sociological or an anthropological study of 'women at war' or 'women after independence'. Nor does it have the pretension to be an all-encompassing account of post-independence nation-building in Algeria or a comprehensive study of memory from 1962 to the present. Instead, by following interviewees' wartime and postwar trajectories, this book aims to write a post-independence history of Algeria beyond the frames of violence, trauma, interminable decline and the Franco-Algerian lens.

At the same time, by examining how interviewees' life stories – what might be termed 'vernacular memory' – are articulated within pre-existing public frames, this book also seeks to make a contribution to wider debates about the relationship between oral history and social memory. Studying the construction of a national past through its artefacts (street signs, monuments and museums) and its formal practices (official speeches, national days and ceremonies) cannot provide a complete picture of its place within a society. Instead, we also need to explore how individuals interact with, respond to and appropriate this past and how and why a dominant narrative resonates and is refracted across different generations and different sections of societies. Research which engages with the question of how memorial discourses are understood and (re)interpreted have so far concentrated on the First World War, the Second World War, the Holocaust in Europe and American history, subject areas at the forefront of the field of memory studies.[32] Moreover, as Paula Hamilton and Linda Shopes underlined in 2008, 'the significant body of interdisciplinary work on the construction of social and cultural memory [has] failed to engage directly with oral history'.[33] This book seeks to take up this challenge for the Algerian case, using oral history to demonstrate that narratives of the nation are not just the product of 'top-down' imposition but also the result of 'bottom-up' engagement, reappropriation or indeed misinterpretation.[34] Moreover, memories which are presented as radically opposed to each other can, on closer inspection, share many points of connectedness. By using the past to debate the present, I argue, Algerians of different ages, genders and social classes have developed a malleable set of codes through which political debate can be conducted without undermining the social importance of the War of Independence as the foundation of Algerian society. Far from being evidence of a nation at war with itself, participating in disputes over the past is also a way of asserting one's belonging to that past, and validating its collective significance.[35]

Structure

This book is divided into six chapters. Chapters 1 and 2 cover the period 1954–62, revisiting key elements of the nationalist construction of the story of the war from the perspectives of some women who participated in it. Central to any nationalist construction of the history of the nation are, firstly, lineage and, secondly, clear dividing lines between who belongs and who does not. Lineage refers not only to the ancestors who can be traced back through blood, language and culture but also to the genealogy of the nationalist movement: that is to say, the events, people and political predecessors which nationalist movements draw upon in order to present their existence as a historical inevitability, the logical culmination of everything which went before. These genealogies require clear distinctions between 'us' and 'them'. Picking a side, especially in times of conflict, is presented as a moral decision between right and wrong, devoid of any other context, and each side is presented as a homogeneous bloc.

By focusing on how interviewees explain their engagement in the FLN and talk about how they negotiated sides during the war, Chapter 1 ('Nationalist genealogies') demonstrates that the complexity and ambiguity of lived experience does not preclude interviewees sharing in an idealised vision of the war. It begins to explore one of the key themes in this book: the social, economic and political reasons which explain why diverse everyday experiences can acquire standardised symbolic meanings.

If we accept that lineage and clear dividing lines between 'us' and 'them' are key to nationalist imaginaries, the importance of gender becomes clear. Nira Yuval-Davis and Floya Anthias set out five key ways in which women have been implicated in nationalism: as biological reproducers of members of the nation, as enforcers of the boundaries of national groups (through restrictions on marriage or sexual relations), as transmitters and producers of the national culture, as symbolic signifiers of national difference and as active participants in national struggles.[36] Algerian nationalism was and is gendered in all five of these ways. Chapter 2 ('Heroines and victims, brothers and sisters') examines colonial and nationalist discourses produced about women during the war, and how interviewees ignored, resisted or appropriated these discourses, then and now. It also considers how potentially seismic social change – increased contact between men and women as a result of war – subsequently has been made less socially disruptive through interviewees' insistence on a language of 'brothers' and 'sisters' when describing interactions between male and female participants.

Chapter 3 ('1962: Continuities and discontinuities') considers
1962 from two perspectives. Firstly, its symbolic importance, as
the end of the war, the birth of a new Algeria, and what is, in many
accounts, the beginning of the end – 'where it all went wrong'. It
explores how interviewees fit into popular narratives about the
'winners' and 'losers' of independence which have developed since
1962, but, secondly, it also examines, on an individual level, the
opportunities which independence presented. In 1962, the Algerian
economy and the country's infrastructure were destroyed. The
desperate need for a qualified, or at least literate, workforce presented new opportunities for educated women and men, although
for many women and men without formal education the new roles
available to them were much more limited.

Chapter 4 ('Embodying the nation') explores how the newly
independent nation was (re)imagined through women under
Presidents Ahmed Ben Bella (1962–65) and Houari Boumediene
(1965–78), though examining official speeches, nationality law,
discourses about marriage and naming, the creation of the Union
Nationale des Femmes Algériennes (National Union of Algerian
Women, UNFA) and the selection of women to act as 'ambassadors'
for Algeria on the world stage. Challenging familiar visions of
1960s and 1970s Algeria as locked in a struggle between 'tradition'
and 'modernity', Chapter 4 argues that a puritanical revolutionary fervour could fuse religious and cultural conservatism with the
desire to build a socialist state, thus 'making safe' women's entry
into the public sphere. As a counterpoint to the obsession with
women in official speeches, Chapter 4 concludes with an explora-
tion of how interviewees resisted 'embodying the nation' by insisting that they were gender-neutral citizens.

Chapter 5 ('From national construction to new battles') examines in more detail urban, educated women's relationship to the
state in the 1960s and 1970s. It looks at how these women participated in what were termed 'tasks of national construction' because
they believed in the necessity of state-building, even if they might
disagree with an authoritarian, and often socially conservative,
political system. It then considers how the relationship between
urban, educated interviewees and the state began to change in the
late 1970s and early 1980s. The reactionary 1984 Family Code
challenged the belief in genderless citizenship, leading some of these
women to use their status as female veterans to produce a new

feminist–nationalist narrative of the nation. Whilst the civil violence of the 1990s forced an accommodation of necessity between urban, educated veterans and the state, the 2010s have been marked by this particular group of women once more reframing their life stories for a new era, presenting themselves as the voices of the weak against the abuse of state power.

Finally, Chapter 6 ('Being remembered and forgotten') explicitly engages with questions about remembering and forgetting which thematically run through Chapters 1–5. It discusses how the end of the single-party state in 1989, alongside the international preoccupation with memory in the 1990s, has led to an explosion of memory about the war – without provoking a major qualitative shift in the language and frames of reference used to discuss it. The war continues to exist as a metaphor of solidarity, self-abnegation and unity of purpose. Exploring how the role of women in the War of Independence has been remembered or presented as 'forgotten' by the state, historians and interviewees themselves, Chapter 6 argues that the war continues to provide a space, albeit a space with shifting and contested limits, within which political criticism can be aired, without undermining the fundamental role of the War of Independence as a social glue. Underlining that remembering is not just a political act, Chapter 6 also examines the economic, social and personal motivations for why women remember their role in the war or omit certain parts of their stories both when invited to official commemorative ceremonies and within more informal networks of family and friends.

Time, myth and taboo:
The difficulties of writing post-independence history

Writing post-1962 Algerian history is challenging. As Malika Rahal underlines: 'in contemporary Algeria, it seems no history is possible after the War of Independence'.[37] In part, this is due to a lack of access to archives: most ministries' post-1962 archives have not been transferred to the National Archives. Those that have are often not yet classified and access to archives held by ministries and state organisations, whilst not impossible, is arbitrary and uncertain. In 2005, at the offices of the UNFA in Algiers, I was delighted when the general secretary said that she would be able to give me access to its archives. These archives turned out to be not dusty internal documents packed with illuminating detail, as I was hopefully anticipating, but two boxes of the UNFA magazine *El Djazaïria*. When I asked what had happened to other archives, I was told that they had been 'lost in a fire'.

The difficulty of writing post-1962 history is also due to the political sensitivities of the post-independence years, which present far fewer opportunities to produce a glorious tale of heroism than the war period. Moreover, many of the historical actors of the past fifty years are not only still alive but still in positions of power. For Algerian historians in Algeria, this is a difficult history to write if you want to hold on to your job. For historians working outside Algeria, embarking on writing this history is an uncertain enterprise, with only a sketchy idea of what sources you will have available or whether eyewitnesses will be willing to talk to you. Whereas for the war, or earlier periods, there is a historiography into which one's approach and argument can be worked, this does not really exist for the post-1962 period. Instead, there are a series of commonly held ideas about post-independence Algeria, perpetuated within and beyond Algeria. Amongst these commonly held ideas we find generalising statements such as: 1960s and 1970s Algeria was a battle between 'tradition' and 'modernity' hence the origins of an ongoing 'identity crisis', women were sent back into the kitchen, contemporary political discourse is obsessed by the past, it was downhill all the way after 1962 ... Such statements are in fact part of politicised narratives, full of coded meanings, allusions and rumours that all is not what it seems – a way of talking about politics typical of a political system which is neither totalitarian nor entirely democratic.[38] Such narratives need to be deconstructed rather than reproduced.

This is not to dismiss the wide range of sociological, linguistic, literary, anthropological and political science studies produced about post-independence Algeria, notably by Algerian scholars, which this book has relied on.[39] I am in no way making the dubious argument that Algeria is a historiographical virgin territory. What I am arguing is that historians have to think about how they are going to construct their sources (oral history is vital), how they might deal with subjects which are politically sensitive (especially if using oral history) and how they might identify an approach where there are plenty of opinions but very few signposts left on the way by previous historical studies.

For the 'squashing down' of history into 1954–62, or into two parallel periods of 1954–62 and the 1990s, is not just an academic or journalistic conceit. It is part of a much broader issue, relating to how time is experienced. This became evident very quickly as I began to carry out interviews. For example, Akila Ouared was born into a family of trade unionists in the eastern Algerian city of Constantine. She was a student activist and organiser in the FLN's metropolitan France branch, the Fédération de France (Federation of France, FF–FLN). Most of her adult life, however, has been spent in politics, campaigning on women's rights issues. I began – or tried to begin – the interview by asking about her current role as president of the Association de Défense et Promotion des Droits des Femmes (Association for the Defence and Promotion of Women's Rights, ADPDF). After a brief response of two and a half minutes, Akila insists: 'Right, me, I'd like to go back to before, how women came to join the National Liberation Front'.[40]

Unlike for the vast majority of my interviews, this one took place at Akila Ouared's place of work rather than in the home and the most substantial part of her political activity was in the post-1962 period. It is therefore significant that *even* Akila Ouared insisted that we must start with the war. This is the dominant event which provides the key chronological marker, overshadowing what follows to the extent that some interviewees, notably those from rural areas, consider the post-1962 period as one in which 'nothing' happened. Seven and a half years of war – or even less for those whose engagement dates from 1955 or 1956 and whose active participation ended in 1960 or 1961 as a result of repression – last an age, punctuated by retellings of the events which marked women the most, whilst decades outside the war period are summarised in a few minutes. Fatima Berci, who cooked for and sheltered rural guerrillas in her village in Kabylia, describes the seven-year war as 'the equivalent of fourteen [years] because day and night we did not stop, every day counted double'.[41] This is an explicit reference to the way in which the war years are experienced in a different time. Chérifa Akache, who carried out a similar wartime role to that of Fatima Berci, makes a similar comment: 'I'd really need two weeks to talk about the revolution'.[42]

For these women, looking at the world from the perspective of the War of Independence is like looking through the wrong end of a telescope: compared to this seismic event, both the 'before' and 'after' shrink in significance. The following passage comes from an interview with Lucette Hadj Ali, a communist of European settler origin from the western city of Oran, who joined the anti-colonial resistance. She described how her uncle, also a communist working with the FLN, managed to escape capture by the French when gendarmes came knocking at a safe house he was staying in near Pointe Pescade, a coastal location a few kilometres outside Algiers. Her uncle's actions also protected fellow underground communists, including Lucette, who were anxiously hiding in the kitchen as he opened the door:

> During the [Second World W]ar, my uncle had been mobilised by de Gaulle or Giraud, I don't know which one. They had organised a departure [from Algeria] to contact resistance networks in France, my uncle had the job of doing it, he left in a submarine, he arrived in Spain, he crossed the Pyrenees and he went to do his thing, after he was decorated. And for this mission, they gave him a good fake French identity card, which he still had. When he presented this card to the gendarmes, one of the gendarmes was from the village [where the uncle had completed the mission], and so it was all really friendly, [the uncle] gave them a drink and they never stepped into the kitchen![43]

Despite being amongst the major global events of the twentieth century, in Lucette Hadj Ali's narrative, the Second World War is reduced to a fairly unimportant background story. This telescoping of time either side of the War of Independence is not specific to women, nor indeed to those whose main political activity was in the period 1954–62. Malika Rahal, who has carried out oral history interviews with mainly male informants on underground political movements after 1962, underlines that: 'Moving through time, elaborating a narrative, arranging events and periods, but also the emotional content, change compared to eyewitness accounts about the colonial period. In the end, it is the very texture of time which appears transformed in the course of these interviews.'[44] Catherine Merridale, an oral historian of Russia, describes her interviewees' difficulties when trying to place private memories without a public framework, that is to say, without an existing shape, order, place and meaning into which an individual can locate his or her story.[45]

Not only are different moments more important than others for the narrator, they also conform to a moral time, that is to say, periods are stacked against each other not only chronologically but also in terms of the differing degrees of moral exemplarity which each period is considered to represent. The war is *the* moral benchmark. This comes through very clearly in women's language of common purpose, idealism and courage when they talk about the war, which is often either implicitly or explicitly a critique of what are perceived to be post-independence or 'today's' values. As Chérifa Akache put it: 'If there were another war, I wouldn't participate. At the time there was solidarity, love, brotherhood, confidence, but it's not the same now.'[46] The value judgements brought upon different periods are remarkably similar across regions, gender and social class.

It would, however, be inaccurate to see women's (and men's) narratives as stuck in the war years. Whilst time is experienced relatively from both moral and chronological perspectives, these perspectives are also in a constant flux. Time contracts and expands and takes on different moral values, because, depending on the present, what once might have been considered bad times can metamorphose into the good old days. Moreover, a period which is not considered important in the life of the interviewee or is skimmed over as potentially controversial and problematic can simultaneously be morally significant in structuring a narrative of 'Algeria' – this became evident in the way women talked about the Boumediene period. Few women talked about him directly, but many expressed sentiments similar to those of Louisette Ighilahriz, a former member of the Algiers bomb network: 'For the black decade which we've just had, that wouldn't have happened with Boumediene'.[47] The interviews in this book were carried out in 2005, just as Algeria was beginning to emerge from the other side of the civil violence of the 1990s, and this inevitably shaped how these women revisited the 1960s and 1970s.

Identifying an object of study, in this case post-independence Algerian history, does not make the study any easier. Restoring chronological time does not neatly fill the gaps in our knowledge. The oral historian is dependent on how interviewees remember: what they consider to be relevant or important to state or conversely unimportant or politically sensitive. Moreover, to differing degrees depending on the individual, the moral prism is always present in shaping interviewees' narratives, and, whilst the interviewer might come to differentiate moral judgement or politicised frames of reference from the recounting of lived experience, this does not necessarily bring us any closer to recreating lived experience. These different 'textures of time', to employ Rahal's expression, account for some of the unevenness in this book – why some periods are given more space then others, why the patchwork of different sources used is different for different periods, why certain women appear to dominate at certain moments, why there are silences around events we would really like to know more about and why sometimes we seem stuck in explaining 'politicised interpretations' without getting down to any 'facts'. When we try to 'stretch out' the period 1962 to the present, inevitably time does not just spring back into shape, parts might remain deformed and misshapen, shadowy and unclear. It is hoped that, with further study and research, more of these shadows will begin to lift.

Terminology and methodology

When writing about Algeria, terms are often loaded with connotations. Word choices to describe individuals, groups or events can be interpreted as a political statement of intent and sometimes no neutral term or definition can be found to the satisfaction of all parties. How to refer to the women and men who participated in the War of Independence is an example of this.

Women who participated in the war are generically referred to in Algeria today as *mujahidat* – the feminine plural of *mujahid*. The religious connotation of this word varies depending on who is using it. During the war, and then in the post-independence period, the vocabulary of jihad, *mujahid*, *shahid* and *fida'i*, which literally translate as 'holy war', 'holy warrior', 'martyr' and 'one prepared to sacrifice his life for a cause', evoked a wider, transnational religious community in order to reinforce the nationalist message. Such terminology is today used by the state, and amongst many of the older generation who fought in the war, as fairly secularised terms: jihad, *mujahid*, *shahid* and *fida'i* are synonyms for war, soldier/veteran, war dead and urban bomber.[48]

In fact, various categories were created after 1962 by the Ministry of Mujahidin (Ministry of War Veterans) to officially classify participants in the war: including *musabbilin*, to refer to members of the civilian support network, and *fida'iyn* as a specific term for urban bombers (feminine plural: *fida'iyat*). There were reportedly

between three thousand and six thousand armed combatants in
Algeria in July 1962, but in subsequent decades the number of
recognised veterans – certified as having either borne arms or
participated in a support role – steadily increased.[49] In 1974, out
of 336,784 officially recognised veterans, 10,949 were women.[50]
Proving one's militancy and acquiring official war veteran status
and its accompanying financial benefits are a complicated, opaque
and corruption-riddled process. 'False *mujahidin*' scandals are
regularly splashed across the Algerian press. If you were in a rural
area in a logistical role or if you are not politically well connected
you are likely to have difficulty obtaining veteran status, and one
might reasonably surmise that the level of women's participation is
underestimated by official figures.

  Some of the women interviewed for this book have official
veteran status; most do not. Interviewees in this book include
women who are nationally and internationally well-known figures
and unknown rural women who have never before told their
story to anyone outside their family. These women accomplished
a variety of roles during the war, from urban bomber in Algiers
to cooking for guerrillas in remote villages. Women in rural and
urban areas today tend to use *mujahidat* to describe themselves
and others, although this is a post-hoc appropriation, and a rural
woman baking bread in her home would not, at the time, have been
considered or have considered her own role as that of a *mujahida*.
This book does, however, use generic terms such as *mujahidat*,
'female combatants' and 'female veterans' to describe all women
who participated in the war whatever their role, as this corresponds
to a lived reality of a guerrilla war with no home front and women's
contemporary forms of self-identification. Chapter 5 explores how,
for one group of women, being part of 'the *mujahidat*' has become
a specific political identity since the 1980s.

  This book is not representative of all the different sociological
profiles of women who participated in the War of Independence.
Notably, uneducated women in the urban guerrilla campaign are
underrepresented, and the wartime roles of women who were in
the FLN in metropolitan France are not explored here in detail,
although this book does pick up the trajectories of some of the
women who were in the FF–FLN when they returned to Algeria
after 1962.[51] Moreover, whilst the ages of the women I interviewed
ranged from early sixties to mid eighties, the median age was

around the late sixties to early seventies mark. This means that most women were in their late teens or early twenties when they participated in the war. This does not mean that this was a young woman's war, although in some ways it was, as Chapter 2 will explore. Clearly many potential informants who were older during the war had died in the forty-three years between the end of the war and the beginning of my research.

These broader methodological questions about how representative this study is exist in a context of highly charged discourses about the linguistic and ethnic identity of Algeria. These are a key feature of contemporary political debate and giving space to or recovering certain voices through oral history might be considered a political act. Looking at the profiles of the women I have interviewed, it could be claimed that I am studying Algerian history from the margins. Of the two main types of profile which I examine, one consists of women from a Francophone ('francisant') urban elite based in Algiers. These women were part of the tiny minority of men and women who received some degree of formal education under colonial rule, and are likely to read and write in French rather than in the classical Arabic (*fusha*) of 'arabisants'.[52] The other group of women are Tamazight (Berber) speakers from the region of Kabylia, who belong to a Berberophone minority, representing approximately twenty per cent of the population, compared to an Arabophone population of eighty per cent. In practice, these politicised linguistic divides are not so clear-cut: in Algiers, for example, 'francisants' use Algerian dialectical Arabic (*derja*) for everyday communication, and, given significant rural to urban migration after independence, especially from Kabylia, many Tamazight speakers living in Arabophone areas would also speak *derja*. The profile of my interviewees was not a deliberate choice when I set out on my research, but rather emerged from the inevitable snowball effect of how networks of contacts develop. However, this is not just a mishap of research methods, and I would make the following additional points about how representative the informants in this study are.

Firstly, we need to be wary of the notion that we can identify a 'real' or 'most representative' Algerian woman. This was a particular concern for Algerian sociologists and ethnographers in the 1960s and 1970s, imbued with the official discourse that Algerianness was about recovering an 'authentic' identity, embodied by Islam, the Arabic language and pan-Arabism. To take just one example,

Nefissa Zerdoumi introduced her 1965 monograph on the education of children in the western Algerian town of Tlemcen – where many Muslims from Al-Andalus fleeing the Reconquista in the Iberian peninsula had settled in previous centuries – by stating that she had chosen this location for her case study because it 'represents in the eyes of all the national culture, with an unceasing belief in its authentic values'.[53] The fact that Zerdoumi sees her study as 'representative' is more a reflection of the dominant identity politics of the time than a factual statement.

The flipside of insisting on one's typicality are claims of exceptionality, which need to be treated with equal caution. From the early days of the French occupation of Algeria, the 'Kabyle woman' was subject to a particular ethnographic obsession, portrayed as more 'liberated' and with more 'rights' than her 'Arab' counterpart. Aside from the political ends of divide-and-rule served by these constructions, the factual basis of such distinctions is questionable, even using measures of 'emancipation' of the time.[54] Nevertheless, representations of the 'Kabyle' woman as benefiting from greater status and rights compared to her 'Arab' counterpart remain potent in the post-independence period, albeit for very different reasons. Writing in the 1990s – thus in the midst of the civil violence of the 'black decade' and in light of events including the passing of the highly conservative Family Code in 1984 and the 1980 Berber Spring (*Tafsut Imazighen*), when the inhabitants of Kabylia rose up against linguistic and cultural oppression – Mohamed Benyahia, a war veteran from the region of Kabylia, argued that 'Kabyle men have never considered women as inferior beings'. He insisted: 'Whilst today a campaign is in full swing for the rights of women, the Kabyle woman does not feel concerned, since the beginning of time, she has been associated with the life of the village and has had full rights'.[55]

Yet whilst recognising and documenting cultural and political differences between regions is entirely valid, assuming or claiming that these differences are inherited, hermetic and unchanging is much more intellectually dubious, and risks falling into an essentialism which is no more legitimate than colonial categorisations constructed to exclude and control colonised populations. Although the profile of each interviewee is an integral part of contextualising and analysing the interview, this profile should not create an expectation that responses will automatically be orientated in a certain way (for example, Kabyle *mujahida* equals resistance to the centralising, homogenising state; French-educated *mujahida* equals secular feminist). Indeed, whilst we are questioning what 'representative' means, we might also question what a 'minority' perspective might be and how we might define this: an interviewee could be in a minority because of her mother tongue, but representative of the majority of women of her generation because she never went to school; a woman might be in a minority because she was in the Algerian Constituent Assembly in 1962, but in the majority because her view of Algeria was broadly in step with the positions of the dominant political faction at the time. At the same time, because the majority of interviewees in this study might, depending on the categories which we employ, be described as in a minority, it makes it even more interesting to explore how they interact with – and indeed find their place within – the dominant discourse.

Notes

1 *Journal d'Alger* (11 October 1957). See also *L'Echo d'Alger* (9 October 1957). All translations are my own unless otherwise stated.
2 Algerian National Archives (hereafter ANA), Algiers, Fonds du GPRA: Ministère des Affaires Etrangères (MAE), Box 252.
3 *El Moudjahid* (1 November 1974).
4 This book refers to the conflict 1954–62 as the Algerian War of Independence. As Sylvie Thénault argues, this term seeks to bridge the different expressions used on each side of the Mediterranean, encompassing all of the following: '"Algerian War" as a war to maintain French sovereignty, "War of Liberation" as a moment of resurrection of an Algerian nation suffocated by colonialism for more than a century, "Revolution" as a radical transformation of the country and its society.' *La Guerre d'indépendance algérienne* (Paris: Flammarion, 2005), pp. 14–15.
5 The works of Benedict Anderson, Eric Hobsbawm and Terence Ranger, Pierre Nora, Ernest Gellner and Anthony Smith, amongst others, have been fundamental in shaping our understanding of nations and nationalism. B. Anderson, *Imagined Communities* (London; New York: Verso, 2nd edn, 2006 [1983]); E. Hobsbawm and T. Ranger, *The Invention of Tradition* (Cambridge: Cambridge University Press, 1983); P. Nora (ed.), *Realms of Memory: Rethinking the French Past*, trans. A. Goldhammer, 3 vols (New York: Columbia University Press, 1996–98); E. Gellner, *Nations and nationalism* (Oxford: Blackwell, 2nd edn, 2006 [1983]); A. Smith, *Nationalism: Theory, Ideology, History* (Cambridge: Polity, 2nd ed., 2010 [2001]).

6 For example, F. Abbas, *L'Indépendance confisquée* (Paris: Flammarion, 1984), H. Aït Ahmed, *La Guerre et l'après guerre* (Paris: Editions de minuit, 1964) and A. Haroun, *Algérie 1962: la grande dérive* (Paris, L'Harmattan, 2005).

7 G. Pervillé, 'Histoire de l'Algérie et mythes politiques algériens: du "parti de la France" aux "anciens et nouveaux harkis"', in C.-R. Ageron (ed.), *La Guerre d'Algérie et les Algériens, 1954–1962* (Paris: Armand Colin, 1997).

8 S. Slyomovics, '"Hassiba Ben Bouali, if you could see our Algeria": women and public space in Algeria', *Middle East Report*, 192 (1995), 8–13; p. 8.

9 D. Amrane, *Les Femmes algériennes dans la guerre* (Paris: Plon, 1991), p. 262.

10 M. El Korso, 'Femmes au combat: hommage à Baya Hocine' paper presented at the Centre National d'Etudes et de la Recherche sur le Mouvement National et la Révolution du Premier Novembre, Algiers, Algeria, 17 June 2002.

11 K. Taleb Ibrahimi, 'Les Algériennes et la guerre de libération nationale: l'émergence des femmes dans l'espace publique et politique au cours de la guerre et l'après guerre', in M. Harbi and B. Stora (eds), *La Guerre d'Algérie, 1954–2004: la fin de l'amnésie* (Paris: Hachette, 2004), p. 314.

12 M. Gadant, *Le Nationalisme algérien et les femmes* (Paris: L'Harmattan, 1995), p. 32.

13 M. Lazreg, *The Eloquence of Silence: Algerian Women in Question* (New York: Routledge, 1994), p. 118, pp. 221–2.

14 C. Enloe, *Bananas, Beaches and Bases: Making Feminist Sense of International Politics* (Berkeley: University of California Press, 2nd edn, 2000 [1989]), p. 44. The view of women acquiring an 'emancipation on loan' during wartime is familiar to historians of non-colonial contexts: for example, this was a common interpretation in the early literature on women and the First World War, which subsequently shifted towards a more complex reassessment of how gendered relations were reordered in the postwar period. See U. Daniel (who coined the expression 'emancipation on loan'), *The War from Within: German Working Class Women in the First World War* (Oxford: Berg, 1997) and, for a more recent approach, K. Canning, *Gender History in Practice: Historical Perspectives on Bodies, Class and Citizenship* (Ithaca: Cornell University Press, 2006).

15 The 'Algerian case' is explicitly referred to as a comparative example in a range of works not specifically focused on Algeria, for example, M. H. Alison, *Women and Political Violence: Female Combatants in Ethno-National Conflict* (London: Routledge, 2009), p. 115, and J. Nagel,

'Masculinity and nationalism: gender and sexuality in the making of nations', *Ethnic and Racial Studies*, 21:2 (1998), 242–69, p. 254.

16 K. Hodgkin and S. Radstone (eds), *Memory, History, Nation: Contested Pasts* (New Brunswick: Transaction, 2006), p. 1.

17 James McDougall's *History and Culture of Nationalism in Algeria* (Cambridge: Cambridge University Press, 2006) explores the contribution of the *'ulama* (doctors of religion) to the construction of national history, including after independence. In a survey which historian Malika Rahal carried out amongst colleagues at ten Algerian universities in 2011–12, there were no doctoral students in a history department working on any topic dealing with post-independence Algeria. In the international research context, the growing interest and increasingly abundant number of publications on the colonial period and decolonisation has not been matched by similar output on the post-independence period.

18 M. Evans and J. Phillips, *Algeria: Anger of the Dispossessed* (London: Yale University Press, 2007), p. xiv.

19 This book uses the term 'civil violence', and not civil war or second Algerian war, to refer to the conflict between the state and Islamist groups in Algeria in the 1990s. In *The Battlefield Algeria 1988–2002: Studies in a Broken Polity* (London: Verso, 2003), Hugh Roberts underlines that it was the FLN as a political party which was defeated with the introduction of multipartyism after 1989, not its political ideas. Arguably, the FIS was simply a development of the Islamist strand which had long existed within the FLN. Moreover, by the end of the decade, the majority of the Algerian population were simply terrified bystanders caught between the violence of radical Islam and state repression.

20 J. McDougall, 'Savage wars? Codes of violence in Algeria, 1830s–1990s', *Third World Quarterly*, 26:1 (2005), 117–31.

21 Historians have begun to look beyond the Franco-Algerian binary for the period of the war, for example, Matthew Connelly's *A Diplomatic Revolution: Algeria's Fight for Independence and the Origins of the Post-Cold War Era* (Oxford: Oxford University Press, 2003). Jeffrey James Byrne's forthcoming monograph explores Algerian foreign policy in the post-independence period. *Mecca of Revolution: From the Algerian Front of the Third World's Cold War* (Oxford University Press).

22 B. Stora, *La Gangrène et l'oubli: la mémoire de la guerre d'Algérie* (Paris: La Découverte, 1991).

23 W. Kansteiner, 'Finding meaning in memory: a methodological critique of collective memory studies', *History and Theory*, 41 (2002), 179–97, pp. 185–6.

24 S. Radstone, 'What place is this? Transcultural memory and the locations of memory studies', *Parallax*, 17:4 (2011), 109–23, p. 117.

25 E. Hobsbawm, *Nations and Nationalism since 1780: Programme, Myth, Reality* (Cambridge: Cambridge University Press, 2nd edn, 1992 [1990]), p. 11. Some more recent publications have sought to take up Eric Hobsbawm's challenge, for example, M. Van Ginderachter and M. Beyen (eds), *Nationhood from Below: Europe in the Long Nineteenth Century* (Basingstoke: Palgrave Macmillan, 2012).

26 M. El Korso, 'Une double realité pour un même vécu', *Confluences Méditerranée*, 17 (1996), 99–108, pp. 100–1.

27 S. Berger Gluck, 'Palestinian women: gender politics and nationalism', *Journal of Palestine Studies*, 24:3 (1995), 5–15, p. 5.

28 L. Abu-Lughod (ed.), *Remaking Women: Feminism and Modernity in the Middle East* (Princeton: Princeton University Press, 1998), p. viii.

29 Combining oral history with historiographical project, this book takes as its starting point Penny Summerfield's argument that hindsight, retrospect and rewriting are not a problem which the oral historian has to see beyond, instead 'these layers of meaning can become part of the object of study'. *Reconstructing Women's Lives: Discourse and Subjectivity in Oral Histories of the Second World War* (Manchester: Manchester University Press, 1998), p. 12. The historian of the Second World War Lucy Noakes insists on the importance of considering constructed discourse alongside the agency of lived experience, and using the former as a framework within which the latter can be analysed and vice versa. 'Gender, war and memory: discourse and experience in history', *Journal of Contemporary History*, 36:4 (2001), 663–72, p. 666. Both authors refer to Judith Butler, who in *Gender Trouble: Feminism and the Subversion of Identity* (London: Routledge, 1990) argues that 'Construction is not opposed to agency; it is the necessary scene of agency, the very terms in which agency is articulated and becomes culturally intelligible' (p. 147).

30 Studies of women and gender in nationalist movements in Morocco, Zimbabwe, Vietnam and Guinea have underlined the importance of understanding women's own frames of reference when taking a gendered approach, notably in terms of what consists of the 'public' and 'private' sphere, religious obligations and the differences in experiences and expectations between rural and urban areas. See A. Baker, *Voices of Resistance: Oral Histories of Moroccan Women* (New York: State University of New York Press, 1998); E. Schmidt, '"Emancipate your husbands!" Women and nationalism in Guinea, 1953–1958', in J. Allman, S. Geiger and N. Musisi (eds), *Women in African Colonial Histories* (Bloomington: Indiana University Press, 2002); S. Ranchod-Nilsson, '"This, too, is a way of fighting": Rural women's participation

in Zimbabwe's liberation war', in M.-A. Tetreault (ed.), *Women and Revolution in Africa, Asia and the New World* (Colombia, SC: University of South Carolina Press, 1994).

31 The Appendix provides brief biographies of interviewees for reference. Interviews with women originating from urban areas were conducted in French and subsequently transcribed and translated by myself. Interviews with women in rural areas were conducted in Tamazight (Berber), which was translated into French by an interpreter present (Badia Benbelkacem or Ouerdia Yermeche), and then transcribed from the recording by a third translator (Mourad Bouchouchi). The subsequent translation into English is my own.

32 For example: J. E. Young, *The Texture of Memory: Holocaust Memorials and Meanings* (London: Yale University Press, 1993); J. Bodnar, *Remaking America: Public Memory, Commemoration and Patriotism in the Twentieth Century* (Princeton: Princeton University Press, 1992), R. Handler and E. Gable, *The New History in an Old Museum, Creating the Past at Colonial Williamsburg* (Durham, NC. and London: Duke University Press, 1997); A. Gregory, *The Silence of Memory: Armistice Day 1919–1946* (Oxford: Berg, 1994).

33 P. Hamilton and L. Shopes, *Oral History and Public Memories* (Philadelphia: Temple University Press, 2008), p. ix. One notable exception which the authors cite is A. Portelli, *The Order Has Been Carried Out: History, Memory and Meaning of a Nazi Massacre in Rome* (Basingstoke: Palgrave Macmillan, 2003). Increasing numbers of works are examining the intersections of social memory and oral history, for example, J. Mark, *The Unfinished Revolution: Making Sense of the Communist Past in Central-Eastern Europe* (New Haven: Yale University Press, 2010).

34 Through its 'bottom-up' approach, this book distinguishes itself from works which analyse the 'top-down' institutionalisation, dissemination and manipulation of a homogeneous and unifying national history, providing key insights into a predominantly male, urban elite. For example, Gilles Manceron and Hassan Remaoun's *D'une rive à l'autre: la guerre d'Algérie de la mémoire à l'histoire* (Paris: Syros, 1993) and Benjamin Stora's *La Gangrène et l'oubli* examine the political uses of memory in post-colonial Algeria. Omar Carlier writes about the figure of the 'mujahid' (resister) in 'Le moudjahid, mort ou vif', in A. Dayan Rosenman and L. Valensi (eds), *La Guerre d'Algérie dans la mémoire et l'imaginaire* (Paris: Bouchène, 2004). Jim House and Neil Macmaster's path-breaking work *Paris 1961: Algerians, State Terror and Memory* (Oxford: Oxford University Press, 2006) combines 'top-down' and 'bottom-up' approaches in its use of oral history to explore the event and memory of 17 October 1961, when an FLN demonstration in

the French capital was brutally suppressed by the police. However, its primary focus is metropolitan France.

35 In *Multidirectional Memory: Remembering the Holocaust in the Age of Decolonization* (Stanford: Stanford University Press, 2009), Michael Rothberg critiques the view of memory as a competition for space in the public sphere – 'a zero-sum struggle over scarce resources'. Exploring the interactions between memories of different events (the Holocaust, slavery and decolonisation), he instead argues that memory is multidirectional, 'subject to ongoing negotiation, cross-referencing, and borrowing' (p. 3). My focus in this book is somewhat different: I examine the interactions of memories of the same event(s), including versions of the past which are often explicitly presented by those articulating them as in competition with alternative accounts. My argument, however, has some parallels with that of Michael Rothberg as I argue that these 'competing' stories are not as diametrically opposed to each other as they claim to be. On the contrary, they are part of the same set of references, thus providing a shared and easily accessible language for public debate in Algeria.

36 N. Yuval-Davis and F. Anthias (eds), *Woman, Nation, State* (Basingstoke: Macmillan, 1989), p. 7.

37 At the start of 2012, Malika Rahal developed the collaborative website *Textures du temps / Textures of time* which seeks to explore some of the issues of writing the history of contemporary Algeria: http://texturesdutemps.hypotheses.org. She has also written about the lack of post-independence history in 'Fused together and torn apart: stories and violence in contemporary Algeria', *History and Memory*, 24:1 (2012), 118–51, and 'Comment faire l'histoire de l'Algérie indépendante?', *La Vie des idées* (13 March 2012), www.laviedesidees.fr/Comment-faire-l-histoire-de-l.html (accessed 19 May 2014).

38 As Hue-Tam Ho Tai highlights in her discussion of late socialist Vietnam, in regimes which are neither totalitarian nor fully democratic 'public discourse often has an oblique quality; it is full of hidden meanings and allusion […] Obliqueness depends on deep cultural familiarity.' *The Country of Memory: Remaking the Past in Late Socialist Vietnam* (Berkeley: University of California Press, 2001), p. 9.

39 There is not space here to cite all the existing works, but in terms of sociological studies there are the works of Lazreg, *The Eloquence of Silence*, and H. Vandevelde-Dallière, *Femmes algériennes: à travers la condition féminine dans le Constantinois depuis l'indépendance* (Algiers: Office des publications universitaires, 1980). Anthropological studies include: C. Lacoste-Dujardin, *Un village algérien: structures et évolution récente* (Algiers: SNED, 1976); N. Plantade, *La Guerre des femmes: magie et amour en Algérie* (Paris: La Boîte à documents,

1988) and N. Zerdoumi, *Enfant d'hier: l'éducation de l'enfant en milieu traditionnel algérien* (Paris: Maspero, 1970). Works on the Family Code include M. Charrad, *States and Women's Rights: The Making of Post-Colonial Tunisia, Algeria and Morocco* (Berkeley: University of California Press, 2001), and L. Pruvost, *Femmes d'Algérie: société, famille et citoyenneté* (Algiers: Casbah Editions, 2002). For women in politics, see Gadant, *Le Nationalisme algérien et les femmes*, and F.-Z. Sai, *Les Algériennes dans les espaces politiques: entre la fin d'un millénaire et l'aube d'un autre* (Algiers: Editions Dar El Gharb, n.d.). There are also a number of journal articles and book chapters by scholars such as Rabia Abdelkrim-Chikh, Christiane Achour and Dalila Morsly, Nadia Aït Zai, Karima Bennoune, Sophie Bessis, Boutheina Cheriet, Baya Gacemi and Marie-Aimée Helie-Lucas, to name but a few.

40 Interview with Akila Abdelmoumène Ouared, henceforth Akila Ouared (13 June 2005).
41 Interview with Fatima Berci (16 June 2005).
42 Interview with Chérifa Akache (21 June 2005).
43 Interview with Lucette Larribère Hadj Ali, henceforth Lucette Hadj Ali (18 December 2005).
44 Rahal, 'Comment faire l'histoire de l'Algérie indépendante'.
45 C. Merridale, *Night of Stone: Death and Memory in Twentieth-Century Russia* (New York: Viking Penguin, 2001), p. 99 and p. 212.
46 Interview with Chérifa Akache (21 June 2005).
47 Interview with Louisette Ighilahriz (8 June 2005).
48 This secularised usage is not universally accepted: in his 1966 publication *Siham al-islam* (Arrows of Islam) Abdellatif Soltani, leader of the *'ulama* movement, rallied against this secular appropriation and nationalist stylisation of such vocabulary, insisting that 'Those who died during the war against the infidels will go to paradise as "mujahidin" if they defended the glory of Islam; for the rest, they can no longer give themselves the title of "shuhada".' J. M. Salgon, *Violences ambiguës: aspects du conflit armé en Algérie* (Paris: Centre des Hautes Etudes sur l'Afrique et l'Asie modernes, 1999), p. 98.
49 R. Branche, 'The martyr's torch: memory and power in Algeria', *Journal of North African Studies*, 16:3 (2011), 431–43, pp. 431–2.
50 Amrane, *Les Femmes algériennes dans la guerre*, pp. 225–7. Djamila Amrane was one of the rare historians to have access to the archives of the Ministry for Mujahidin; she herself is a former combatant. In the 1995 census of war veterans, the figure of 26,078 female participants was put forward – double Djamila Amrane's figure. The Ministry of Mujahidin's official explanation was that the registration of women from Kabylia was not included in the 1974 census. See R. Seferdjeli, '"Fight with us, women, and we will emancipate you": France, the FLN

and the struggle over women in the Algerian war of national liberation, 1954–1962' (PhD dissertation, London School of Economics, 2004), pp. 148–51.

51 For a discussion of women in the FF–FLN during the war see N. Macmaster, 'Des révolutionnaires invisibles: les femmes algériennes et l'organisation de la Section des femmes du FLN en France métropolitaine', *Revue d'histoire moderne et contemporaine*, 59:4 (2012), 164–90. In addition, none of the women interviewed for this book represent the profile of the small minority of Algerian Jews (often communist) who participated in the War of Independence. For an account of a woman of Jewish–Berber origin who participated in the anti-colonial struggle see H. G. Esméralda, *Un été en enfer: Barbarie à la française. Témoignage sur la généralisation de la torture, Algérie, 1957* (Paris: Exils, 2004).

52 According to the 1966 census, 63.3% of men were illiterate and 85.9% of women were illiterate. 9.5% of men and 1.5% of women could read and write only in Arabic, and 12.5% of men and 5.4% of women only in French. 14.3% of men and 6.9% of women could read and write in both languages, suggesting that the literate minority was more likely to be literate in French. The census, however, does not define what 'literate' means – knowing the alphabet, or being able to read a newspaper article. Statistics in A. Mazouni, *Culture et enseignement en Algérie et au Maghreb* (Paris: François Maspero, 1969), p. 213.

53 Zerdoumi, *Enfant d'hier*, p. 27.

54 For example, whilst France decried Muslim inheritance law as giving daughters only half of that given to sons, in Kabylia women inherited nothing until a decree of 1931, which gave them some inheritance rights. See D. Sambron, *Femmes musulmanes, guerre d'Algérie 1954–1962* (Paris: Autrement, 2007), p. 60. Moreover, for every representation of the Kabyle family as more 'liberated', one might counter a representation of the uncompromising 'moral code' in Kabylia, in which defending women's honour was a matter of life and death, and 'dishonoured' women were potentially put to death. See for example M. Feraoun, *Journal, 1955–1962* (Paris: Editions du Seuil, 1962), p. 185.

55 M. Benyahia, *La Conjuration au pouvoir: récit d'un maquisard de l'ALN* (Algiers: ENAP Editions, 1999), p. 224.

1

Nationalist genealogies

Men in hooded cloaks

On 1 November 1954, a series of co-ordinated bomb attacks, assassinations and acts of sabotage took place in locations across Algeria. The targets were symbols of colonial repression – barracks and police stations – and its economic infrastructure – power stations, telecommunications and transport links. These seventy incidents were accompanied by a statement from a newly formed organisation calling itself the Front de Libération Nationale which demanded 'The restoration of a sovereign, democratic and social Algerian State within the framework of Islamic principles' and 'The respect of all fundamental freedoms without distinction of race or confession'. Achieving independence must have been difficult to imagine in 1954. Algeria was not just a colony, but, from 1848 onwards, three departments of France (Oran, Algiers and Constantine), from 1881 placed under the authority of the Ministry of the Interior. This was a unique feature in the French empire, as was the large number of settlers in Algeria. These settlers came from across the Mediterranean basin, and included people of Spanish, Italian and Maltese, as well as French, origin. In 1954, there were around one million 'Europeans' for 8.5 million 'French Muslims'. Political, economic and social domination by settlers was entrenched through legal frameworks which excluded the autochthonous Muslim population from full citizenship rights.

The FLN's most successful attacks on 1 November 1954 were in the mountainous regions of Kabylia, to the east of Algiers, and further south eastward in the Aurès massif. Here, steep terrain and dense Mediterranean vegetation provided cover for a few hundred armed men (*maquisards*) who formed a rural guerrilla movement (the *maquis*). The FLN's numbers and access to weapons, however,

remained small and the French government and press were quick
to minimise the incidents of 'bloody All Saints' Day' as a law and
order problem which would be dealt with internally, with foreign
influence from Tunisia or Egypt possibly to blame. In the Algerian
nationalist calendar, 1 November 1954 has acquired enormous
retrospective significance: it is depicted as both the culmination of
more than a century of unceasing resistance to French rule and the
beginning of the final collective struggle to overthrow the colonial
oppressor.

Yet in the village of Agraradj, near the small town of Azazga in
Kabylia, Fatima Benmohand Berci's war began with the visit of an
aunt looking for her son:

> My cousins had gone underground. Amar Ouamrane, he had left
> [i.e. had joined the *maquis*]. My aunt Hassina, *Allah yarahma* [may
> God accord her paradise], came to see my husband saying 'I no
> longer see my son'. My husband said to her 'Your son is a man, don't
> go looking for him'. Krim Belkacem came and he gave an outfit to
> everyone. They all had a *burnus* [a long hooded cloak made out of
> coarse fabric]. Nobody knew. They forbade tobacco and chewing
> tobacco. Only people they trusted knew. Very few women knew,
> apart from those who were in on the secret, the ones who they really
> trusted. During the night, they came in the houses, they took all the
> shotguns of civilians.[1]

This wayward son and the man distributing hooded cloaks were
in fact two of the key military and political figures in the War of
Independence. Both Krim Belkacem (born in 1922 in the village of
Aït Yahia Moussa, Kabylia) and Amar Ouamrane (born in 1919
in the village of Frikat, Kabylia) had been soldiers in the French
army during the Second World War. On their return to Algeria,
both had become involved in nationalist parties, notably the Parti
du Peuple Algérien (Algerian People's Party, PPA), created in 1937,
and its later incarnation, the Mouvement pour le Triomphe des
Libertés Démocratiques (Movement for the Triumph of Democratic
Liberties, MTLD), created in 1946. The legalistic MTLD participated in elections in the post-Second World War period, but also had
a clandestine wing, the Organisation Spéciale (Special Organisation,
OS), which advocated revolutionary insurrection. Members of the
OS would go on to form the Comité Revolutionnaire pour l'Unité
et l'Action (Revolutionary Committee for Unity and Action, CRUA)
in March 1954. Five members of the CRUA – Mohamed Boudiaf,

Larbi Ben M'Hidi, Mostefa Ben Boulaïd, Mourad Didouche and Rabah Bitat – were given the task of co-ordinating the move to armed action. In summer 1954, Krim Belkacem joined them and in October the CRUA adopted the name 'FLN'. Until early 1957, Krim was military leader of the *wilaya* III (the region of Kabylia) in the FLN's Armée de Libération Nationale (National Liberation Army, ALN). For much of the war, he would be one of the most powerful figures in the FLN–ALN. Within the *wilaya* III, Ouamrane had responsibility for the area around Mirabeau (today Draâ Ben Khedda) and then the area of Azazga before taking command of the *wilaya* IV (Algiers region) in August 1956.

Fatima Benmohand Berci, however, is talking about a period before the creation of the FLN. Krim and Ouamrane had been living clandestinely in the mountains of Kabylia since 1947 when, in separate incidents, both were condemned to death *in absentia* for shooting agents of law and order. Fatima Benmohand Berci is not describing her first contact with the FLN–ALN, but rather her first meeting with a two-man, or at most few-men, *maquis* unit before the FLN came into existence. Between 1947 and 1954, these 'bandits of honour', loosely held together by the belief that independence would be fought for through armed struggle, were moving about the isolated rural areas surrounding their home villages, gradually gathering men, arms and support.[2]

The contact which these clusters of resisters built with the local population initially remained firmly anchored in extended family networks. The bonds of blood guaranteed loyalty before political adhesion was concretised. Local populations accepted them as relatives. The message of rejecting colonial rule could also be located in the experiences of their day-to-day lives and, in many cases, past anti-colonial uprisings which ancestors had participated in. Fatima Benmohand Berci was a few months old when she first came back to Kabylia and the village of Agraradj. She was born in Tunisia in 1926. Two generations previously, her family had fled across the border following the failed insurrection against French colonialism led by El Mokrani in 1871.

The directives of this latest uprising were nevertheless viewed with circumspection even by those let in on the secret: Fatima Benmohand Berci's brother-in-law was initially reluctant to part with his shotgun. The ban on cigarettes and tobacco plug – initially motivated by a desire to deny the colonial state tax revenues, and

later seen as part of a purifying religious zeal – found few adher-
ents: 'people didn't follow it that much'.[3] If there was a transmitted
memory of anti-colonial resistance, there was also a memory of
its failure and ensuing repression which tempered hasty commitment to the latest clandestine cause. A turning point in Fatima
Benmohand Berci's account was, even if she does not use the date,
1 November 1954: 'The action really started when they burned
down a cork factory in Azazga'.[4] This act of arson was one of the
All Saints' Day attacks.

Yet this real action in fact started over a number of months following 1 November. Fatma Yermeche is Fatima Benmohand Berci's
neighbour in Agraradj. According to her, the war began when she
was twelve years old – that is to say, in 1955:

> We didn't see the *mujahidin* at first, they came in secret, because they
> were scared that someone in the population would sell them out [...]
> Those that worked with the *caïds*, with the French [i.e. autochtho-
> nous men working for the local colonial administration], they started
> by eliminating them. Once they'd got rid of everyone who could
> denounce them, who were of course imposed by the French, we saw
> them.[5]

Chérifa Akache, from the village of Aït Abderrahmane in the
Ouacifs, also emphasises the initially mysterious nature of the rural
guerrillas' presence: 'At the start I didn't know anything. In general
in Kabylia, women don't get involved in what men do. They spoke
amongst themselves, but I didn't get involved. The women started
to get involved the day French soldiers came to the village.'[6] Both
Chérifa Akache and her husband were eighteen years old at the
time. When he first joined the *maquis*, he did not say anything to
his wife. Chérifa began to have what she describes as her 'woman's
suspicions' – and pushed her husband to explain his suspect behaviour. He then began bringing men back to eat.

Ferroudja Amarouche also remembers the burning of the cork
firm in Azazga. In 1954, she was living in the neighbouring village
of Bouzeguene, with her husband and three children. But for her
too, the start of the war happened a number of months later:

> It was the day that the French soldiers came to the village of
> Bouzeguene, in 1955, it was during the month of Ramadan
> [this began mid-April in 1955]. The *maquisards* had burnt down the
> cork firm, to show their rejection of the French. My father-in-law had

fought in the war with France [the First World War], and when they announced this fire, he said 'It's a declaration of war'. My father-in-law died just after, at Azazga, he had a café there.[7]

Ferroudja's father-in-law, like Krim and Ouamrane, was a veteran of the French army. From India to French West Africa, colonised men who had fought in the British and French armies in the First and Second World Wars could be problematic demobbed subjects for the colonial authorities. Having come into close contact with political ideologies such as communism and nationalism on their travels, they often returned to their villages deeply dissatisfied with the colonial status quo. Ferroudja's father-in-law, who was wounded in the 1914–18 conflict, had immediately seized upon the symbolic importance of the FLN's attacks and explained this to his family. At this point in the interview, Ferroudja's husband Tahar joined in, to explain how the death of his father accelerated his and his wife's adhesion to the FLN–ALN. The French administration in Azazga refused to allow Tahar to inherit the café, claiming that he was an enemy element. Excluded from his business, he was then named – according to him, without consultation – head of a group of *maquisards* in the region. He was initially reluctant, worried about who would look after his wife as he had no brothers and only one sister. Considering nevertheless that 'France' had attacked him first by taking the café off him, he accepted the role.

A long history, going back into the previous century, of resistance and repression in the region, as well as more recent events, such as the two world wars, provided a framework through which villagers could locate events unfolding around them – 'even' women, who would not usually be part of political discussion. Women's active involvement in the struggle began, however, with a straightforward set of practical instructions rather than a political discourse. Fatima Benmohand Berci describes the first time she was asked to cook for the *maquisards*. A group of men came to the house, including Amirouche, Si Haoues[8] and 'an old man called Si Ali, with rosary beads':

> They asked my husband to buy meat, bread and couscous. [They said] 'In two, three days you will make food, twelve men are going to come and eat here'. My husband did the buying and me and another woman prepared the food. Around nine in the evening a group of *mujahidin* came and ate at the house.[9]

Thus began the wartime activities of rural women. They washed the *mujahidin*'s clothes, cooked for them, gathered medicinal plants to heal their injuries and, crucially, informed them of the movements of the French army. The logistical support provided by these women was crucial to the survival of the rural *maquis*. The FLN was inspired by the methods of Mao Zedong and Ho Chi Minh, and in direct contact with both by 1959.[10] The organisation took to heart Mao's much-quoted revolutionary dictum: the guerrillas' relationship to the rural population is that of the fish to water – the latter is crucial to the survival of the former.

As the rural guerrilla movement grew and women became increasingly implicated, they were targeted by male *maquisards* with a generic (as opposed to gendered) discourse, aimed at reinforcing the patriotic dimension of their actions. Fatma Yermeche describes local meetings for men and women during which, she says, the *mujahidin* told them: 'This is our country, we want independence, we want to run our country, not foreigners, you need to be brave, you need to stay strong'.[11] Ferroudja Amarouche says: 'We knew that we were going to war for Algeria. Even the children knew. The little ones, when they [the French soldiers] said to them "Have you seen the *fellagas* [pejorative term for rural guerrillas]?," they knew, they said "No, we haven't seen them."'[12] For Fatima Benmohand Berci the message was just as straightforward and clear: 'They grouped us together, they said "You have to work with us" and we said "OK" [...] We knew what we were doing, they'd explained it to us, it was for the liberation of the country. We accepted giving our lives and our strength.'[13]

Alongside this straightforward and accessible message of freedom from colonial rule, these rural interviewees also imply that they caught a glimpse of an egalitarian post-independence state. Fatima Benmohand Berci recalls one incident in which the *mujahidin* came to eat and there was no food to give them: 'One day Si Abdallah[14] came to my house with twelve people. There were only six dates [to eat]. Si Abdallah cut each date in two and said, "*In sha'allah* [God willing], I hope that our struggle will lead us to independence where everyone will have a share."'[15] Allegory as much as anecdote, this reminds us that the war is also being revisited by these women through the knowledge of nearly fifty years of independence and the suspicion that the dates have not been fairly distributed.

From event to metaphor

Concrete descriptions and symbolic representations of food are a key theme in these rural interviewees' accounts. Apart from the obvious dangers of living in a war zone, hunger was one of the major issues facing them. In March 1956, the French National Assembly, led by the Socialist Prime Minister Guy Mollet and his Republican Front government, voted Special Powers to the army, effectively giving it a free hand to quell the growing revolt in Algeria. Yet a cycle of violence and counter-violence only entrenched the crisis. In May 1958, a coalition of settlers and army generals in Algiers, doubting the resolve of politicians in Paris to maintain Algeria under French rule, staged what looked very much like a coup. The Fourth Republic collapsed, and de Gaulle returned to power. De Gaulle launched a two-pronged programme of, on the one hand, socio-economic and political reform and, on the other hand, a massive military offensive against the FLN–ALN. General Maurice Challe oversaw the campaign to 'pacify' Algeria from west to east. This resulted in wide-scale destruction of the rural economy, as well as significant population displacement, as sections of the rural population were forcibly removed to prevent them assisting the ALN. By 1 March 1959, at the high point of the Challe offensive, 429,000 French army soldiers were in Algeria.[16]

Ferroudja Amarouche explains how a drought made shortages even worse:

> There was nothing to eat, there wasn't any water, and even sometimes we ate grass. And the French soldiers said to us: 'There isn't even enough grass for you to eat, serves you right'. One Ramadan, there was nothing to eat, it was grass we tried to eat. And even the grass was difficult to find. [There was] nothing, nothing.

Bread made with barley has since the Middle Ages been connoted as the bread of the very poor, like grass, an animal foodstuff adopted in extreme circumstances. There is a clear sense of abasement when Ferroudja describes what local populations were reduced to gleaning for sustenance, accompanied by a strong sense of how this symbolically differentiated them from the French army soldiers with food in their stomachs: 'One day the French killed two young people, and these two youths had a little bit of bread made with

barley on them. They took it out of their pockets and they placed on
their stomachs to say, "There, that's what they eat.""[17]
Rural interviewees carry the food metaphor over into the post-
independence period. No longer representing colonial humiliation,
it metamorphoses into a symbol of what these women see as the
failure of the post-colonial state to live up to expectations about
the creation of a more equal society. Describing successive Algerian
post-independence leaders, Fatima Berci declares: 'Whoever is
in power eats, and when his belly is nice and full, he's no longer
hungry and off he goes.'[18] As Chapter 6 explores further, rural
women's stories of suffering might be read through a similar lens –
they are at once descriptions of very concrete pain and loss, and a
critique of a perceived lack of recognition for their wartime sacrifice in the postwar period. The event is often remembered through
material deprivation and physical and emotional suffering, but such
memories also serve as metaphors, they are post-hoc morality tales.
If we consider that memories recall both the events and their
metaphorical significance in the present, it is worth returning to
women's stories about how they became involved in the nationalist movement. On the one hand, these are stories about local and
family networks bringing women into a guerrilla struggle. Famous
men such as Amirouche, Krim Belkacem, Ouamrane and Si Haoues
are mentioned because the interviewees actually met them. With
little or no access to the press, radio or televised news during
the conflict, the war experience of these women was local. After
independence, language (their being Tamazight/Berber speakers),
literacy (these women were never taught to read or write) and geographical barriers (living in a village, although Chérifa Akache and
Ferroudja Amarouche moved to Algiers after 1962) have limited
these women's exposure to published history in French or Arabic,
and the audio, if not the visual, narratives of Arabic-language
documentaries and films shown on state television. We might reasonably expect less knowledge of, and thus less borrowing from
or construction against, national frames of memory amongst these
rural women than amongst literate Francophone or Arabophone
women in urban areas. Interviewees' references to the religious calendar, local events, family networks and family history in shaping
how they understood the conflict seem to have a separate existence
alongside a post-hoc nationalist calendar of big dates to which these
women make no explicit references.

Yet this is not an unfiltered memory. If these women tell me the names of Amirouche, Krim Belkacem, Ouamrane and Si Haoues, it is because they expect me to recognise them as historical figures. Chérifa Akache talks about cooking for Amirouche 'amongst others' – it is Amirouche who matters. When I asked Chérifa Akache if she knew Amirouche she told me: 'I know him, I served him [food], I even washed his feet'.[19] Washing someone else's feet is a profound mark of respect. Normally a woman would do this only for her husband, or a member of her family.

Since the 1980s, Amirouche and Krim have their place in national history as wartime heroes in a much-edited form, but in addition they also have a regional history. This regional history is not necessarily separatist, rather it often uses local or regional heroes as examples of national alternatives, more inclusive, fairer and freer post-independence paths not taken. The circumstances of the deaths of Amirouche and Si Haoues have played a key role in shaping this oppositional dimension.[20] In 1959, angry at what they perceived to be the failures of the FLN–ALN leadership stationed in Morocco and Tunisia to supply rural guerrillas inside Algeria with arms, the two men headed to Tunis to meet with members of the Gouvernement Provisoire de la République Algérienne (Provisional Government of the Algerian Republic, GPRA). The GPRA was created as the executive organ of the FLN in 1958, presented as a sovereign government-in-exile in a bid to strengthen the FLN's international negotiating position. On the way, Amirouche and Si Haoues were killed in an ambush by French soldiers who seemed remarkably well informed of their movements, possibly by their enemies within the FLN–ALN. In this perspective, the story of Amirouche can be seen as part of a narrative of the good fight gone bad; the revolution betrayed. This is certainly the view of the politician and author of *Amirouche: Une vie, deux morts, un testament* (Amirouche: a life, two deaths, one testament, 2010) Saïd Sadi, whose village of birth, Aghribs, is adjacent to Agraradj, where Fatima Benmohand Berci, Fatima Berci and Fatma Yermeche all live. Born in 1947, Sadi is a long-time activist on questions of cultural pluralism and secularism and at the time of writing the biography was the president of the party Rassemblement pour la Culture et la Democratie (Rally for Culture and Democracy, RCD). In *Amirouche*, Sadi sought to challenge both French army caricatures of 'the bloody Amirouche' and the denigration of Amirouche during the presidency of Boumediene (1965–78), when Amirouche was depicted as brave, but in thrall to purging paranoia and anti-intellectualism. For Sadi, recovering the memory of Amirouche – whom he describes as an 'autodidact, unsurpassed leader, whom our mothers were already singing about when he was alive'[21] – is about much more than righting a wrong done to an individual reputation, it is also about saving the honour of Algeria from crooks who manipulate history.[22] This celebration of local heroes as a national alternative is not specific to Kabylia. As Thomas DeGeorges argues, as the popular legitimacy of the war generation was increasingly challenged in the 1980s and early 1990s, war veterans from the eastern, central and western parts of the country began to emphasise local aspects of their identity thus 'reinforcing their historical legacy on both the national and regional levels'.[23]

The history of protest in Kabylia nevertheless does lend itself well to alternative national futures read through regional pasts. Another famous son of the region is the FLN founding member Hocine Aït Ahmed, who with the Front des Forces Socialistes (Front of Socialist Forces, FFS) led an armed rebellion in Kabylia in autumn 1963 against the seizure of power in Algiers by the political alliance of Ben Bella, a leading figure of the wartime FLN who would become first president of Algeria (1962–65), and the ALN's Etat Major Général (general staff, EMG), headed by Boumediene. Within a year, the FFS rebellion was crushed, its leaders arrested and around four hundred rebels – mainly veterans of the War of Independence – killed. The nationalist (rather than separatist) dimension of this regional memory is highlighted by recent attempts by some members of the contemporary FFS to ensure that those who died during the failed 1963 rebellion are counted amongst the martyrs of the War of Independence.[24]

It is hazardous to try and read this oppositional narrative – i.e. the idea that Kabylia is a heartland of anti-authoritarian protest – into the ways in which the rural women whom I have interviewed recount their encounters with regional heroes. Only Fatima Berci makes a brief reference to the 1963 FFS uprising, in response to the question 'Can you remember when independence was declared?':

> FB: Yes, I can remember. The French chased us out [of the village, threatening] 'Otherwise we'll kill you'. In the end I left here [the village of Agraradj] and I spent two years in Algiers before independence. My

husband worked with the *mujahidin* [i.e. was in the *maquis*] and he
couldn't leave otherwise they would have killed him.
NV: So you were in Algiers on independence day [5 July 1962]?
FB: I went [to Algiers], just for a short time to rest. I had a child
who was forty days old, now he's forty and he's got seven children.
There was the ceasefire [17 March 1962], independence, I came back
[to Agraradj] and I stayed here. Then after the war with the French,
there was the war with the Arabs. I could talk until the morning and
I wouldn't have finished telling you everything we did.[25]

The expression 'the war with the Arabs' does not imply an
ethnic conflict, but rather is a reference to the fact that the 1963
FFS uprising, which began in Kabylia because this is where Aït
Ahmed's political support base was strongest, led to soldiers from
the newly created Armée Nationale Populaire (National People's
Army, ANP), which replaced the ALN after independence, coming
to the region. This included men from outside the region, who were
Arabic speakers. In any case, Fatima Berci dismisses 'the war with
the Arabs' in one sentence, before returning to her main narrative
thread: her actions and suffering during the war against the French.
The other key reference structuring her story is her family, and
discussion of her husband, son and grandchildren push the national
picture to the periphery. National dates are replaced by children's
ages and the forty days' confinement that many women in Algeria
adhered to after the birth of a child.

Rather than being specific to Kabylia, the way in which Fatima
frames her account has parallels with histories of rural women
involved in guerrilla wars across the world: the importance of
family and local networks in shaping the nature of women's experiences is foregrounded and the emphasis in women's accounts
is on suffering and multiple pressures which they feel have not
always been fully recognised. Ferroudja Amarouche declares:
'This was really a region very hostile to France, we really resisted
and it was really known [at the time] that we were resisters.
Other people said: "Do you think that it's you who are going to
make the new Algeria?"'[26] In the small Indian town of Chauri
Chaura, the historian of Indian nationalism Shahid Amin uncov-
ered similar critiques when interviewing Naujadi, the widow of
a man imprisoned for the burning down of a police station in
1922 during Gandhi's campaign of civil disobedience. Naujadi

complained that her husband's political pension did not come to her, but instead was intercepted by local politicians, who paraded the relatives of rioters in Luknow and Dehli for their own political ends: 'Everybody has got their raj, our raj never came', explained Naujadi, 'It's us who created the turmoil, and look what we got – nothing!'[27]

Family histories and histories of nationalism

We will now turn to consider women who in many ways have very different profiles to those of Fatima Berci, Fatma Yermeche, Fatima Benmohand Berci, Chérifa Akache and Ferroudja Amarouche. These are women who were from urban areas, often the capital, Algiers. During the war, these women were nurses in the *maquis*, notably joining rural guerrilla units after leaving their desks and books during the student strike of spring 1956, or they were liaison agents and urban bombers in Algiers in what became known as the 'Battle of Algiers'. The beginnings of the 'Battle of Algiers' were in August 1956, when the FLN decided to launch a campaign of urban bomb attacks and assassinations, in an attempt to take some of the pressure off an increasingly embattled rural *maquis*. In January 1957, Prime Minister Mollet handed civil and military control of Algiers over to General Jacques Massu and his tenth paratrooper division, which sought to restore order by any means.

Many, but not all, of the urban interviewees under consideration here had had the opportunity to acquire some degree of formal education. In 1954, ninety-one per cent of the Algerian or 'French Muslim' population was illiterate. Only 4.5 per cent of women could read and write, and thirteen per cent of men.[28] Of the fifteen women of 'Muslim' origin examined here who began their action in towns (four of whom then moved on to join the *maquis* and three of whom went to France and joined the FF–FLN), fourteen had received an education at least until the end of primary school in the French education system. A number of them had passed the baccalaureate and/or were in further or higher education when the war interrupted their studies.[29]

The women under discussion here thus have had much more exposure to published national history, and indeed films and television documentaries, since the end of the War of Independence compared to rural women. These urban women's awareness of the structure, content and style of this history is reflected in the course of interviews. In most cases, even if the detail might be particular to the interviewee, the frames of reference which these urban women use are much more easily recognisable for the historian: they fit with published accounts of the development of Algerian nationalism and they use a familiar chronology. You do not have to calculate when the war began by working out when the month of Ramadan was in 1955. Instead, interviewees are much more likely to locate themselves in the genealogy of Algerian nationalism in the same way that Fadéla Mesli does.

Fadéla Mesli was born in 1936 into a middle-class family from the western Algerian town of Tlemcen. When she was eight, her family moved to the Algiers Casbah, site of the Ottoman-era citadel and traditional district surrounding it. In this 'Muslim' quarter of Algiers, her father opened a *hammam* (bath house). Referred to as the 'pearl of the Maghreb', Tlemcen is often characterised – and caricaturised – as the cradle of a 'pure' and 'authentic' Algerian and Maghrebi culture, defined as Arabo-Andalusian and Muslim. This image has been studiously maintained by the Algerian state since independence, twinning the town with Kairouan in 1969, the Tunisian home of North Africa's most prestigious mosque, and Granada in 1989. In 2011, Tlemcen was named Capital of Islamic Culture. Until his recent rehabilitation, the Algerian state has been less forthcoming about celebrating Tlemcen's most famous son, Ahmed Messali, otherwise known as Messali Hadj. Born in 1898, Messali was a founding figure of modern Algerian nationalism. He was the first to demand outright independence and he established Algeria's early nationalist movements, the Etoile Nord Africaine (North African Star, ENA) in 1926, the PPA in 1937 and the MTLD in 1946. However, after the Second World War, Messali's authority was increasingly challenged by a younger generation of activists keen to accelerate the move to armed action. Messali not only rejected the creation of the FLN in 1954 but from that point on was also – and this explains his subsequent marginalisation – leader of a rival movement, the Mouvement National Algérien (Algerian National Movement, MNA).[30]

Transmitted echoes and lived experiences of this political, social and cultural history inflect how Fadéla Mesli depicts her first encounters with Algerian nationalism.

My grandfathers – maternal and paternal – were part of the first intake of teacher training students. France tried to draw from well-known middle-class families, whose children were talented, to get them to go to the Ecole Normale d'Instituteurs d'Alger [Algiers teacher training college, opened in 1865]. The objective was to train them in French language and culture so that after they could instrumentalise them to win over the rest of the population. [My grandfathers] did not fall into the trap and they kind of rebelled, they did the opposite of what they were meant to do. They taught their Muslim pupils the true values of our country, our culture and our identity. My maternal grandfather even thought it important to preserve musical heritage. He created an association of Andalusian music. He said, 'We must not let ourselves be deculturised, because a people without culture is a dead people. A people without roots is a dead people.' [The French authorities] expelled him to Morocco – he was a teacher in Oujda [fifteen kilometres west of Algeria in the French protectorate of Morocco] – and that's why I was born in Morocco. My paternal grandfather died when I was a little girl, I was five or six, so I couldn't ask him what misery colonialism subjected him to, but he suffered to such an extent that – and it was a silly reaction – he forbade his children to study in French. It was a rejection. That's why my father couldn't continue his studies. As soon as [his children] arrived at the primary school leaving certificate [my grandfather] withdrew them.

From tentative initial contact with the colonial state, Fadéla Mesli's grandfather renounced subversion from within for economic and cultural withdrawal. That he had been a teacher – that is to say, a state employee – whereas his son ran a privately owned *hammam* is significant. Fadéla's father was clearly not entirely convinced of the benefits of this isolation. He sent his daughter to a French school and carried out a nationalist education at home. Fadéla insists on the role of her mother, father and older brother in this: 'At school they taught us one thing, and at home our parents were there to remind us that we were not French, we were colonised, and that we had a nation'. As a very young teenager, Fadéla Mesli attended meetings of the Union des Femmes Musulmanes d'Algérie (Union of Muslim Women of Algeria, UFMA), the women's branch of the PPA–MTLD run by Mamia Chentouf. Fadéla sold the MTLD journal *Algérie libre*: 'We discussed, amongst ourselves, very timidly, the liberation of our country and the nationalist movement'.[31] This women's wing – in reality a handful of women – was founded in 1947, eleven years after the creation of the Union

Musulmane des Femmes de Tunisie (Muslim Union of Women, UMFT), a much larger and well-established movement linked to the Tunisian nationalist movement Neo-Destour, and three years after Malika El Fassi signed the Moroccan Independence Manifesto.[32] Regardless of who ruled the country, Fadéla Mesli's parents had social aspirations for their daughter. In 1954, she was studying to be a nurse: 'The dream of my mother was that I study to be a midwife so I could open a birthing clinic. At the time, that was the done thing in families – in what we might call the notable families – to have a daughter who was a midwife who had a birthing clinic.' Around the same time as beginning her nursing studies, Fadéla Mesli also began to carry out activities for the FLN in Algiers, carrying weapons and messages, collecting money from local inhabitants and participating in youth meetings. In spring 1956, Fadéla participated in a student strike called by the FLN. This was part of a series of strikes through which the organisation sought to build a mass movement, by obliging populations to show themselves to be for or against them. For Fadéla, this strike was the trigger for a whole new level of action: 'I was more or less known I suppose by the [French] intelligence services. They [the FLN–ALN] needed medical personnel in the *maquis* so I took the opportunity to go up to the *maquis*, with Mrs Zerdani and Mrs Safia Baazi.' The three young women joined a rural guerrilla unit in the countryside surrounding Algiers, in the *wilaya* IV. This was not as banal a decision as Fadéla Mesli makes it sound, as Chapter 2 will explore. Only her brother knew that she was planning to abandon her studies to join the *maquis*: 'My parents would not have accepted me joining the *maquis*, to tell you the truth. It wasn't in our culture.'[33] Her parents would have been horrified by the idea that their daughter was mixing with men in a culture and society where the sexes were meant to be strictly separated in respectable families.

Although the trajectory of Fadéla Mesli's family is suggestive of fluctuating modes of resistance and accommodation between the colonial authorities and prominent Algerian families in the late nineteenth century and first half of the twentieth century, the way she structures her story foregrounds the theme of permanent and continuous cultural difference and resistance. This idea of a separate, distinct culture of the colonised makes more sense if seen as a symbolic value rather than the lived reality of a family zigzagging between Tlemcen, Oujda and Algiers. Socially, linguistically and culturally, the colonised population of Algeria was diverse. Apart from when she talks about her family's reaction to her joining the *maquis*, Fadéla Mesli's account of her political engagement in many ways plots the same trajectory as the narrative promoted by the post-independence nation-state. The failure of assimilation, the importance of cultural resistance when colonial repression crushed armed struggle, the primordial difference of the colonised: Fadéla's reference to 'our country, our culture, our identity' evokes, in a more inclusive form, the oft-quoted declaration 'Algeria is our country, Islam is our religion, Arabic is our language'. The latter statement is attributed to Abdelhamid Ben Badis, leader of the Association des '*Ulama* Musulmans Algériens (Association of Algerian Muslim '*Ulama*, AUMA), a religious and cultural organisation founded in 1931 which sought to 'purify' Algerian Islam from pre-Islamic practices and construct a collective identity distinct from that of the colonial power. After 1962, 'Algeria is our country, Islam is our religion, Arabic is our language' became a guiding tenant for the writing of nationalist history. For a very different set of references, produced in a very different context, we might turn to the diary of Baya Hocine, written during the War of Independence.

Baya Hocine was a seventeen-year-old urban bomber, condemned to death in December 1957. She was one of six female members of the FLN to receive the death penalty, although no woman was executed and all were released from prison following the 1962 Evian Peace Accords.[34] I did not have the opportunity to interview Baya Hocine, for this book – she died in 2000, a few days short of her sixtieth birthday. She was however, interviewed by the historian and fellow *mujahida* Djamila Amrane (Danièle Minne) in the 1980s. Baya Hocine also left behind one of the rare personal documents written by a woman during the war: her prison diary. This diary found its way into French army archives after being seized in a cell search of Barberousse prison in April 1958. The document in the archives is a typed-up version of the diary, presumably considered by the cell searchers as potentially useful in anti-nationalist psychological warfare. The four men alongside whom Baya Hocine had been arrested were guillotined. This was a fate that Baya Hocine, and fellow teenage bomber Djoher Akrour, eventually escaped, although Baya did not know this when she was writing her diary. If Fadéla Mesli tends to reach for her rose-tinted glasses, Hocine saw the world through much greyer lenses.

The profile of Baya Hocine is also markedly different from that of Fadéla Mesli. She was born in 1940, in the Casbah, the youngest of three children. Her brother Mohamed was twelve years older than her, her brother Ahmed eight years older. Baya Hocine's family were landless peasants, from the village of Ighil Imoula in Kabylia. Her mother was a cleaner. Her father held various unskilled jobs from junk dealer to porter, but was also an activist in the PPA, and as a result was often in prison. In her prison diary, one of the influences cited by Baya Hocine to explain her politicisation is the first film she ever saw, aged fourteen. *Los Olvidados* (The Forgotten Ones / The Young and the Damned, Luis Buñuel, 1950) tells the hopeless story of juvenile delinquents in the slums of Mexico City in the 1950s. In this Latin American film – which won the Cannes Film Festival prize for best director in 1951 – Baya Hocine saw plenty of comparisons with the Algerian situation: 'Our young people are shaped by a foreign government, which debases a people and encourages debauchery in order to exploit a country without resistance'.[35] This rather moralistic, lofty tone, is tempered by episodes in her diary recounting the grinding daily existence of a poor family in the Casbah – Baya Hocine's father died from malnourishment in 1946; before he died he forced her brother Mohamed to marry in what was clearly an unhappy union, Baya's niece went blind from measles when she was nine months old owing to a lack of medical treatment, Mohamed sometimes got drunk and beat his sister, wife and daughters and when Baya was suspected of writing a love letter to a boy she was beaten by both her brothers.

Yet alongside these harsh realities, a political education was taking place. Baya Hocine declares that 'My political maturity is due to my brother who is a Marxist. I am too. But my time in prison has made me a big anti-communist. I am ~~allied~~ [*sic*] atheist and anti-racist.'[36] In his *Histoire intérieure du FLN*, Gilbert Meynier cites the exceptional case of Baya Hocine, who declared herself '"atheist and anti-racist"'.[37] By declaring herself an atheist, Baya Hocine's frames of reference in 1957 are strikingly different from those of the women whom I interviewed in 2005, not because the latter insist on religious readings of their engagement but rather because it is difficult to imagine many Algerians publicly declaring themselves atheists today unless very deliberately choosing to adopt a position of radical opposition to societal norms. In the context of this private diary, written by a teenager expecting to be put to death and who declares herself a Marxist, the reference to atheism is coherent. Yet my incessant staring at the crossed-out word, wondering if a mistake had been made when the diary was typed up, reveals how much expectations about what 'Algerianness' entails – or at least, what can safely be declared in the public space and remain within the acceptable limits of the national community – might have shifted between the war and the 2000s.

Baya Hocine's father did not want his daughter to go to French primary school. For him, as for Fadéla Mesli's grandfather, this was a form of anti-colonial resistance. However a mixture of persuasion by her older brother and the return of her father to prison meant that Baya did go to school. It is here that she received the education necessary to combat colonialism with its own language. Writing in her prison diary in January 1958, she declared that from a young age she had been taught the principles of the French Revolution of 1789, Liberty, Equality and Fraternity:

> The history teaching I received at high school clearly showed me that nationalist and revolutionary movements were in no way considered subversive, on the contrary, all my textbooks spoke with admiration and respect of those who sought to shake off the yoke of foreign domination. France herself, who recognises in her constitution the 'right of peoples to self-determination', has always prevented our people from emancipating themselves.[38]

Adopting the French language and the revolutionary vocabulary of 1789 to reject twentieth-century colonialism was common amongst the tiny, but slowly growing, post-Second World War generation of Algerian students educated in French.[39] As the writer Kateb Yacine declared in 1962, 'To write in French is almost, on a much more elevated level, to snatch the gun from the hands of a paratrooper'.[40]

Nationalist engagement, prison and a death sentence were not how Baya Hocine's much-loved mother had envisaged her daughter's future. If the political convictions of Baya Hocine's father made him reject a French education for her, her mother's social and educational aspirations for her daughter worked in the opposite direction. When Baya left school in 1956 to pursue the armed struggle full time, one of her saddest memories, in an interview she gave in the 1980s, is that of her mother's disappointment: 'She dreamt to see her daughter with the baccalaureate [...] Every prize I won [at school] was an immense joy for her. She did not understand why

I would stop studying, freeing the motherland was the job of the father, not that of a young girl still in school.'[41] Her brothers were also fairly indifferent to their sister's desire for action. In May 1956, Ahmed gave his sister a leaflet demanding that students leave their desks and join the *maquis*, but when she declared her intention to follow this call he shrugged and handed her some books to read.[42] After a brief spell transporting medicine and leaflets, in early 1957, Baya Hocine entered a bomb commando unit. The bombs planted by Baya Hocine and Djoher Akrour, at the stadiums of Alger and El Biar on 10 February 1957, resulted in ten deaths and thirty-six people injured.[43]

To Fadéla Mesli's cultural resistance, Baya Hocine brings the argument of the rights of man; to Baya Hocine's atheistic Marxism, Fadéla Mesli's early associations with nationalism were in its populist, religiously impregnated forms associated with Messali Hadj and the *'ulama*. To Fadéla Mesli's Arabo-Andalusian classical music, Baya Hocine brings Mexican social realism. What both women have in common, however, are mothers who have educational aspirations for their daughters. For it is not war alone which brought these women into the public sphere. In many cases, it was the confluence of the conditions of total war with the unexpected consequences of the social aspirations of urban families in the 1940s to educate their daughters within the slightly increased educational provision made for girls by the late colonial state. Through their emphasis on education, Mesli and Hocine's mothers inadvertently equipped their daughters with the skills and knowledge to go beyond the role of 'the woman at the door' and become active agents of revolution. School also put these young women in contact with a non-familial milieu where they could make political contacts. It is no coincidence that women in urban bomb networks – and particularly those who went on to plant bombs or join the *maquis* – had disproportionately high levels of literacy compared to the French Muslim population as a whole.

When she joined the FLN, Djamila Boupacha was working as an auxiliary nurse: in contrast, her mother did not speak French, and although her father spoke French he had received no formal education.[44] Louisette Ighilahriz describes herself as coming from a whole family of nationalists: 'My maternal grandfather was a gunsmith; in secret, he made arms for local revolutionaries'. Louisette describes her mother as 'illiterate but hyperpoliticised'.[45] Mimi

Maziz transported bomb-making materials in Algiers before joining the FLN's European network. She owes the fact that she was able to go to school to her mother's basic literacy. Mimi's mother had taken her daughter to register for school and was told that it was already full – children signed up in alphabetical order. However, her mother could see the list, and could see that a 'Meyer' had been signed up – she insisted that 'Ma' was before 'Me', and Mimi got her place.[46] Within some urban families a generational shift was taking place. It was a shift that many families did not easily accept and which left many behind, but it was nevertheless happening.

Alternative roots

Both Fadéla Mesli and Baya Hocine trace out clear political genealogies. For Fadéla Mesli, interviewed in 2005, a rich cultural heritage protected her family from losing its collective identity in the late nineteenth century, she paraphrases the 1930s *'ulama* and their insistence on language and culture, she was a member of the PPA–MTLD's UFMA before joining the FLN and going up to the *maquis*. Baya Hocine, writing in 1957–8, presents a different path, albeit one leading in the same direction: it is poverty, Marxism and her French education, perhaps even more than her father's engagement in the PPA–MTLD, which lead her to the FLN and the Algiers bomb network.

Other women, however, describe their engagement in the FLN as much more accidental. They do not insert themselves and their family histories into the established outlines of resistance trajectories stretching from the nineteenth century to the present day. During the War of Independence, there was not always a direct correlation between level of politicisation and the level of armed action women engaged in; within a highly secretive operation with necessarily difficult admission procedures, contingency could play a significant role in determining whom women would come into contact with, and what kind of roles they would be given.

Malika Koriche began our interview by underlining that before independence Algerians had nothing. They could not be educated in Arabic, only a tiny minority got an education – now, she points out, Arabic is Algeria's official language. Born in 1926, Malika attended school for only three years between the ages of seven and ten. At the age of fifteen, she was forcibly married by her parents, but divorced shortly afterwards.[47] Her brother was a member of the Scouts Musulmans Algériens (Algerian Muslim Scouts, SMA). The Muslim Scouts movement was established in Algeria in the interwar period, and played a key role in the spread of nationalist ideas amongst youth. The massacres in the Constantine region in May 1945, when thousands of Muslims were killed in a wave of brutal colonial repression, was triggered by the death of a Scout, Bouzid Chaal, in Sétif on 8 May 1945, during a demonstration to celebrate the liberation of Europe and demand Algerian independence.

Malika Koriche's initial emphasis on the importance of the Arabic language and the Scout movement locates her motivations within the familiar contours of the top-down state story of Algerian nationalism: the importance of cultural resistance and the framing of movements such as the SMA as a stepping stone on a linear path leading to the FLN. However, as Malika's story unfolded, it became clear that contingency and chance also played an important role in shaping her nationalist engagement.

It was Malika Koriche's brother who brought her into the nationalist movement in August 1956 by asking her to transport two revolvers, one of which belonged to her brother-in-law and the other to her neighbour who lived opposite and was 'like family'. Then her brother and his group were arrested. Malika Koriche confided in a female neighbour, Kheria, who lived in the apartment downstairs from her aunt, how upset she was. What Malika did not know was that Kheira's family was embedded in the Algiers urban guerrilla network. A week later, Malika was contacted by a FLN–ALN cell, that of Ali le Tailleur and Ramel. When Ali le Tailleur's cell was dismantled, Malika Koriche pretended to be his sister and visited him in prison to check if her new contact, Saïd Bakel, could be trusted. Reassured, Malika Koriche joined Saïd Bakel's cell and in June 1957 she planted two bombs at the Pointe Pescade seaside resort just outside Algiers.[48] In Malika's case, family networks and chance meetings brought her into contact with and gradually deepened her implication in the FLN's clandestine networks.

The fact that Malika Koriche had very little opportunity for formal education puts her to a certain extent in a similar situation to that of rural interviewees. As in rural areas, family and neighbours provided key points of access and guarantees of loyalty. But as we have seen in the accounts of Fadéla Mesli and Baya Hocine, for women who had been to school – which provided the location

for socialisation outside of the family based on political affinity –
different webs of contacts meshed together, crossing between old
and new modes of sociability. Therefore, when educated, urban
interviewees emphasise the contingency of their engagement, rather
than its roots in a recognisable nationalist genealogy, we need to
ask why.

Djamila Bouazza was a high-school student when she joined the
Algiers bomb network. She explained that her family were small
business owners who had no particular political activities. She
described studying history at school, listening to the radio, seeing
injustices and 'realising that we were colonised' but insisted that 'I
don't know what politics is', that she 'went to war as a civilian' –
she was given orders about where to plant bombs and she followed
these orders.[49] Arrested and put on trial in July 1957, Djamila
Bouazza and her co-accused Djamila Bouhired were condemned to
death. Djamila Bouazza's depoliticisation of her wartime engagement needs to be placed in the context of her husband's postwar
oppositional political activities which led to his whole family
being hounded. For Bouazza, insisting on patriotic apoliticism is
a long-practised form of protection from political persecution, as
Chapter 6 explores further.

Amongst some European women who joined the FLN and who
still live in Algeria today, the emphasis in their accounts is on the
inevitability of their engagement in the anti-colonial struggle – even
though their actions put them in a tiny minority compared to the
vast majority of the European population of Algeria, which was
characterised by varying degrees of hostility to independence.[50]
Precisely because the participation of these European women in the
nationalist movement was not obvious at all in the 'classic' trajectory of cultural resistance leading to armed uprising, these women
insist on their participation in the war as the logical conclusion of
their political beliefs and everyday experiences.

Annie Steiner's grandfather was a European settler, arriving in
Algeria from Italy in 1870. Her mother was of French origin. Unlike
many women of European origin who joined the anti-colonial
resistance, Annie was not from a Communist Party background.
When I asked her how she came to join the Algiers FLN network,
her reply was 'I came gradually, for lots of reasons' – although she
began to work for the FLN as early as 1954. In trying to understand the reasons for Annie Steiner's engagement, she talks about

realising how narrow-minded the settler population was. She had been to Paris and had seen that the city was 'much more open' compared to the 'very oppressive' European community in Algiers.[51] When she was arrested in October 1956 she was working for the Centres Sociaux, a social work project to improve education, health and professional training for French Muslims, created by the French resister and ethnologist Germaine Tillion in October 1955. This role exposed Annie Steiner to the misery of the lives of the colonised population, although not all social assistants in the Centres joined the FLN and Tillion herself was critical of both French abuses of power and FLN terrorism.[52]

The context of colonial discrimination and socio-economic misery inexorably leading individuals to joining the FLN is also a theme in Jacqueline Guerroudj's account. Jacqueline had arrived in Algeria from France in 1948, and worked as a teacher near Tlemcen. The headteacher of the school, Ahmed Triqui, was a communist, who according to Jacqueline helped her understand colonialism. But above all, Jacqueline Guerroudj says she saw the injustices of colonialism all around her, and, alongside a number of other communists, she joined the Algiers bomb network. Following her arrest and trial, Jacqueline Guerroudj was the only woman of European origin condemned to death.

Jacqueline Guerroudj euphemistically states that communists did not join the FLN 'like anyone else' but that individuals within the FLN welcomed them with varying degrees of enthusiasm or hostility.[53] The positions of the Parti Communiste Français (French Communist Party, PCF) and Parti Communiste Algérien (Algerian Communist Party, PCA) were, to say the least, ambiguous on the colonial question. The PCF leader Maurice Thorez maintained the view of Algeria as a 'nation in the process of formation'[54] and in March 1956 PCF deputies in the French National Assembly had voted the Special Powers Act, effectively handing control of Algeria over to the army. By 1 November 1954, the PCA had a firmly nationalist tone under the influence of prominent members such as Sadek Hadjeres, Larbi Bouhali and Abdelhamid Benzine, but much of the European working-class rank-and-file remained hostile to any notion of Algerian independence. Fear that the PCA might try to hijack the movement, or by their very presence scare off potential support from the Western bloc, meant that the FLN leadership was suspicious of the communists. They resisted the overtures of some

PCA members to form an FLN–PCA pact and sought to ensure that communists joined the front on an individual basis.

There is a kind of apolitical determinism in both Annie Steiner and Jacqueline Guerroudj's accounts. Other European settlers saw the same misery and discrimination and did not make the same choices as these two women. We might explain this depoliticisation and apoliticism in a number of ways. Firstly, although Annie Steiner was not a member of the PCA, or its post-independence clandestine successor, the Parti de l'Avant-Garde Socialiste (Avant-Garde Socialist Party, PAGS), she was close to it – in negotiations between the PCA and FLN she acted as a liaison agent. In order to protect the party from colonial oppression, and then from the repression of the post-independence state, secrecy and discretion have been the *modus operandi* for Algerian communists or communist sympathisers for at least seventy years. Secondly, the emphasis on circumstances dictating that they had to act – there was no other choice – in part helps these women to make sense of very difficult personal sacrifices. Both were mothers: Annie Steiner had two daughters, with whom she lost contact for a long time after the war as a result of her imprisonment. Jacqueline Guerroudj was the mother of five children when she was condemned to death. Lucette Hadj Ali had two boys whom she did not see for almost the entirety of the war. The marriages of both Lucette and Annie ended in the course of the war. The overriding moral and political imperative is important: it had to be worth it.

Insisting on the inevitable nature of their engagement is first and foremost, however, about insisting on their Algerianness. Some other – Muslim – interviewees express their respect for European women who joined the FLN through statements such as 'they didn't have to do it' – which implies they were not morally bound to join the struggle in the same way that it was a duty for Muslims.[55] This is a double-edged act of recognition: it turns the War of Independence into an ethno-cultural conflict, pitching Muslims against Europeans instead of anti-colonialists against partisans of French Algeria. By insisting that they *did* have to participate, these non-Muslim women of European origin are rejecting such a reading of the war: they too were morally obliged to act. Annie Steiner makes this case in my 2005 interview with her, in light of forty-three years of independence, the 'rediscovery' of Algeria's 'Arabo-Islamic collective identity' and the 1990s civil violence during which people of European origin were particular targets of Islamist terrorism and stigmatised as internal enemies: 'People who say that they are "Algerian", what does that mean? I'm profoundly Algerian. The Algeria of today, it's not the Algeria that I would have wanted, but I don't regret anything. Even during the terrorism [of the 1990s] I never thought that I could live otherwise.'[56]

This desire to insist on an (almost) primordial belief in Algerian independence, dating from long before 1 November 1954, can also be found in the account of Lucette Hadj Ali. Lucette says that the 1 November attacks came as no surprise: 'We [in the PCA] said to ourselves, right, it's starting!' Her grandfather was one of the founders of the Communist Party in Oran. Her father imbued his children from a young age with Marxist and anti-racist ideas. However, whilst Lucette was very aware of the struggle for social justice in terms of class, she admits that 'I had no idea what colonisation was'. In Oran, the European and Algerian populations lived separate existences: 'The only Algerians I saw was when I went to the market'. It was when Lucette went to Algiers to continue her studies during the Second World War that she says she really saw for the first time the misery in which Algerians lived, and 'what the colonial regime really was'.

Lucette was a member of the PCA and its Union des Femmes d'Algérie (Union of Women of Algeria, UFA). At first, the activities of the UFA entered little into the world of Muslim women. During the Second World War, the UFA organised housewives' committees to try to deal with the high price of food – but in many Muslim families, it was men, not women, who went to the market. After the Second World War, Lucette and her colleagues would demonstrate outside schools, demanding that Muslim children be allocated places in schools, and campaigning for Muslim women to be given the right to vote:

> In 1947, there were debates about the Statut d'Algérie [Statute of Algeria], and French women had had the right to vote for a year, and Algerian women didn't have it. So we organised demonstrations for the right to vote for Algerian women. We filled up a theatre to demand the right to vote for Algerian women.[57]

At this point, Lucette Hadj Ali's friend Naget Khadda, who was sitting in on the interview, interjected with a question about the

Statute of Algeria and the UFA campaign. The Statute of Algeria
sought to redefine the political structures of Algeria. Algeria
remained three departments of France with the Governor General
in Algiers reporting to the Minister for the Interior in Paris. An
Algerian Assembly (1948–56), possessing limited budgetary powers
and tasked with applying legislation, was elected through two
electoral colleges, each selecting sixty representatives. The first
electoral college was composed of 460,000 Europeans and 58,000
Muslims judged to be assimilated, the second college was made
up of 1,400,000 unassimilated Muslims.[58] Naget Khadda asked
Lucette Hadj Ali whether the demand for votes for Algerian women
was made on the same basis as the second college for men, that is
to say, remaining within the boundaries of this 'improved' electoral
system, which gave more colonised men the vote, but ensured that
the settlers retained majority rule despite being the demographic
minority.

> LHA: Oh yes, of course.
> NK: So that wasn't contested.
> LHA: It was at the time when the Statute hadn't yet been finalised, it
> was just afterwards that it was finalised.
> NV: In the UFA, were you more for greater equality, or explicitly for
> Algerian independence?
> LHA: Both at the same time. There was discrimination in welfare
> and social rights between French and Algerian, and therefore we
> demanded equality.
> NK: But the PCF was for a more equal France, not for an independ-
> ent Algeria.
> LHA: Yes, the PCF wanted Algeria to remain French, but we [the
> PCA] said 'we need an independent Algeria'. It wasn't said openly,
> they talked about liberation.
> NK: Maybe Algerians in the party like Bachir [Hadj Ali] said that.
> But the Europeans, they only came round later.
> LHA: Of course, of course.[59]

Indeed, the kinds of changes which the UFA was demanding –
votes for women and greater welfare and social rights – were
present in various colonial reform projects between 1944 and
1947, and would be actively implemented by the French authorities after May 1958 in an attempt to gain the support of Muslim
women for the maintenance of French rule in Algeria. It was
also in 1958 that Muslims – men and women – were accorded

political representation more in proportion with the size of the population. This discussion between Lucette Hadj Ali and Naget Khadda is an exchange between women of two different generations. Lucette was involved in politics before the War of Independence; her friend was not. Naget Khadda is looking back to pre-1954 political activity from the perspective of what happened next: independence through armed conflict. She tries to fit Lucette's earlier activities into a binary divide – of being 'for' or 'against' independence. This does not fit the context of 1945–54, when reformism could be a real challenge the colonial system, and not just a last-ditch attempt to uphold the status quo, as it became in 1954–62, and especially after 1958. However, by trying to understand whether the PCA was 'for' or 'against' independence, Naget Khadda reveals something interesting about Lucette Hadj Ali's account. Lucette does not deny the shifting positions of the PCA on the question of Algerian independence, nor the divergence of opinions within the party. However, in Lucette's initial presentation of the story, socio-economic campaigns and demands for women's voting rights are reframed as part of the build up to 1 November 1954. In this reframing, Lucette creates a communist pathway into the genealogy of anti-colonialism, pushing at the edges of an exclusive form of cultural nationalism to make it more inclusive.

Depoliticised unity in prison

By the end of 1957, the French army had 'won' – militarily at least – the 'Battle of Algiers'. Nevertheless, publicity surrounding the methods that they had used to do so, including torture and summary execution, provoked public outrage, notably amongst French intellectuals who launched a series of anti-torture and anti-colonial campaigns.[60] The political damage to French claims of moral authority and political legitimacy in Algeria was significant. Nevertheless, the FLN urban bomb network had been largely destroyed, with large numbers of its members, including – amongst the women I have interviewed – Djamila Boupacha, Djamila Bouazza, Zohra Drif, Baya Hocine, Zhor Zerari, Jacqueline Guerroudj and Malika Koriche, put on trial, sentenced and imprisoned. 'Justice' was a summary affair, steamrolling over usual legal processes using

exceptional legislation.[61] The first prison in which FLN activists
in Algiers were usually confined – later they would be transferred
to French prisons – was Barberousse, which had women's and
men's wings. Barberousse prison was built by the French in the
nineteenth century on the edge of the Casbah. During the War of
Independence, it was the location of fifty-eight executions, including the first two FLN militants guillotined in June 1956, Ahmed
Zabana and Abdelkader Ferradj.

The promiscuity of prison, its forced cohabitation and the
psychological pressure of being either condemned to death or
surrounded by people who were inevitably led to frayed nerves.
In Baya Hocine's prison diary, there are regular accounts of disputes with fellow inmates. At one point, talking about Djamila
Bouhired, Djamila Bouazza and Djoher Akrour, she wrote: 'I hate
them, as much as colonialism, more'[62] – such hyperbole reflects the
potent encounter between collective nationalist fervour and the
realities of individual personality clashes and moments of personal
despair.

The interest of Baya Hocine's diary lies not in these fiery
arguments – which were often quickly dissipated – but in the ways
in which Baya Hocine's disappointment that her nationalist co-
detainees did not live up to her idealised expectations of a nationalist movement were aggravated by class and political tensions:
'When I frequented daughters of pashas [high-ranking notables in
the Ottoman empire], muftis [senior Islamic scholars] and sectar-
ian communists, I had a cruel awakening'.[63] Hocine complained
about the 'bourgeois' attitudes of some of her co-detainees whom
she saw as having little conception of the war being 'for the people'.
On Christmas Day 1957, a heated discussion with 'D.B.' (probably
Bouhired) about God led Baya to call D.B. a 'fanatic' and D.B.
to call Baya a 'communist'.[64] Communist, though, Baya was not:
'Outside I hated reactionaries, here I learn to disdain communists
[...] Deep down, a European woman remains the same, deep down
they are all paternalist.'[65] This sense of 'paternalism' comes from
Baya feeling at times belittled as a result of the communist women's
supposedly greater political experience and more established organ-
isational structure than the 'FLN girls'. At the same time, it was
Eliette Loup, a communist, and, moreover, the daughter of a rich
landowner, who often comforted Baya. Baya Hocine's entry for
29 February 1957 read:

We are many. We have all fought for a common cause, each in her own way. We have students, doctors, law graduates, professors of literature, pharmacists, union leaders, and old Muslim women. All these people belong to different parties: FLN, PCA, PC (Christians) and MNA anarchists [*sic* – the MNA was not an anarchist movement, but rather a rival nationalist movement to the FLN]. It is difficult to unite them. A scission is slowly deepening.[66]

On 1 July 1957, Baya tried to initiate a discussion about how detainees would mark 5 July, the date of the French invasion of Algeria in 1830, which would later become Algerian independence day:

Total failure. Communists were neutral, one anarchist [anarchist is perhaps used here as an ideological description, rather than as a pejorative term for the MNA] said 'we haven't got any lessons in civics to receive, and we've had enough of following the crowd'. I had a confrontation with a *Messaliste* [supporter of the MNA] over the bomb attacks. In the evening, in the dormitory, the communists do their self-criticism.[67]

These groups of women clearly had very different ideas about what independent Algeria should look like, with wide-ranging arguments about the nationalist calendar, the place of religion and the type of socio-economic system which should be adopted. To further complicate this, these women were not recognised as political prisoners and were imprisoned alongside common-law detainees. Fadéla Mesli explains:

Me personally, I had no problem accepting the misery of the *maquis*, what was more difficult was being confronted with the common-law prisoners. Criminals and prostitutes ... we were well brought up young women. But we reacted quickly – they were humans like us, it was misery which pushed them to become what they were, and we quickly accepted them. We even worked to win them over to our cause.[68]

A similar argument was made in the 1961 publication *L'Aliénation colonialiste et la résistance de la famille algérienne* (Colonial alienation and the resistance of the Algerian family), part sociological study, part anti-colonial propaganda. Under the pseudonym Saadia-et-Lakhdar, Salima and Rabah Bouaziz, both leading members of the FF–FLN at the time, described prostitutes and dancers who participated in the nationalist struggle. For one woman quoted, this was a morally purifying experience: 'I am free from this dirty job, thanks to God and the trust which our brothers give us'.[69] In an interview in the 1980s, Baya Hocine reflected on the FLN's moralising drive with less certainty: 'They rounded up the prostitutes, the brothers had tried to ban prostitution, sometimes they picked them up. They beat them ... I didn't agree, but I had no power because what [these women] did was not pretty, at least according to the morals of the time.'[70]

These moments of division, doubt and social difference in prison co-existed alongside moments of great solidarity – making flags, shouting slogans in French and Arabic, fasting whether Muslim or not, singing the Free French resistance anthem *Le Chant des partisans* to enrage prison wardens, and using phrases such as 'France assassinates patriots', 'the ALN leads the Algerian people' and 'the warden hit the prisoner' to teach co-detainees to read and write Arabic.[71] The main opponent remained the prison administration, and the women put their differences aside to make their demands heard. In remembering Barberousse, however, many women skim over the political debates and instead present an almost ahistorical vision of feminine solidarity.

Writing in her memoirs, Jacqueline Guerroudj, whose husband Abdelkader was also in prison and also condemned to death, argues that political differences showed themselves in a much more pronounced way amongst men in prison than amongst the women.[72] When I interviewed Jacqueline, she did add, however, that Baya Hocine and Djoher Akrour were always 'at each other's throats'.[73] When, in the 1980s, Baya Hocine revisited a political schism in her own family described in her diary, which pitched her FLN father and brothers against her MNA uncle, she stated: 'It was men's business, there's lots of political talk amongst men. That is what is amazing amongst women, they don't talk about politics but they understand everything, and suddenly this silent mass can become an active player in a particular event.' In the 1980s, she referred to prison as a 'bad memory', nothing more, and then added that she had probably read too many books on the French resistance, which showed only the positive side of prisons and therefore had not prepared her at all for the reality.[74]

Yet reading Jacqueline Guerroudj's memoirs, *Des Douars et des prisons* (Villages and prisons, 1991), or listening to contemporary interviews with women who were imprisoned in Barberousse might have the same effect for subsequent generations. This romanticisation and gendered essentialism ('women don't talk about that') can in part be explained by the effects of time passing, and also as a coping mechanism to make painful memoires safe. Towards the end of her memoir, Jacqueline Guerroudj states: 'I reread and I realise with consternation that, without having lied about anything, my story is not entirely true. I have involuntarily applied the reflexes of survival: bury the intolerable, cultivate the supportable, savour the agreeable or the positive, dust the lot with a bit of humour and serve up warm.'[75] We also need to take into account, however, the post-independence context and the impact of this on firstly, the idealisation of the war years as a political critique of the present and, secondly, the need to depoliticise the war, to bury differences that might be divisive or dangerous for society as well as the individual, to ensure that the war remains a social glue. This is a central theme of Chapter 6.

Confusing sides and the enemy within

For Fatima Berci:

> The women who joined the *maquis*, they were luckier than us who stayed, they were less exposed. We were defenceless – at any moment they [the French army] could come, break down the door [...] The French came, they surrounded us, they made us come out, they smashed the roofs, and then the *mujahidin*, they came and they made us rebuild our houses.

In her village of Agraradj, Fatima is recognised locally as one of the leading organisers of women's logistical support during the war and she emphatically states 'we were ready to die for our country'. However, she stresses that the villagers had little room for manoeuvre whomever they might have wanted to support: 'There was too much pressure,' she says, 'we were caught between two fires. There was France and there were the *mujahidin* who made us stay.'[76]

In February 1958, the populations of Agraradj, Ibeskeine and Tazerout Bou-Amar – around 2,200 people – were 'regrouped', or, less euphemistically, forcibly displaced, into the villages of Aghribs, Taguercift and Ikherbane where an army-run Section Administrative Spécialisée (Specialised Administrative Section, SAS)

Figure 1 French soldiers patrol homes in the *douars* (villages)
of Kabylia, 1957

could keep close control over their movements and activities.[77]
Before this effective 'shutting down' of the village, Agraradj was
subject to regular French army operations. To take just one four-
week period: on 8 August 1956 the village was sealed off and all
houses searched; on 4 September 1956 French soldiers once again
sealed off the village with the aim of capturing two 'notorious
fellagas'; three days later, on 7 September 1956, soldiers once again
set out to Agraradj to capture 'HLL [Hors-la-loi, or outlaw] BERSI
[*sic*] el BACHIR' and 'to destroy his home in reprisal'.[78] Fatima
Berci regularly evokes Bachir Berci's name as part of a litany of
male relatives killed during the war which punctuates her account
at regular intervals: 'Berci Bachir, Berci Mohand, Berci Saïd, Berci
Rezki ...'.[79]

Fatima Berci says her home was burnt down three times by French soldiers. In the same village, Fatma Yermeche's family home was also burnt down twice. In Bouzeguene, the home of Ferroudja Amarouche's parents was destroyed when the French discovered she was cooking for the *mujahidin* there. The women talk about soldiers pouring petrol and defecating into their grain supplies and forcing women to gather stones to rebuild bridges blown up by rural guerrillas. When the villagers saw the French soldiers coming, any men left ran off into the forest to avoid being shot or arrested – leaving the women to face up to the interrogations. Fatma Yermeche explains:

> When they [the French soldiers] asked me questions [such as], 'Have you cooked for the *mujahidin*?' I denied everything, I said, 'I haven't seen them and I haven't cooked for them.' They beat us. They made us drink soapy water, [they used] electricity [to torture us], the women too, especially those who were suspected of having cooked.[80]

Rural women willingly hid, fed and carried out other tasks for the *mujahidin*, but had no illusions about their fate if they stopped doing this. In the words of Fatima Berci: 'If you left, it was like you were betraying your country. We were beyond being scared.'[81] In the village Aït Abderrahmane, Chérifa Akache was arrested by the French army, who then began to torture her to try and extract information. Chérifa Akache says she could stand the pain because 'I preferred to die a heroine for the revolution than be killed by the *mujahidin* as a traitor'. Under torture, however, men and women did break and give the French army information. 'Traitors' are a shady presence in these rural women's accounts – very much present but always anonymous or living in another village. Chérifa Akache said she had to change village seven times because her activities were denounced. When I asked her who the informers were, she said it was often young people who had helped the *mujahidin*, running errands or keeping lookout: 'When [the French army] caught the young ones ... [*she trails off*] it was especially the very young ones whom [the *mujahidin*] sent to bring food [who informed]'.[82] In the incident that led to Chérifa Akache's arrest in January 1959, soldiers broke down her door at midnight, accompanied by a woman from another village who had cooked for the *mujahidin* alongside Chérifa Akache, but who Chérifa Akache said had subsequently become a denouncer.

Yet, if we read this woman's story though Chérifa Akache's account, this 'denouncer' becomes a much more ambiguous figure. Chérifa Akache says she herself was tortured with electricity and had her stomach pumped with soapy water. It is likely that the woman who informed on her had received similar treatment. When Chérifa Akache refused to say anything, the soldiers confronted the two women. The informer then denied that she knew Chérifa Akache and started contradicting herself. She was beaten as a result. The two women were taken to a forest where the *mujahidin* were thought to be. The informer started seeing *mujahidin* everywhere, literally shouting 'I can see one over there'. It seems clear that by this point the informer was so terrified she was hallucinating. Can this frightened woman, who cooked for the *maquisards*, really be classed as a traitor? For the *mujahidin*, there was no room for doubt. Soon after this incident, they slit her throat.

All the rural women whom I interviewed expressed a particular disdain for *goumiers* or *harkis*, two terms generically used by these women to describe Muslims from Algeria who served as auxiliaries in the French army. In 1961, there were an estimated 120,000 Muslim auxiliaries. They joined the French army for a variety of reasons – some to escape poverty, some as an act of opposition to the FLN, some were pro-French, others were coerced – and they fulfilled different kinds of roles.[83] Chérifa Akache remembers the night she was arrested: 'There were *harkis* with them, and they shouted at us in Kabyle [Tamazight] "donkey, open the door"'.[84] Her interrogator – who was a *harki* – rapidly dismissed her attempts to adopt the identity of her sister not only because he could speak the same language as her, but also because he was familiar with the region and in all likelihood her family. Fatima Berci says: 'It was a clean war as long as there were no *goumiers*. The *goumiers* did a lot of harm.' She reiterates, 'When it was the French [soldiers], it was OK. But as soon as they brought in the *harkis*, they knew the population and the problems began.'[85]

Clearly we should be very wary of concluding that Muslim auxiliaries were more likely to cause 'problems'. That these women single out *harkis* as particularly brutal could be a post-hoc reading, transposing the popular insult that *harki* has become in independent Algeria – a synonym for traitor – on to an archetype of the basest of men. The local knowledge which *harkis* possessed made them more dangerous because they could identify and more effectively interrogate women suspected of supporting the FLN, but this does not make them more likely to be violent. Fatima Berci's association of the *harkis* with 'problems' could also be because of the kinds of roles which Muslim auxiliaries were assigned. Notably, they were used as part of shock troop units (*Commandos de chasse*) which tracked down *maquisards* from village to village over extended periods of time during Challe's Jumelles operation (June 1959–March 1960). This meant that they were physically present in villages to a far greater extent. Operations Jumelles was also the most intense moment of the war for these rural interviewees – daily life consisted of aerial bombardment, harassment from the French army and a worsening food crisis.

Moreover, distinguishing between collaborator and resister during the war was not easy, and switching sides happened in both directions. The line between 'supporter' and 'opponent' was one that it could be all too easy for civilians to cross. The French army sought to pressurise captured FLN soldiers into enlisting, and the FLN deliberately targeted the wives of Muslims enrolled in the French army to get them to persuade their husbands to desert. In Bouzeguene, local women targeted the wives of *moghaznis* – the term used to refer to Muslim auxiliaries working for the SAS – to try to persuade them to get their husbands to desert.[86] The actions of those whom interviewees describe as *harkis* could also be more than ambiguous. After her arrest and three months in prison, Chérifa Akache became very ill. The French army provided a helicopter for her to Tizi Ouzou, not as a humanitarian gesture but in order to bring her to court in the regional capital of Kabylia. She was asked to identify faces in a series of photographs, but she remembered the same version of events which she had previously provided and was released. By this point, Chérifa Akache was seriously ill and wanted to join her parents in Algiers. She states that she went to Algiers under the identity of the wife of her brother-in-law who was 'with the French army': 'They [the *mujahidin*] asked him to get me some identity papers'. When I asked Chérifa how her *harki* brother-in-law came to work with the *mujahidin*, she explains that he was a double agent, although she defines this as being 'with one lot and then with the other', rather than being on one 'side' throughout and just pretending to be with the other: 'This *harki* accompanied me. The *mujahidin* said [to her] "You should go to Algiers, because you keep getting arrested and it's better that you go." Once I arrived in

Algiers, I went to stay with my parents at El Harrach and I stopped all activity.'[87]

By 1960, Fatima Berci, Fatma Yermeche, Fatima Benmohand Berci, Chérifa Akache and Ferroudja Amarouche had lost their homes and livelihoods and numerous members of their families had been killed. The *mujahidin* in their region had largely been defeated. These women had been displaced, or they had moved to stay with family in other regions. Their active participation in the war was over. The *harki* metaphor, however, remains a powerful way in which they structure their lives, with the interior enemy which they see as still amongst them blamed for a host of post-independence difficulties.

Conclusion

The dominant nationalist genealogy in Algeria today is that of the armed resistance led by figures such as the Emir Abdelkader, Fatma N'Soumer and El Mokrani after the 1830 invasion giving way to cultural resistance from 1871 onwards. Then, in the 1930s, religious reformist movements such as the *'ulama* gave a political impetus to this cultural resistance, and movements such as the Scouts and the ENA–PPA–MTLD provided the training ground necessary for the creation of the FLN. In this dominant nationalist genealogy, the FLN is depicted as the culmination of, and necessary improvement upon, everything that went before, destined to lead Algeria to independence through armed struggle.

When we compare this linear narrative with how interviewees in 2005 explain their motivations for joining the anti-colonial struggle, its imprint is traceable, notably amongst urban, educated interviewees, who have been exposed to it to a significant degree both during the war and after independence. The desire to belong to this narrative of the nation also explains why interviewees of European origin weave their political and personal trajectories into the same end point – the FLN and armed struggle – if not the same cultural beginnings.

Baya Hocine's 1957–8 diary, produced in a very different context, when it was far from certain that the author, or Algeria, would ever see independence, suggests much more heterogeneous paths into the anti-colonial struggle, with enduring differences of political opinion amongst women continuing, and, indeed, being exacerbated, in prison. Yet even amongst urban women interviewed in 2005 who reproduce a familiar nationalist genealogy, the messiness of experience emerges. Some educated women's engagement was the unintended consequence of the limited educational opportunities offered by the late colonial state. Families – and especially mothers – of activists had conflicting aspirations: they wanted to support the anti-colonial struggle, but also demanded that their children seize rare opportunities for social mobility. Chance, contingency and accident also explain the kinds of roles that interviewees came to play in the conflict.

The way in which rural interviewees explain their engagement in the anti-colonial struggle does not conform to the classic nationalist narrative because they evade a recognisable chronology. This does not mean that their accounts are without structure: interviewees have told their stories to each other and their families many times before, leading to some degree of standardisation. But there is no 1 November 1954 or 5 July 1962. Instead, there are local events, local men, the religious calendar and births, marriages and deaths. These local and regional frames of reference neither confirm nor contradict the national memory, rather they co-exist alongside it. Rural, illiterate women also arrive at the same end point as urban, educated women: they fought for Algeria, and they talk about doing it willingly, whilst also making it understood that refusal was not really a choice.

Yet when interviewees attribute meaning to the individual, complicated stories they tell, they are unequivocal. For rural women, the war is a symbol of their unrecognised sacrifice for Algeria. For both rural and urban women, the war is a symbol of collective purity of purpose. As Chapter 2 will demonstrate, if boundaries were crossed – and notably gender boundaries – this was rendered licit by the greater ideal. Thus while these oral histories undermine certain elements of the glorified national discourse, in that they introduce the messiness of experience, the mismatch and sometimes incoherent co-existence between the personal, local, regional and national, they also reproduce its abstract, idealistic reading of the past.

Rather than talking about 'official history', which is often set up in opposition to 'vernacular' memory, it might be more useful to talk about a dominant history, or at least dominant moral reading, generally held to be true in its broad strokes. This dominant narrative is important because for each of these women it is what ties her to the nation-state. For rural women with very little contact with the state, it is a social contract based on a blood debt. This view would be reinforced by the post-independence system of pensions and privileges for *mujahidin* and widows and children of *shuhada* (martyrs of the war). For European women, it is proof of their Algerianness. This view would be reinforced by the 1963 Nationality Law, which adopted an ethno-cultural definition of Algerianness, with exceptions made for Europeans who had participated in the War of Independence and who were thus considered to have 'earned' the right to be Algerian. For some of the urban, educated Muslim *mujahidat* who from the 1980s onwards would lean on their wartime role to campaign on women's rights issues, the war would provide irrefutable proof of their belonging to the nation – they were not 'Westernised' outsiders. This is why, when they tell their war stories, these women simultaneously undermine the myth and reinforce it. During the war, the men and women who fought for independence were not a monolithic bloc. But everyone wants it to have been so.

Notes

1 Interview with Fatima Benmohand Berci (17 June 2005).
2 As Gilbert Meynier underlines, 'In the first months of the war, the reality of the FLN on the ground in Algeria was that of networks of connivance and clientelism which had their origins in the pre-[Second World] war period, mainly from MTLD radicalism, the dismantled pro-independence party'. *Histoire intérieure du FLN 1954–1962* (Paris: Fayard, 2002), p. 258.
3 Interview with Fatima Benmohand Berci (17 June 2005).
4 *Ibid.*
5 Interview with Fatma Yermeche (16 June 2005).
6 Interview with Chérifa Akache (21 June 2005).
7 Interview with Ferroudja Amarouche (10 December 2005).
8 Amirouche Aït Hamouda joined the *maquis* in 1954 and was head of the *wilaya* III (Kabylia) 1957–59. Si Haoues, the *nom de guerre* of Ahmed Ben Abderrezak, rallied to the FLN in 1957, having been in the rival nationalist movement, the MNA. Si Haoues became head of the *wilaya* VI (south).
9 Interview with Fatima Benmohand Berci (17 June 2005).
10 J. J. Byrne, 'Our own special brand of socialism: Algeria and the contest

of modernities in the 1960s', *Diplomatic History*, 33:3 (2009), 427–47, p. 430.
11 Interview with Fatma Yermeche (16 June 2005).
12 Interview with Ferroudja Amarouche (10 December 2005).
13 Interview with Fatima Benmohand Berci (17 June 2005).
14 Si Abdallah, the *nom de guerre* of Mohamed Salah Maghni, was a captain in the *wilaya* III (Kabylia), killed in 1959.
15 Interview with Fatima Benmohand Berci (17 June 2005).
16 For an oral history of soldiers in the French army, see J.-C. Jauffret, *Soldats en Algérie 1954–1962* (Paris: Autrement, 2nd edn, 2011 [2000]). For a history of the 'regroupment camps' which displaced large sections of the rural population of Algeria, see M. Cornaton, *Les Camps de regroupement de la guerre d'Algérie* (Paris: Harmattan, 1998).
17 Interview with Ferroudja Amarouche (10 December 2005).
18 Interview with Fatima Berci (16 June 2005).
19 Interview with Chérifa Akache (21 June 2005).
20 An opponent of Ben Bella and the EMG's seizure of power in 1962, and Boumediene's coup in 1965, Krim Belkacem was assassinated in Frankfurt in October 1970, strangled with a tie in a hotel room. However, it is much more difficult to cast Krim as a wartime democrat. With Abdelhafid Boussouf and Lakhdar Ben Tobbal, Krim Belkacem formed the '3B', a formidable power base within the FLN–ALN for a large part of the war. The 3B are widely suspected of being implicated in the December 1957 murder of rival Abane Ramdane, the man credited with turning the FLN–ALN into an effective organisation from November 1955 onwards. A. M. Amer, 'La Crise du Front de libération nationale de l'été 1962: indépendance et enjeux de pouvoirs' (PhD dissertation, Université Paris Diderot (Paris 7), 2010), p. 19.
21 S. Sadi, *Amirouche: une vie, deux morts, un testament* (Paris: L'Harmattan, 2010), p. 24.
22 *Ibid.*, pp. 15–16.
23 T. DeGeorges, 'The shifting sands of revolutionary legitimacy: the role of former mujahidin in the shaping of Algeria's collective memory', *Journal of North African Studies*, 14:2 (2009), 273–88, p. 274.
24 *Le Matin DZ* (4 October 2010) www.lematindz.net/news/9759-abd elhafidhyaha-les-martyrs-du-ffs-de-63-ne-sont-pas-a-vendre.html (accessed 19 May 2014).
25 Interview with Fatima Berci (16 June 2005).
26 Interview with Ferroudja Amarouche (10 December 2005).
27 S. Amin, *Chauri Chaura, Event, Metaphor, Memory* (Berkeley: University of California Press, 1995), p. 190.
28 Amrane, *Les Femmes algériennes dans la guerre*, p. 27.
29 Using a questionnaire given out to twenty-five *fida'iyat* registered in the

Ministry of Mujahidin, Djamila Amrane found similar statistics: only three of them were illiterate. *Les Femmes algériennes dans la guerre*, p. 91.

30 For more on Messali Hadj and the MNA, see the pioneering biography of Benjamin Stora, *Messali Hadj: pionnier du nationalisme algérien, 1898–1974* (Paris: L'Harmattan, 1986), as well as the more recent work by Nedjib Sidi Moussa, 'Devenirs messalistes (1925–2013): Sociologie historique d'une aristocratie révolutionnaire' (PhD dissertation: Université Paris 1 (Panthéon-Sorbonne), 2013).
31 Interview with Fadéla Mesli (20 December 2005).
32 F. Sadiqi, *Women, Gender and Language in Morocco* (Leiden, Boston: Brill, 2003), p. 93. As Fatima-Zohra Sai underlines in *Mouvement national et question féminine: des origines à la veille de la Guerre de libération nationale* (Algiers: Editions Dar El Gharb, 2002), between the 1920s and 1940s in Algeria, there was a national struggle and a class struggle but no specific women's struggle.
33 Interview with Fadéla Mesli (20 December 2005).
34 Amrane, *Les Femmes algériennes dans la guerre*, p. 159. In total, around 1,500 FLN activists received the death penalty during the War of Independence. It is estimated that between 198 and 222 men were executed. S.Thénault, *Une Drôle de justice: les magistrats dans la guerre d'Algérie* (Paris: La Découverte, 2001), pp. 313–14, and F. Malye and P. Oudart, 'Les Guillotinés de Mitterrand', *Le Point* (31 August 2001).
35 Service historique de la défense, Paris (hereafter SHD), 1H1246/D2: Journal de Baya Hocine.
36 *Ibid.*
37 Meynier, *Histoire intérieure du FLN*, p. 236.
38 SHD, 1H1246/D2: Journal de Baya Hocine.
39 Guy Pervillé discusses how the interwar generation of French-educated Algerian students viewed France as a monolithic bloc, whereas the post-1945 generation made a distinction between 'ideal' France (the values of 1789) and 'legal' France (France of colonial repression). See 'Le Sentiment national des étudiants algériens de culture française de 1912 à 1962', *Relations internationales*, 2 (1974), 233–59, and *Les Etudiants algériens de l'université française* (Paris: Editions du CNRS, 1984).
40 Interview in 1962 reproduced in K. Yacine, *Le Poète comme un boxer: entretiens 1958–1989* (Paris: Editions du Seuil, 1994).
41 Amrane, *Des Femmes algériennes dans la guerre d'Algérie* (Paris: Karthala, 1994), pp. 143–6.
42 SHD, 1H1246/D2: Journal de Baya Hocine.
43 SHD, 1H1245.
44 G. Halimi and S. de Beauvoir, *Djamila Boupacha* (Paris: Gallimard, 1962), p. 47 and p. 227.

45 L. Ighilahriz with A. Nivat, *Algérienne* (Paris: Fayard and Calmann Lévy, 2001), pp. 27–8 and p. 78.
46 Interview with Mimi Maziz (18 December 2005).
47 *Pour toi ma patrie: Combattantes de la lutte armée, les femmes aussi écriront leur histoire* (*El Djazaïria* publication, c. 1974).
48 Interview with Malika Koriche (18, 21 and 22 December 2005).
49 Interview with Djamila Bouazza (3 and 9 June 2005).
50 Although men and women of European origin who participated in the anti-colonial struggle in Algeria were a tiny minority, they are relatively well represented in the autobiographical literature. Most famous is Henri Alleg, whose exposé of the use of torture by the French army in Algeria in *La Question* (first published in 1958 by Editions de minuit) had a wide impact within and beyond France. His *Mémoire algérienne* was published in 2005 (Paris: Stock). Women of European origin who joined the FLN have also published their memoirs: J. Guerroudj, *Des Douars et des prisons* (Algiers: Bouchène, 1991), H. Ameyar, *La Moudjahida Annie Fiorio-Steiner, une vie pour l'Algérie* (Algiers: Association les amis de Abdelhamid Benzine, 2011) and E. S. Lavalette, *Juste algérienne: comme une tissure* (Algiers: Barzakh, 2013). See also the monograph by A. Dore-Audibert, *Des Françaises d'Algérie dans la guerre de libération* (Paris: Karthala, 1995).
51 Interview with Annie Steiner (22 June 2005).
52 G. Tillion, *Les Ennemis complémentaires* (Paris: Editions de Minuit, 1962 [1960]).
53 Interview with Jacqueline Guerroudj (15 and 18 December 2005).
54 Maurice Thorez speaking in Algiers in March 1939, quoted in M. Evans, *Algeria: France's Undeclared War* (Oxford: Oxford University Press: 2012), p. 75.
55 This is not only a common discourse amongst women. After the communist militant Henri Maillot's death in the *maquis* in June 1956, admiring comments often took the form 'He's more Muslim than us', despite Maillot's insistence that he was Algerian of European origin and that Algeria was also his motherland. S. Hadjeres, '1956: FLN et PCA: Rencontres et premiers accords', *Quotidien d'Oran* (1 July 2009).
56 Interview with Annie Steiner (22 June 2005). In this context of insisting on one's Algerianness, it is no surprise that the subtitle to Steiner's mémoires is 'a life for Algeria', or that the title of Eveline Safir Lavalette's autobiography is 'Just Algerian'. Lavalette, whose background was in Catholic youth movements and the journal *Consciences maghribines*, also presents her affiliation with the FLN as the logical conclusion of her previous activities – 'I read the 1 November declaration, and I make it mine' – despite being, as Ghania Mouffok, who prefaces the

autobiography, underlines, a 'European woman of good family', *Juste algérienne*, p. 41 and p. 17.
57 Interview with Lucette Hadj Ali (18 December 2005).
58 Evans, *Algeria: France's Undeclared War*, p. 102.
59 Interview with Lucette Hadj Ali (18 December 2005).
60 The role of French intellectuals in campaigning for an end to the Algerian War has a large literature. See for example, J. D. Le Sueur, *Uncivil War: Intellectuals and Identity Politics during the Decolonization of Algeria* (Lincoln: University of Nebraska Press, 2nd edn, 2005).
61 See Thénault, *Une Drôle de justice*.
62 SHD, 1H1246/D2: Journal de Baya Hocine, entry 23 February 1958.
63 SHD, 1H1246/D2: Journal de Baya Hocine, entry 11 October 1957.
64 SHD, 1H1246/D2: Journal de Baya Hocine, entry 25 December 1957.
65 SHD, 1H1246/D2: Journal de Baya Hocine, entry 8 September 1957.
66 SHD, 1H1246/D2: Journal de Baya Hocine, entry 29 February 1957. Hocine's dismissal of the MNA as 'anarchists' might be understood more as a critique of what she sees as their role in creating disorder within the anti-colonial struggle.
67 SHD, 1H1246/D2: Journal de Baya Hocine, entry 1 July 1957.
68 Interview with Fadéla Mesli (20 December 2005).
69 Saadia-et-Lakhdar, *L'Aliénation colonialiste et la résistance de la famille algérienne* (Lausanne: La Cité, 1961), p. 140. The study was also published in *Les Temps modernes*.
70 Amrane, *Des Femmes dans la guerre d'Algérie*, p. 146.
71 SHD, 1H1246/D2.
72 Guerroudj, *Des Douars et des prisons*, p. 65.
73 Interview with Jacqueline Guerroudj (15 and 18 December 2005).
74 Amrane, *Des Femmes dans la guerre d'Algérie*, p. 144.
75 Guerroudj, *Des Douars et des prisons*, p. 85.
76 Interview with Fatima Berci (16 June 2005).
77 Archives Nationales d'Outre Mer, Aix en Provence (hereafter ANOM), 5/SAS/5: Aghribs.
78 *Ibid.*
79 Interview with Fatima Berci (16 June 2005).
80 Interview Fatma Yermeche (16 June 2005).
81 Interview with Fatima Berci (16 June 2005).
82 Interview with Chérifa Akache (21 June 2005).
83 C.-R. Ageron, 'Le "drame des Harkis": mémoire ou histoire?', *Vingtième siècle*, 68 (2000), 3–15, p. 3. The French army had a long history of recruiting local men to conquer and control its colonial empire: *goumier* is a general term to describe Muslim auxiliaries in the French army during the whole colonial period, particularly from the Second World War onwards. *Harkis* were a category of Muslim auxiliaries in

the French army, brought together in units called *harkas*, who were participated in military operations. Since 1962, both terms, but especially the term *harki*, are generically used in Algeria to refer – pejoratively – to all types of Muslim auxiliaries to the French army and administration. See F.-X. Hautreux, *La Guerre d'Algérie des Harkis, 1954–1962* (Paris: Perrin, 2013).

84 Interview with Chérifa Akache (21 June 2005).
85 Interview with Fatima Berci (16 June 2005).
86 SHD, 1H1532 and ANOM, 5/SAS/18: Bouzeguene.
87 Interview with Chérifa Akache (21 June 2005).

2

Heroines and victims, brothers and sisters

Gendered discourses and national identities

The Algerian War of Independence was a battle to win 'hearts and minds' as much as a military conflict. Between 1954 and 1962, in the struggle to prove who had the popular legitimacy and political credibility either to maintain French Algeria or to create a new independent state, the image, role and rights of 'the Muslim woman' were a key area of confrontation.

Using 'the Muslim woman' as a measure of the possibilities and limitations of the French 'civilising mission' or as the last bulwark against colonial interference in the autochthonous family was not a wartime innovation. In nineteenth-century Algeria, the attention paid by French military personnel, social scientists and political lobbyists to detailing Muslim women's dress, morals, social status and cultural practices was intimately linked to both justifications for French rule and the creation of a state of exception.[1] A law passed on 14 July 1865 declared that the indigenous Muslim man was French, and thus subject to military service and able to join the civil service, but that he could not benefit from the full rights of French citizenship unless he rejected his 'Muslim personal status' in matters of family law. This 'personal status' consisted of customs considered to be at odds with the French civil code, notably the prerogative of fathers to choose the spouses of their children, polygamy, the right of husbands to unilaterally dissolve their marriage (repudiation), the theory of the 'sleeping child' which allowed children born between ten months and five years after the end of a marriage to be recognised as legitimate, and the privileging of male descendants over female in matters of inheritance. In short, what the French state saw as the distinctive features of the way in which Islam regulated relations between men and women was what made

Muslim men unassimilable into the French nation.[2] In practice, this was a convenient way for a numerical minority to justify the political exclusion of the majority, in what was meant to be an integral part of French territory, where, in theory, all male citizens benefited from universal suffrage.[3]

The status of Algeria as three departments of France and the presence of a significant settler minority meant that the political, economic, social and cultural effects of colonisation were inescapable. By the late nineteenth century, armed opposition to colonial rule had given way to cultural resistance. As we have seen in Chapter 1, families migrated to Morocco, Tunisia, Syria, Palestine and Egypt, or refused to send their children to French schools. Given the colonial obsession with categorising, painting and photographing the Muslim woman, hiding her from the European gaze (through veiling, or confining her to the home) and resisting attempts at 'Frenchification' were politicised acts. If religion became, in the words of Jacques Berque, a 'bastion of withdrawal' for the colonised population,[4] the Muslim woman – through the invisibility of her body and her proclaimed moral purity – was the symbol of its impenetrability.[5] Whilst this was a common response to European domination across North Africa and the Middle East in the late nineteenth and early twentieth centuries, the duration and scale of colonisation in Algeria meant that the Algerian Muslim woman acquired a particularly acute symbolic importance. This left much less political space for Algerian reformers to question the status of women within their own societies. Although his ideas travelled to Algeria, there was no Algerian equivalent of Egyptian intellectual Qasim Amin, who in the late nineteenth century argued that it was in the interest of the 'nation' to educate women, transform their dress and bring them into public sphere of work and politics.[6] When the Tunisian writer Tahar Haddad published in 1930 *The Status of Women in Islamic Law and Society*, which criticised practices such as veiling, forced marriage, seclusion, polygamy and repudiation, he was attacked by the leading Algerian religious scholar Ben Badis, who accused Haddad of promoting 'Francisation' and 'de-Islamisation'.[7] Such binary oppositions between 'Muslim women' and 'French culture' were inevitably much more pronounced in nationalist and colonial discourses than in the everyday experiences of men and women, for whom the boundaries between 'us' and 'them' could be much more blurred.

The 1947 Statute of Algeria extended citizenship rights to all Muslim men, but a single electoral college in which European and Muslim votes had equal weight was introduced only in 1958, in the lead up to the referendum on the new constitution of the Fifth Republic. In 1946, French women in France and European women in Algeria acquired the vote for the first time. This right was not extended to Muslim women, supposedly out of respect for 'custom' and 'tradition'. As in 1865, under the cloak of cultural sensitivity, Muslims – this time Muslim women – were excluded from political rights. The hypocrisy of this situation did not escape contemporary observers. In 1951, Marie-Hélène Lefaucheux, former member of the French resistance and founding member of the Commission on the Status of Women at the United Nations, pointedly highlighted the incongruity of not extending the right to vote to Muslim women in Algeria when many members of the Arab League were in the process of granting women's suffrage.[8]

The War of Independence created the conditions to reshape how women were used to imagine the nation – or rather, a series of competing nations. From 1955 onwards, with efforts intensifying after 1958, rather than using the 'difference' of the Muslim woman to exclude Muslim men and women, the French state made concerted efforts to appeal to Muslim women, through whom, it was hoped, the 'hearts and minds' of the Muslim family could be won. In a burst of last-ditch welfare colonialism, a raft of measures were introduced to try and prove that only France could 'emancipate' Muslim women from the oppression of tradition and cloistering. These included implementing voting rights for women in 1958, installing a Muslim woman in government office, establishing new schooling and healthcare programmes, encouraging women to unveil in public ceremonies and, in 1959, effectively ending the 'Muslim personal status' by bringing marriage under civil rather than religious jurisdiction. Liberty, equality and fraternity, or, to be more precise, becoming 'modern' mothers and housewives, meant not only being ruled by France but becoming Frenchwomen. This tardy, and ultimately doomed, nation-building project was aimed as much at external observers of the Algerian issue – that is to say, validating claims that Algeria was France to the international community – as at domestic audiences in Algeria.

The FLN's response was equally sensitive to international opinion. Through tracts, newspaper articles and photographs of

uniformed women bearing arms in the *maquis*, nationalists insisted
that emancipation from colonial rule was the essential precondi-
tion to women's liberation. In January 1961, the FLN sent three
delegates to the Afro-Asian Women's Conference in Cairo. Mamia
Chentouf, Djamila Rahal and Leila Benouniche were experienced
representatives of the nationalist movement, and they took with
them to Egypt a message from Ferhat Abbas, president of the
GPRA:

> In Algeria, the Woman's contribution in the armed struggle is not
> limited to a secondary part. She is taking part in this struggle arms
> in hand, just like her fighting brothers. However, in Algeria – like in
> other Afro-Asian countries, the role of women could not possibly be
> limited to this first stage of the liberation struggle. In these countries,
> women are the symbol of the new generation and it is therefore
> towards the process of shaping the new societies that their efforts
> should be guided. It is in this line [*sic*] that the woman could really
> free herself and be considered as an essential element of progress.[9]

Before joining the FLN, Abbas had been a founding member of the
Union Démocratique du Manifeste Algérien (Democratic Union of
the Algerian Manifesto, UDMA), a reformist, middle-class organisation created in 1946 whose ideas about women were influenced
by intellectuals such as Qasim Amin. Abbas's words also echo those
of a writer from a very different era and political and cultural background: the Martiniquais psychiatrist, writer and anti-colonialist
Frantz Fanon.

From 1957 onwards, Frantz Fanon was a journalist for the
FLN's clandestine newspaper *El Moudjahid*. He wrote extensively
on the role of Algerian women in the independence struggle, declaring that 'the liberty of the Algerian people can be identified with the
emancipation of women and their entry into history'.[10] Women's
active participation in the struggle was depicted as revolutionary
and revolutionising: 'Algerian society reveals itself not to be the
womanless society that has been so well described. Side-by-side
with us, our sisters upset a little more of the enemy's plan of attack
and definitively liquidate old myths.'[11] This was an important
weapon in combating the French government's depiction of the
nationalist struggle as a minority movement led by religious fanat-
ics and backed by Gamal Abdel Nasser, portrayed as 'a "Muslim
Mussolini"' with a pan-Arab imperialist agenda.[12] The new model

of the 'liberated Algerian woman' counteracted racial stereotypes
of both the submissive Arab woman and the barbarous Arab man.
In the FLN narrative, this was the birth of the new Algeria and the
birth of the new Algerian woman.

These wartime discourses about women have been a fruitful area
of research in recent years.[13] Less documented is how the women
who were the targets or subjects of this discourse responded to it,
appropriated it, rejected it or ignored its very existence.

The SAS, the FLN and rural interviewees

The importance of the role of rural women in the nationalist struggle was emphasised at a conference held on 20 August 1956 in the
valley of the Soummam in Kabylia. This grouped together some
of the key figures in the FLN, including Krim Belkacem and Amar
Ouamrane, to produce a – not uncontested – political platform
on the aims of the movement and its military and psychological
methods. The Soummam conference gave the FLN a parliament,
the Conseil National de la Révolution Algérienne (National Council
of the Algerian Revolution, CNRA) and an executive, the Comité
de Coordination et d'Exécution (Co-ordinating and Executing
Committee, CCE). The CCE would be replaced by the GPRA in
1958. The minutes of the Soummam conference identified 'the
women's movement' as a particular area of importance: 'Immense
possibilities exist and are increasingly numerous in this domain'.[14]

Yet Fatima Berci, Fatma Yermeche, Fatima Benmohand Berci,
Chérifa Akache and Ferroudja Amarouche were actively participating in the war long before the Soummam conference. Rather than
propaganda aimed at women being used to rally them, a glorified
version of the contribution of rural women was used in tracts to
persuade urban women to support the independence movement.
In the *wilaya* IV (Algiers region), a tract seized by the French army
on 7 August 1961 addressed to 'patriot sisters' paid homage to the
'Algerian peasant woman', described as 'sublime in her resolve': 'A
poignant spectacle is offered by the Algerian peasant women who
have remained alone in entire *douars* [villages] because all the men
have been taken to prisons from where they never return, or killed
in cold blood before their eyes by the criminal occupier.'[15]

In 1959, *El Moudjahid* serialised extracts of what was described
as the 'Diary of a *maquisarde*'. The anonymous author, who stated

that she was based in the *wilaya* IV and then in the *wilaya* III (Kabylia), wrote:

> What struck me upon my arrival in the *maquis* was the order and discipline which reigned. The extraordinary morale of our populations. The women are particularly admirable. They are the ones who stay in the *douars*, alone with the children and old people, as the men come and serve in our troops [...] After battles, when the enemy has gone, these women are the ones who welcome us with smiles, despite us knowing that they have just suffered the worst cruelty: torture and rape. I never heard them complain. On the contrary, although they had to put up with much more than us, it was they who encouraged us, who blessed us. I often saw them bury their dead – husbands, sons – and each time they repeated these words: 'We do not mourn them. Why cry, since they died for the motherland, they died the most beautiful and glorious of deaths.'[16]

Given mass illiteracy and problems of distribution, it is hardly surprising that rural women were more likely to be the subjects of FLN printed propaganda about women than its intended audience. The FLN's gendered discourse – be it celebrating the heroic misery of the rural woman patriot or declaring that in independent Algeria the contribution of women would open up 'radiant perspectives of fulfilment and emancipation in keeping with our times'[17] – does not seem to have reached women's ears in Agraradj, Bouzeguene and Aït Abderrahmane, the villages of the rural interviewees under consideration here. Their engagement predates any such strategy and what these women remember are more general, non-gendered rallying words, which emphasised the fight for freedom, equality and socio-economic redistribution.

These rural women were much more likely to hear promises of women's emancipation from the French army and administration. Fatima Berci, Fatma Yermeche and Fatima Benmohand Berci's village of Agraradj and Ferroudja Amarouche's village of Bouzeguene both came under the administration of a Section Administrative Specialisée, respectively the SAS of Aghribs and the SAS of Bouzeguene. The SAS were civil administration bodies run by members of the army, created across Algerian territory between 1955 and 1956 under the impulsion of Algeria's Governor General Jacques Soustelle. By the end of 1961, there were seven hundred SAS in Algeria, in addition to twenty Sections Administratives Urbaines (Urban Administrative Sections, SAU) in urban areas, notably in the Casbah.[18] The SAS were presented as a response to the under-administration of large parts of Algerian territory. This was seen as having facilitated the FLN's implantation as a state-within-a-state and its organisation of parallel political, economic and social structures. Across Algeria, French Muslims were refusing to engage with the French state on an unprecedented scale. Whilst there was a long tradition of rural populations refusing to officially register births, marriages and deaths, it was estimated that the number of people 'missing' from official records – i.e. who had no legal existence – had risen from 100,000 in 1913 to 230,000 in 1959. Indeed, the 1959 marriage law, presented as a cornerstone measure of late colonial reformism, was largely ignored, including in urban areas, with a majority of families eschewing civil marriage for unregistered religious ceremonies.[19]

The role of the SAS was to create an administrative infrastructure and provide basic healthcare and education facilities – that is to say, create the beginnings of an effective state in rural areas 125 years after the French invasion. The first task of a new section would be to construct a fortified building to house its activities. The construction of SAS buildings was carried out by men drawn from the local population who were supposedly benefiting from these employment-creating 'public works'. In many cases, however, labour was requisitioned from recalcitrant populations. The SAS also played a role in patrols, surveillance and indeed military operations. Fundamentally, the task of the SAS was to prevent local populations in rural areas supporting *maquisards*, through close surveillance and psychological warfare.[20] Images of devoted SAS officers helping out smiling local populations were produced for national and international media consumption. A television report in June 1956, filmed in Kabylia, showed SAS officers helping out a 'young Kabyle woman' who had fallen ill, by evacuating her from her village to the town of Tizi Ouzou: 'A direct contact has been re-established; the reconquering of hearts has commenced', the audience was told. 'This will be the victory of officers, efficient collaborators of the administrators, teachers and doctors of the *bled* [countryside]. The French Algeria of tomorrow is being born.'[21]

The attitude of the FLN towards the SAS was unsurprisingly hostile. Local populations were instructed not to use their facilities; SAS personnel were assassination targets. An ALN document from the *wilaya* III (Kabylia) in 1959 proudly – and rather predictably –

declared that 'the population shows a negative reaction towards the paternalism of the SAS. All other psychological action of the enemy in no way attacks the morale of the people, it leaves them phlegmatic.'[22] Whether using the facilities available equalled buying into the propaganda is highly questionable. Read against the grain, the SAS archives for the areas of Bouzeguene and Aghribs provide an alterative set of insights, suggestive of women's ability to instrumentalise the SAS message, rather than simply remaining coolly aloof.

At the Bouzeguene SAS, responsible for twenty villages in the surrounding area, a daily record was kept of activities, the number of visitors and their 'state of mind'. On 3 August 1959, three hundred people were recorded as having visited the local SAS – to put this into context, each SAS area on average covered about ten thousand inhabitants.[23] These three hundred people included eighty who were ill, notably skeletal children suffering from malnutrition. The SAS personnel were described as having undertaken psychological action amongst its mainly female adult visitors, on the theme of the social conditions of women. Other psychological action sessions had evocative titles such as 'France, protector of children' and 'The rebellion brings misery and death'. The healthcare and food aid provided by the SAS was clearly used by inhabitants of the surrounding villages – after all, these were the only medical facilities available in regions where the intensifying war and its ensuing food shortages increasingly threatened the lives of local populations. The Bouzeguene SAS officers' log claimed some success in associating the provision of services with psychological action:

> 7 August [1959]. Friday. The détente is very clear, some women in the course of psychological action openly spoke out against the rebels, and some shouted 'It's the fault of the *fellagas*.' It is disappointing to not be able to follow up on all these demands, due to a lack of resources.
> 8 August [1959]. Saturday. A delegation, designated by all the women, came to find the Captain. To summarise [what the women said] – 'We trust you again, you must not let us down. Protect us, we have discussed at length what you said to us, our children are sick, we are sick, we know you want what's best for us, you are our father, don't disappoint us, have patience and you will win.'[24]

The optimistic author of these entries seems to have taken these women's declarations of loyalty at face value. Yet one may well question whether the Bouzeguene SAS was carrying out psychological action on women – or vice versa. The female delegation of 8 August clearly had the ability to adopt a language which would speak to promoters of paternalistic welfare colonialism, taking on the subservient role of foolish children led astray by the bad influence of bandits. Having drawn the SAS captain in with the lure of a successful mission, the women then made it clear that their support was conditional on the continued provision of food, healthcare and other facilities.

On the basis of its internal records, including logs and correspondence with the regional and national hierarchy, the officers of the Bouzeguene SAS appear to have been entirely convinced by the argument made by these women. Officers constantly complained that the section was unable to carry out effective psychological action because it was understaffed and underfunded. They struggled to meet demand for medical care, and could not satisfy women's requests to accept their daughters at the new school owing to a lack of space and qualified personnel. The SAS lorry was incapable of negotiating the mountainous terrain. Medical supplies which had been ordered did not arrive. The women soon became tired of speeches about the benefits of French rule when supplies ran low. On 15 August 1959, just a week after such apparently promising signs of success in psychological action, an entry in the SAS log recorded that 'patience is wearing thin within the population, we cannot make the women understand that we lack personnel'. For the SAS officers, this was an argument in favour of more material means to keep up the campaign to 'win hearts and minds' – but such attitudes might be more revealing of the superficial effects of the propaganda. Indeed, implicitly, the author of the log was perhaps conscious of women's instrumental use of the SAS facilities. An entry for 11 August 1959 reads 'We give them the Good Word, but that does not feed you!'[25]

If the SAS could be a source of food, medical assistance and, on a few occasions, redress for acts of violence committed by the regular French army during its incursions, there is little evidence to suggest that any of its language of 'emancipation' filtered down to rural women. The oblique references that interviewees make to attempts by the SAS to provide professional training or household management workshops, or to get them to vote, are framed in the language of the French trying to make them do something which they did not want to do. In Bouzeguene, Ferroudja Amarouche recounts a failed attempt by 'the French' – these seem to be SAS officers – to get young women to come to a sewing workshop. Following a flat refusal from the inhabitants of the village, 'they' returned early the next day with army reinforcements to round up the women. To resist, the women tied their belts together. The brightly coloured woven belts worn by women in the region of Kabylia are considered to be a symbol of fertility. In this instance, they served to build a human wall, in Ferroudja's words, 'the belts were really tough'.[26] The army backed down. In Ferroudja's account, this workshop supposedly to promote her and other women's 'social evolution' is seen simply as a form of forced labour.

In Aghribs, there were requests for the army to come and help SAS officers as women resisted attempts to take their photographs to create identity cards.[27] In Bouzeguene, Ferroudja Amarouche describes the women of the village pulling faces to sabotage the images – a more comic version of the sullen and defiant women in military photographer Marc Garanger's now iconic identity shots taken in the village of Bordj Okhriss, just inside the western border of the *wilaya* III (Kabylia).[28] As Neil Macmaster underlines in his discussion of Garanger and the women of Bordj Okhriss: 'French welfare intervention was always under the immediate or imminent sign of the gun'.[29] Getting women to vote, following the introduction of the right to vote for French Muslim women in 1958, also involved physical violence. In Kabylia, interviewees once again tied their belts together to avoid being dragged off to vote. This was not only a principled stance – it was also a matter of life and death, as Ferroudja Amarouche explains: 'If you went to vote, the *mujahidin* would kill you. Even the labourers that the French forced to come and build their camps, the *mujahidin* said, "If you build camps we will kill you".'[30]

The shock of the 'civilisées': urban women appropriating – or not – discourse about them

One of the most documented aspects of the Algerian War of Independence is the FLN–ALN's tactical use of stereotypes and assumptions about 'the Muslim woman' in urban areas. Unveiled women dressed in Western clothes were used to carry out bomb attacks within the European quarter of Algiers, their physical appearance presumed to be a symbol of their level of 'civilisation' and therefore pro-French sentiment. Using veiled women wearing the traditional *hayk* – a loose white cloth covering the body and head with a triangle of material covering the nose and mouth – to transport weapons, medicine and letters played on the stereotype of the passive, submissive Muslim woman who knows nothing of politics and who should not be touched.

The purported ability of Muslim women to transgress the male and European spheres during the war fascinated and frightened both at the time and subsequently. In 'Algeria Unveiled', Frantz Fanon summarises the activities of rural women in a few short sentences before describing at length the revolutionary role of urban women: 'Carrying revolvers, grenades, hundreds of false identity cards or bombs, the unveiled Algerian woman moves like a fish in the Western waters'.[31] The most striking visual representation of these women's ability to melt into the crowd can be seen in Gillo Pontecorvo's 1966 film *The Battle of Algiers*, in the much-discussed scene in which three women 'disguise' themselves to go and plant bombs in the European districts, dyeing and cutting their hair and putting on Western clothes to the pounding beat of the *qarqabou* (castanets). In reality, many of the women in the urban bomb network were students and young women who already dressed in 'Western' clothes, had been in contact with Europeans either in school or the workplace and, on the basis of crude judgements of their physical appearance, could 'pass' as European without any dressing up. What they were disguising when they transported weapons and planted bombs was not their physical appearance or cultural identity but their political engagement.

For the French army and colonial authorities, the participation of these 'Westernised' Muslim women in the nationalist movement was a source of stupefaction. Considered *évoluées* (evolved women) or *civilisées* (civilised women) to use the colonial terminology of the time, these women should have been leading supporters of 'French Algeria' which had, supposedly, given them the tools to emancipate themselves from the weight of oppressive traditions, superstition, cloistering and the veil. The colonial press went into overdrive to try and explain the 'uncharacteristic' behaviour of these women. Boyfriends were often blamed for leading girls astray. In July 1957, FLN members Djamila Bouhired and Djamila Bouazza were tried by a military tribunal, accused of planting bombs in Algiers. The trial was salaciously reported on the front pages of the colonial press, complete with photographs and daily updates on their outfits. Bouazza, it was reported, had been described as 'docile and gentle' in her school reports, but nevertheless had fallen 'in thrall to the myths of Ali la Pointe and [the leader of the FLN–ALN in Algiers] Yacef Saadi'. In court, Bouazza was supposedly 'slovenly, frenzied, comical and pathetic, crude and childish', laughing insolently whilst nervously rolling her skirt belt around her wrist, playing the 'class idiot' to Bouhired's 'good pupil' and shouting out 'They say I'm a whore'.[32]

A decade after Algerian independence, the 1972 memoirs of Colonel Yves Godard, one of General Massu's officers during the 'Battle of Algiers', reflect his enduring bafflement as to why young women, so 'European' in their dress, language and manners, would join the outlaws. Djamila Bouazza, who had been a post office employee before joining the FLN, is depicted by Godard as 'very de-Islamised and, to be trendy, had her shoulder-length hair lightened'.[33] Describing Hassiba Ben Bouali, a student member of the Algiers bomb network, he declares that 'nothing in her language or her attire differentiates her from a young European woman of bourgeois background'. Godard's attempts to explain these women's actions depoliticises their engagement: he continually returns to what he describes as the 'curious' case of bomber Zohra Drif, the daughter of a *qadi* (judge of 'indigenous affairs') who had been a law student before she was arrested in the Casbah in September 1957 alongside Yacef Saadi. The only reason that Godard can come up with for why this young woman of 'French education and culture' who could 'pass for a colonist's daughter' joins the 'outlaws' is that some 'idiots' at university made fun of her Muslim name.[34]

The FLN and its sympathisers created their own gendered discourse about these women, and in particular about the 'three Djamilas': Bouhired, Bouazza and Boupacha. Jacques Vergès, the controversial French-Vietnamese lawyer who would later go on to represent the Khmer Rouge and the Nazi war criminal Klaus Barbie, led Bouhired's defence. When Bouhired and Bouazza were both found guilty and condemned to death, Vergès published an impassioned *J'accuse*-style defence of his client entitled *Pour Djamila Bouhired* (For Djamila Bouhired). In this, Vergès and his co-author Georges Arnaud condemned the torture Bouhired had been subjected to at the hands of the French army, including

Figure 2 The arrest of FLN militant Zohra Drif by the French army,
24 September 1957

placing electrodes in her vagina and on her nipples, and questioned
the legality of the military court in which she had been tried.[35]
Bouhired rapidly became a symbol of anti-colonial struggle, not
just in Algeria but also across the Arab World and the Third World.
In 1958, she was the subject of a film supporting the independence struggle by the Egyptian director Youssef Chahine, *Gamila
al-Gaza'iriyya* (Djamila the Algerian). British diplomatic reports
from India reveal FLN envoys distributing leaflets appealing to
the Indian people on behalf of 'two young Algerian girls [...] Miss
Djamila Bou[h]ired aged 23 years and Miss Djamila Bouazza aged
19 years [...] two young patriots', with sympathisers summoned to
'save the lives of those young girls'.[36]

In 1960, another 'young girl' and member of the FLN's Algiers
network who needed saving was Djamila Boupacha. The brutal
torture and rape with a bottle which Boupacha endured at the hands
of the French army provoked a scandal in French and international
opinion largely through the campaigning of Boupacha's lawyer,
French-Tunisian Gisèle Halimi (later a leading figure in the French
pro-choice movement), and Simone de Beauvoir.[37] Boupacha's

violated virginity was the focus of much attention, as Judith Surkis underlines: 'If in *The Second Sex* [de] Beauvoir denounced the fetishisation of virginity as the product of paternalistic ethics, here she nonetheless mobilised that figure for the sake of political argument'.[38] In December 1961, Pablo Picasso sketched a portrait of Djamila Boupacha, who at the time was imprisoned in France, her wide-eyed innocence staring out from the canvas.

Whether for or against the nationalist movement, all of these descriptions place the bodies and sexuality of these women on display for public consumption. Women were depicted as politically conscious militants using their bodies in 'new' ways to defeat the (male) enemy by charming or tricking their way into colonial society. Or they were innocent, pure victims, their bodies martyrised and honour defiled by (male) soldiers. Or they were revolutionary whores, foolishly allowing themselves to be led astray by manipulative men.

These women, however, were not just subjects of gendered propaganda, and some were also called upon to be active agents in the war of words. In 1961, whilst still in prison, Zohra Drif wrote *La Mort de mes frères* (The death of my brothers). In this pamphlet, she declared that women's participation in the anti-colonial struggle was completely natural because 'Algerian women have seen their brothers, their husbands and their sons tortured and massacred before their eyes. Young girls have been raped in the houses of the Casbah, and across all of Algeria, in front of their brothers and fathers, who are powerless under the threat of the gun.'[39] *La Mort de mes frères* is full of classic nationalist stereotypes – women's engagement is linked to their status as wives, mothers and sisters, they are victims of death, violence and rape and they are depicted as participating in the conflict in order to restore a threatened masculinity. Yet, during my interview with her in 2005, Zohra Drif suggested that at the time she was quite conscious that she was writing a piece of propaganda, for a specific audience:

There was a French fringe which supported the struggle of Algerians, and they had asked me to write what I wanted to say for the review [Jean-Paul Sartre's] *Temps modernes*. I wanted first of all to bear witness to the most terrible aspect of prison [...] the execution of very young patriots. Secondly, I wanted to share the experiences and the positions of Algerians in the struggle, in a magazine which would have an impact on a certain section of the [metropolitan French] population.[40]

Zohra Drif suggests that she knew her audience for having been imprisoned alongside activists of French and European origin, and she knew that they were more likely to be convinced by arguments against the death penalty and violence than by images of female warriors. She was using stereotypes for political purposes.

The *maquisarde* Fadéla Mesli also talks about appropriating propaganda made about her. She describes how the head of her rural guerrilla unit in the region around Algiers (*wilaya* IV) took a whole film of photographs of her, Safia Baazi and Meriem Belmihoub, who were among the first three nurses to join the *maquis*. The purpose of the photos, says Mesli, was to show a forthcoming meeting of the United Nations that the FLN was not just a group of outlaws, as they were stigmatised by the French state and in the colonial press, but a whole people fighting for independence. In fact, the photographs came to serve another purpose. Shortly after they were taken, Mesli, Baazi, Belmihoub and the roll of film were captured by the French army. Sensing the possibility of a propaganda coup, the army passed on to the French press a selection of images of the three women in uniform, brandishing guns. On 11 August 1956, the magazine *Jours de France* published the photographs under the headline, 'These smiling nurses are "killers"'.[41] The choice of language sought to provoke shock at the way in which these women had transgressed their nurturing role as both women and nurses, highlighting the unsettling contrast between their youthful attractiveness and their violent acts, not to mention their profound ingratitude in turning the nursing skills provided by the French education system against the motherland. Fadéla describes how the local press reported that they were Egyptian women: 'they could not believe that Algerian women were taking to the *maquis*'.[42] At the same time, 'Many people [men] joined the *maquis* when they saw these photos', Fadéla recounts. 'They said to themselves, "how is it that women can fight and we are like 'women' – in inverted commas – staying at home?"'[43]

Zohra Drif, a lawyer by training and at the time of the interview a member of the Algerian Senate, and Fadéla Mesli, a medical professional and deputy in the Constituent Assembly of 1962 and in the National Assembly 1977–82, felt at ease appropriating these gendered stereotypes in 2005. They turned them into stories which are valorising by revealing their conscious manipulation of images projected on to them. Other female veterans similarly take control of their image when talking about how they used their physical appearance to extract information or escape dangerous situations. Born in Bougie (today Béjaïa), Fadila Attia was recruited in 1956, aged twenty, to work in the Algiers offices of the Governor General Robert Lacoste. This role gave her a privileged position to spy for the FLN and she transported documents across Algeria and to FLN bases in Morocco. According to Fadila, her blonde bobbed hair and 'European' appearance meant that she was regularly mistaken for a Frenchwomen and in her administrative post she was on good terms with her boss, who did not suspect in the slightest her political sympathies. Fadila expresses pride at how her youth and beauty enabled her to transport documents from Algiers to Morocco without arousing suspicion, surprising even members of the FLN based in her destination, the Moroccan town of Tétouan: 'They didn't believe me, they thought I was a spy, even the Algerians. They asked how, a girl like that, did she manage to cross all of Morocco, without having problems?'[44]

In rural Kabylia, some women also used engrained colonial stereotypes about the patriarchal authority of 'the Kabyle man' as a form of defence in French army interrogations. Interviewees describe evading questions by playing the role of the 'traditional' submissive woman, bound by religion and custom and ignorant of the world outside their front door. Chérifa Akache told the French army soldiers who arrested and interrogated her that she had 'accidentally' helped the *mujahidin* because she had confused them with the French army. When the French soldiers demanded to know where her husband was, she played the role of the abandoned wife to hide the fact that he had joined the *maquis*: 'I said that I didn't know anything, if he was alive or dead or anything [...] I said "you know amongst Kabyles, when the husband leaves, the wife returns to her family. I was with my family when you arrested me and I don't know where he is."'[45]

Maquisardes in the *wilaya* V (Oran region), Yamina Salem, El Hora Kerkeb and Habiba Chami talk about being inspired by Djamila Boupacha, Djamila Bouazza and Djamila Bouhired during the war. Yamina Salem explains: 'the first name, "Djamila" was a synonym for heroine during the war because there were three

Djamilas who for us were extraordinary, who for others were terrorists because they planted bombs [...] We used to say "We are all Djamilas!"'[46]

For the 'three Djamilas', appropriating their image is not so easy. These women cannot control the way their pasts are used in the public space in the same way that other *mujahidat* can select anecdotes and stories about themselves. Tied up with the representations of abstract idealism surrounding them, the beauty of struggle (Djamila means 'beautiful' in Arabic), are very public discussions of physical, sexual and psychological violence inflicted on them. This is not only a painful past, it is also a painful past to remember publicly. Djamila Boupacha says that she has never been able to read Gisèle Halimi and Simone de Beauvoir's book about her. Fifteen years ago, however, she was going to be interviewed and as she was getting muddled up in the dates she decided to read the book 'so I wouldn't say anything silly'. Yet in doing so, she 'felt like I was being strangled'.[47] Djamila Bouazza describes herself as 'traumatised' by the months she spent in a cell with Djamila Bouhired, condemned to death. She says that she is often solicited for interviews, but that she rarely accepts, 'sometimes I can't even speak'.[48]

As Chapter 4 will discuss, the way in which Djamila Boupacha and Djamila Bouhired relate to their wartime image also needs to be viewed in relation to each woman's post-independence trajectory. After 1962, both women continued to be the subjects and agents of nationalist discourse, but in a context where this discourse was no longer a critical part of a defence strategy to get them off death row or secure their release from prison. Djamila Bouazza's postwar trajectory took a different path. She was obliged to use her revolutionary credentials to try to protect her family from political persecution when her husband, Abboud Boussouf, entered into clandestine opposition. As Chapter 6 will explore, this has profoundly shaped how Bouazza relates to being a nationalist symbol.

Brothers and sisters, then and now

Gilbert Meynier and Mohamed Harbi have argued that, on the ground, most leaders and members of the FLN–ALN were a long way off promoting or believing in the public discourse which the nationalist movement maintained about the new Algerian woman. Harbi, a leading member of the FLN during the war who later became a post-independence opponent of the single-party state as well as a renowned historian, argues that the theme of women's participation in the nationalist movement was promoted for the benefit of foreign observers. He underlines that no woman ever held a leadership position within the FLN between 1954 and 1962.[49] Having exhaustively studied the internal documents of the FLN, including its – relatively few – documents on women, Meynier demonstrates that marriage in the *maquis* was tightly controlled by the military hierarchy, there were instances of young female recruits being subjected to virginity tests, women accused of adultery risked the death penalty and, at the end of 1957, the decision was taken to remove women from rural guerrilla units and send them to the Tunisian and Moroccan frontiers. Meynier concludes that for the leaders of the FLN: 'In 1962, everything was in place for women to go back into the cocoon of their homes, which they had been drawn out of by the parenthesis of the war'.[50] In a order issued on 2 November 1960, in the *wilaya* V (Oran region), Commander Si Allal insisted: 'I am reminding you for the last time that it is forbidden to recruit female soldiers and female nurses without the authorisation of the zone. In independent Algeria, the liberty of the Muslim woman ends at the threshold of the door. Women will never be the equals of men.'[51]

Nevertheless, given the ideological heterogeneity and geographical spread of the FLN, we need to question how representative such orders were of wider attitudes and the extent to which there was the desire – or the ability – to apply them on the ground. Ryme Seferdjeli underlines the importance of taking into account the diverse attitudes of individual men and women, as well as regional, class and family differences, when exploring the experiences of the *mujahidat* in the *maquis* and women who came into contact with *mujahidin*.[52] Individual itineraries of women in the *maquis* show that the removal of women was often not put into practice. Interviewee Khadjidja Belguembour remained in her *maquis* unit in the *wilaya* II (Constantine region) until the end of the war. In French army files of ALN members captured or killed, we find a number of examples of women killed – and indeed recruited into the *maquis* – long after women were supposedly withdrawn. Internal records of how the FLN dealt with real-life transgressions of a strict moral code separating men and women provide examples of both harsh punishment (unauthorised marriages punished by death) and the pragmatic turning of a blind eye (extra-marital relationships begrudgingly accepted as long as consensual).

For example, Sergeant Olkma, who joined the *wilaya* II in 1957, was subject to an internal investigation after it transpired that he had acquired a series of 'wives', who subsequently fell pregnant, as his *maquis* unit travelled through villages in the region. He had apparently persuaded a series of women to 'marry' him in secret, thus avoiding formal requests to his unit leader or the women's fathers, with the words: 'Between me and you, there is the vow of twelve million Algerians, and that is our vow'. The FLN investigators were clearly hesitant about punishing Olkma – the report pointed out that he was a good soldier and that his sexual relations were consenting.[53]

The 'Zakia affair' in the *wilaya* III (Kabylia) was of a very different nature. Zakia Hammadi arrived in *wilaya* III from Cap Aokas (near Béjaïa) in March 1959, motivated to join the *maquis* after political discussions with her cousins. The disappearance of this nineteen-year-old, who spoke excellent French and 'dressed in the French way' initially provoked consternation from French gendarmes who struggled to believe that she had joined the *maquis* of her own free will. Unfortunately for Zakia, an officer in the ALN, 'H'Mimi', forced her to marry him, despite the fact that he was already married with two children. Remaining nevertheless suspicious of his educated, French-speaking wife from the town, he put her under the constant surveillance of a chaperone.[54] In his memoirs, Mohamed Benyahia, a *maquisard* in the *wilaya* III who knew – and disliked – H'Mimi, describes himself and his fellow *maquisards* as disgusted by H'Mimi's behaviour, to the extent that the 'Zakia affair' was a major topic of conversation and was unequivocally viewed by the men as rape.[55] Archival documents show that H'Mimi was summoned to an extraordinary meeting on 13 September 1959 where he was accused of 'family abandonment, marriage with a girl aged thirteen, acts against Qur'anic law and various financial questions' – which were presumably irregularities in the collection and spending of funds.[56] Although these very specific individual cases cannot be generalised, the language of the discussion suggests that there were leaders within the ALN hierarchy who made a distinction between an – unenforceable – blanket ban on relations between men and women outside of officially approved marriages, and the absolute necessity of acting in situations where men had abused their position of power to force women to marry or into exploitative sexual relations.

For all the FLN propaganda to the outside world about women fighting alongside their brothers, having women living alongside men in clandestine units, be they underground urban networks or rural *maquis* units, was nevertheless potentially problematic. The potential impact on discipline of sexual relations between combatants is an issue for any armed force and explains the reluctance of armies the world over to allow mixed fighting units. In addition to this, having men and women who were not related to each other in the same space broke with what was understood in Algeria to be a key organising principle of Islam: the separation of the sexes. Writing in mid-1957 in the *wilaya* V (Oran region), the officer cadet Ben Ali euphemistically refers to 'the laws of nature' troubling men and women otherwise courageously fighting alongside each other: 'The result of this is that the presence in the *maquis* of young women can create very problematic concerns'. Ben Ali suggests that rather than trying to keep men and women separate, temptation should be removed through the sanctifying ties of marriage. *Mujahid* and *mujahida* could get married in the *maquis* or 'sisters' could be evacuated to the Moroccan and Tunisian frontiers, 'where they will be settled down, trained, and married to Algerians in the revolution'.[57]

The anxiety to separate the sexes was amplified by the fact that *maquisardes* were in many – although by no means all – cases educated women of the town, mixing with the illiterate men of the village. Louisette Ighilahriz does not have particularly fond memories of her two-month period in the *maquis* in 1957. She was the only woman in the unit, and the men were suspicious of her. In her memoirs, she writes: 'for them I remained a women of the town who, horror of horrors, even knew how to use a pen'.[58] Louisette Ighilahriz strikes a (slightly) discordant note in an otherwise consensual memory of mutual respect and chaste relations between men and women. When Fadéla Mesli arrived in the *maquis*, the head of the *wilaya* Slimane Dehiles, known as Si Sadek, was unimpressed. She explains:

I was young and I looked much younger that I was. The colonel of the *wilaya* had been told that he was going to get a competent nurse, and how he was disappointed when he saw a kid before him! I had a little fringe, bunches and he said 'That's the nurse? She's still bottle feeding, send her back to her mother.' But there was a battle, he saw me at work and he was reassured.

After Si Sadek's initial doubts, Fadéla Mesli describes an uncomplicated relationship with male *maquisards*: 'It didn't create any problems. No problems, and that's what was surprising. When you want to impose yourself [*she trails off*] It gave the male combatants a boost to see women there too.'[59] Other interviewees similarly minimise the significance of what was in reality a sea change in forms of social contact between men and women. From a small village in the mountains of Jijel, Khadjidja Belguembour joined the *maquis* in the *wilaya* II (Constantine region) as a teenager to avoid being rounded up in a French 'regroupement' camp:

> I found myself amongst men who I'd never seen before, who I did not know. I felt safe straightaway. I wasn't afraid that I would be sold out, or that anyone would do anything to me. I struggled to get used to sleeping and there was a man who said to me 'Here, you don't have a mother, you don't have a father, you have nothing. You have brothers [in arms], and the father, it's the one wearing the uniform. You take a piece of cork, you put it under your head and you lie down next to the fire. That's all there is.'

Later on in the interview she insists:

> I need to add a very important detail. Us in the *maquis*, we didn't live with the male soldiers under the same roof. In the countryside, where there was a refuge, the men were separate, the women cooked, did the logistical stuff, separately. I never saw the *maquisards* eat, unless we were on the move. I never saw a *maquisard* sleep. There wasn't any discussion. The only discussion I had sometimes, if I had the time, was with the injured. Otherwise each of us had our job to do.[60]

When women who were in the *maquis* talk about the war now, many of them describe it as a completely desexualised period, in which they lost all sense of their femininity. For Yamina Salem, a nurse in the *wilaya* V (Oran region), men and women really did live alongside each other like brothers and sisters. Romantic thoughts were the last thing in her head – in any case she was too dirty and she had lice.[61] Louisette Ighilahriz might have felt that she was seen as a woman, but, like Yamina Salem, she did not feel like one: 'I was no longer really a woman. The war had transformed me, I had become lacking in all feeling and had basically forgotten my femininity.'[62]

The post-hoc consensus on the wartime moral order can be found also in rural women's accounts. Cooking, washing and healing were in many ways 'traditional' gendered roles. Yet the clandestine wartime context in which women were accomplishing these tasks and the responsibility and potential punishment which they entailed represented a radical break with the past. As increasing numbers of younger men joined the *maquis*, or moved to industrial towns in Algeria and France to find work amid the deepening socio-economic crisis, those left in the countryside were women, children and old men. Fatma Yermeche was married aged thirteen. Her husband Ali was a migrant worker in France and an activist in the Montpellier branch of the FF–FLN. As a result of this activism, between February 1960 and April 1962 he was imprisoned. Ferroudja Amarouche's husband Tahar joined the *maquis* in 1955, and was captured and imprisoned between 1958 and 1962. Fatima Berci's and Fatima Benmohand Berci's husbands were also *mujahidin*, as was the husband of Chérifa Akache when he was killed in 1961. During the war, these women nominally became 'heads of the household'. This both was and was not a break with the past: before the war, men in rural areas would often migrate to France to work for long periods. Wives would be left behind to take care of farming, with the support and under the authority of the extended family. When I asked Ferroudja Amarouche what life was like for her in the absence of her husband, she states that she 'worked in the fields to feed my children', and that her mother-in-law, her father and her brothers all supported her, including two brothers who were migrant workers in France, who likely supported her by sending money back home.[63]

What was a radical change was that many rural women came into direct contact with men from outside their families for the first time. In Aït Abderrahmane, Chérifa Akache explains:

CA: I considered [the *mujahidin*] my brothers. I went into the room where they were without any reticence because they were brothers. When they stayed for a long time in the mountains they used to come with their feet in a bad state, dirty and with sores. I'd look after them without complexes, and I considered them my brothers. I wasn't alone. There were eleven, twelve women who did it together.
NV: Would you have done this before the war?
CA: Before the war, I wouldn't have seen them and they wouldn't have seen me. But my husband told me 'If a *mujahid* comes, he is your brother, whether I'm there or not.'

NV: Were you surprised?

CA: *C'est normal!* [*in French, with all the connotations of 'natural' and 'to be expected' that the word 'normal' has in French, before switching back to Tamazight*] I felt responsible, and I felt that in a way I was replacing him when he wasn't there. Everyone did what they could. There were my sisters and mother too.

NV: And what were your relations like with the *mujahidin*?

CA: They always came as good as angels. Never did they have any other intention. The older women, they called them 'my mother' and the women who were the same age as them, they called them 'my sister'.[64]

Beyond the extraordinary conditions of war, Chérifa's adaptation to these new forms of contact was helped by the fact that they were accepted by her husband and always carried out within the safety of the group: women might have entered into contact with men outside the family, but a woman, in Chérifa's account, never entered into contact with a man. Moreover, the fraternal language of brothers and sisters with its religious connotations of the *umma* (the community of believers) helped combatants and the civilian populations which they relied on to create a safe, familiar environment – a pseudo-family sphere – in radically changed conditions.

These women's uniform post-hoc accounts of brotherly and sisterly relations between men and women contrast with the patchier picture that emerges from the archives. Even if we consider the documents detailing sexual abuse on the part of individual *maquisards* and illicit relations as isolated incidents, the very fact that FLN–ALN report writers were discussing relations between men and women suggests the difficulties of maintaining the moral order and mutual respect which was publicly declared. The fact that marriages took place, and that the FLN sought to create its own codes and rituals to sanction these marriages, are also indicative of an attempt to adapt to forms of social contact which did not fit the brother/sister construction.[65] Khadjidja Belguembour was married two months before the end of the war, to a man whom she had nursed: 'They asked for my hand in marriage in the traditional way. It was the leaders who did the deal'.[66] By this, Khadjidja means that the head of her unit wrote to her parents, which was not really 'traditional', but it was traditional in the sense that the young man did not ask her directly.

Interviewees also hint at social resistance to these new forms of contact between men and women when urban women describe the less than positive reaction of their families to their engagement in the urban bomb network or the *maquis*, or when rural women talk about the 'older women' who were always there, watching over, when *maquisards* came to eat. Suspected of spying for the FLN–ALN within the Lacoste administration, Fadila Attia was arrested and held, although not charged, on a number of occasions. Following one period during which she had been tortured for a number of days, Fadila returned home to her family in the Algiers suburb of Kouba to a far from sympathetic reception: 'They had another go at me because I had disappeared from the house: "Where was I? A young woman who stayed out all night!" And I was dirty! I was full of fleas. "Who told you to go and work for the brothers?" And I said, "No, I was arrested, I didn't do anything."' When, in summer 1957, she travelled by train across Algeria to take documents to the ALN in Morocco, she was accosted on the train by a French army major and a group of soldiers. After they insisted on knowing her name, Fadila Attia presented herself as 'Françoise'. In a burst of gallantry, the soldiers shared their lunch with her, carried her suitcase between changes and, on arrival, the major insisted that two of his men accompany Fadila Attia to her uncle's house in Casablanca: 'When my uncle saw me arrive with two French soldiers he thought that I'd sold out'. Fadila's uncle was not primarily concerned that his niece had betrayed the nationalist movement. For him, the fact that her companions were male was much graver than the fact that they were French: 'He wrote to my mother [asking] "What is this you're sending me, a girl from the streets"'. A few days later, Fadila Attia moved out of her uncle's home and spent the rest of the war as a courier for the FLN in Morocco. She had no contact with her family back in Algeria: 'My family didn't know about anything. For them I had vanished for seven years. [Afterwards] everyone understood. My mum thought that I was dead. For seven, five years she hadn't seen me. But', Fadila Attia adds with a note of surprised relief, 'she didn't criticise me'.[67]

Conclusion

Seeking to use oral history to evoke women's responses to the wartime propaganda about them and aimed at them involves a tricky triangulation of sources. Firstly, there are archival sources. These include pamphlets, texts, images and film produced by the

French and nationalist men and women, the internal archives of the French administration and army and captured FLN–ALN documents. The anxieties and wishful thinking contained within these sources can potentially be read 'against the grain' to gain a glimpse into how women responded to them at the time.

These sources and these against-the-grain readings then need to be cross-referenced with women's oral accounts, in which they remember French army attempts to win them over and the reaction of male nationalists to their presence in the struggle many decades later. This testimony has been filtered through subsequent life experiences, political events, social change and, in some cases, exposure to public narratives about the role of women in the war. The two main discourses about the impact of the war on women which have emerged since 1962 are, on the one hand, the view of the war as a revolution in gender relations, encouraged at least by some men within the FLN–ALN, whether or not this was reflected in the institutional structures and social attitudes of post-independence Algeria. On the other hand, there is the alternative view of the FLN–ALN as an inherently patriarchal, and at times misogynistic, nationalist movement which inevitably strangled at birth any potential change.

There are, therefore, a series of interpretative lenses: that of the authors of primary sources about women, the 'recovery' of the voices of women written about though these sources, women talking about themselves later in life, and the dominant explanatory frameworks elaborated after the event which potentially shape the form that women's recollections take. Then there is the lens of the historian. Applying a gendered reading to the oral histories of women who do not necessarily view their lives, aspirations and problems as part of a wider context of power relations between men and women demands a careful balancing act, to avoid skewed results in which the analytical method obscures women's own ways of seeing their world.

Some urban, educated women do use gender as a category of analysis. Fadéla Mesli, who joined the *maquis* as a student, describes the war in the following terms:

> We had two struggles to lead, the struggle against colonialism, and the struggle in our families. A woman who lived amongst men, there were dangers, there were our customs. We led two revolutions, one

against colonialism, the other against taboos, and I would say that the latter was even more difficult.[68]

Ferroudja Amarouche, who was married with three children before the war, and who had six more children after 1962, frames her life in very different terms.

> He [her husband] did his duty, I did my duty [during the war] and [after 1962] we brought up our children in decent conditions, *al-hamdulillah* [Thanks to God]. The most important thing is that he [her husband] came back, and in good health. If he had died, I would never have come to Algiers, and I couldn't have had more children![69]

To argue that the war years were a period of relative freedom for rural women such as Ferroudja, in which they had more opportunities to enter into the public sphere and mix with men, which in turn led to either a permanent change in attitudes or a return to male dominance and separate spheres once the war ended, is to adopt an analysis that rural interviewees would not use themselves.

Exploring the connections between wartime discourses about women and their lived experiences, we see that urban, educated women both were active agents in the strategic creation of propaganda about themselves and could also be trapped by its narrative constraints. Rural women could be unaware of, ignore or strategically use gendered discourses about their lives and aspirations. The metaphor of brotherly and sisterly common purpose is one of the key points of connectedness between the wartime nationalist and later state-promoted discourse on women during the war, feminist counter-narratives from the 1980s onwards and women's own stories. In Chapter 6, we will explore in more detail the broader political and social purposes that this narrative of fraternity and mutual respect serves postwar; in the context of this chapter we can see the important role it plays in rendering publicly acceptable relationships which had the potential to be socially disruptive. Indeed, when interviewees move away from the brother/sister trope and recount more personal experiences which reflect their families' suspicions about these new relations, the disruption to the established order becomes more visible.

How might we expect these wartime discourses and experiences to translate into the post-independence period? Did the war pave the way for a brave new world of gender relations? Or was change still superficial, couched in a familiar language to make a 'return' to normal both likely and not that noticeable? In fact, emphasis on evaluating whether or not the war marked a new era or parenthesis is a problematic approach. To a certain extent, it has been encouraged by a tendency to read history backwards to discover the origins of the perceived successes or failures of the post-independent state. Yet we can only judge if we are looking at a 'new era' or a 'parenthesis' not from the standpoint of today, fifty years after independence, but by returning to the context of the 1960s. And we can only really think about the gender question by locating it in a broader view of political, socio-economic and cultural change in these first years of independence.

Notes

1 There is a significant literature on the creation of colonial categories, including P. Lorcin, *Imperial Identities: Stereotyping, Prejudice and Race in Colonial Algeria* (London: I. B. Tauris, 1995), and L. A. Stoler, *Carnal Knowledge and Imperial Power: Race and the Intimate in Colonial Rule* (Berkeley: University of California Press, 2002).

2 Between 1865 and 1870, the 1865 law also applied to the Jewish population of Algeria – full citizenship was offered only if the individual renounced Jewish family law. The 1870 Crémieux decree naturalised en masse the Jewish population of Algeria, and legally Jews were counted in the category of 'Europeans'. However, the Jewish presence in Algeria long predates colonisation, and there were some notable exceptions to the Crémieux decree: for example, it did not extend citizenship to Jews in the M'zab region, which was conquered in 1882. Jews were not settlers, but they came to be classed as *pieds noirs*, notably after their 'repatriation' to France in 1962. The Jewish population of colonial Algeria is a growing field of research: see, for example, a special issue of *Archives Juives* on 'Français, juifs et musulmans dans l'Algérie coloniale', 45:2 (2012), and a special issue of *Journal of North African Studies* on 'Jews and French Colonialism in Algeria', 17:5 (2012).

3 P. Weil, *Qu'est-ce qu'un Français? Histoire de la nationalité française depuis la Révolution* (Paris: Gallimard, 2004), pp. 354–5. Non-citizens were also subject to the 1874 indigenous code, a list of twenty-seven infractions additional to the penal code; the number of infractions was increased in 1876 and 1877.

4 Cited in G. Meynier, *L'Algérie révélée: la guerre de 1914–1918 et le premier quart du XXe siècle* (Geneva: Librairie Droz, 1981), p. 245.

See also D. Rivet, *Le Maghreb à l'épreuve de la colonisation* (Paris: Hachette, 2009).

5 For more on this, see J. Clancy-Smith, 'Islam, gender and identities in the making of French Algeria, 1830–1962', in Clancy-Smith and F. Gouda (eds), *Domesticating the Empire: Race, Gender and Family Life in French and Dutch Colonialisms* (Charlottesville: University Press of Virginia, 1998).

6 S. Joseph (ed.), *Gender and Citizenship in the Middle East* (New York: Syracuse University Press, 2000), p. 6.

7 S. Bakalti, *La Femme tunisienne au temps de la colonisation 1881–1956* (Paris: L'Harmattan, 1996), pp. 57–9.

8 ANA: Box 549: Report of Mme Lefaucheux, French delegate and President of UN Commission on Women, July 1951.

9 ANA: Fonds du GPRA/MAE/78: *The First Afro-Asian Women's Conference, Cairo 14–23 Jan 1961: Reports, speeches, resolutions* [pamphlet].

10 F. Fanon, *Sociologie d'une révolution (l'An V de la révolution algérienne)* (Paris: Maspero, 1972 [1959]), p. 93.

11 'Les Femmes dans la révolution', text published in FLN newspaper *Résistance algérienne* on 16 May 1957 and reproduced in an annexe to Fanon's *Sociologie d'une révolution*.

12 Evans and Phillips, *Algeria*, p. 60.

13 See the work of N. Macmaster, *Burning the Veil: The Algerian War and the 'Emancipation' of Muslim Women* (Manchester: Manchester University Press, 2009), R. Seferdjeli, '"Fight with us, women, and we will emancipate you"', and Sambron, *Femmes musulmanes*.

14 Plateforme de la Soummam, www.elmouradia.dz/francais/symbole/textes/soummam.htm (accessed 19 May 2014).

15 SHD, 1H1646: Salut à nos soeurs patriotes!

16 *El Moudjahid* (12 June 1959). It is worth pointing out that the widely available (French language) version of wartime *El Moudjahid* was published in three volumes in Yugoslavia and is not identical to the printed material published in Tunisia. The Yugoslavian version was adapted (or 'purified') to win over international opinion; articles such as the 'Diary of a female guerrilla fighter' would be seen as particularly useful in achieving this aim. Thanks to James McDougall for underlining this point. The Arabic version of *al mujahid* was, according to Meynier, 'more on the left and more secular than *El Moudjahid* [in French]' because the authors did not feel a constant need to demonstrate Algeria's Arabo-Islamic origins. Meynier, *Historie intérieure*, p. 235.

17 SHD, 1H1646: Front et armée de libération nationale, Etat major *wilaya* 4, Salut à nos sœurs patriotes! (undated – seized 7 August 1961).

18 J. Fremeaux, 'Les SAS (Sections administratives spécialisées)', *Guerres mondiales et conflits contemporains*, 208 (2002), 55–68.

19 N. Macmaster, 'The colonial "emancipation" of Algerian women: the marriage law of 1959 and the failure of legislation on women's rights in the post-independence era', *Stichproben: Wiener Zeitschrift für kritische Afrikastudien*, 12 (2007), 91–116, pp. 100–1.

20 Much of the activity of the SAS was therefore inevitably aimed at women in villages. Also aimed specifically at women, but roving rather than static and directly attached to the French army, Equipes Médico-Sociales Itinérantes (Itinerant Medical-Social Teams, EMSI), created in 1957, sought to fulfil similar tasks to the SAS.

21 'Les Officiers SAS', report for *Journal Télévisé de 20h* (4 June 1956), www.ina.fr/economie-et-societe/vie-sociale/video/CAF94072992/les-off iciers-sas.fr.html (accessed 19 May 2014).

22 SHD, 1H1619: Etat major de guerre, *wilaya* III, Questionnaire politique.

23 Fremeaux, 'Les SAS', p. 58.

24 ANOM, 5/SAS/18: Bouzeguene, Journal de marche.

25 *Ibid.*

26 Interview with Ferroudja Amarouche (10 December 2005).

27 ANOM, 5/SAS/5: Aghribs: Rapport trimestriel (15 September 1959).

28 M. Garanger, *Femmes algériennes 1960* (Paris: Contrejour, 1989 [1982]).

29 Macmaster, *Burning the Veil*, p. 212.

30 Interview with Ferroudja Amarouche (10 December 2005).

31 Fanon, *Sociologie d'une révolution*, p. 41.

32 *Echo d'Alger* (12 July 1957); *Journal d'Alger* (12 July 1957).

33 Y. Godard, *Les Trois Batailles d'Alger Tome I: les Paras dans la ville* (Paris: Fayard, 1972), pp. 342–3 and p. 346.

34 *Ibid.*, pp. 340–1.

35 G. Arnaud and J. Vergès, *Pour Djamila Bouhired* (Paris: Editions de minuit, 1957).

36 National Archives, London (hereafter NA): FO371/131697: Officer of High Commissioner for UK in Dehli, Distribution of propaganda by FLN in Algeria (1958).

37 Halimi and de Beauvoir, *Djamila Boupacha*.

38 J. Surkis, 'Ethics and violence: Simone de Beauvoir, Djamila Boupacha and the Algerian War', *French Politics, Culture & Society*, 28:2 (2010), 38–55, p. 45.

39 Z. Drif, *La Mort de mes frères* (Paris: François Maspero, 1961), pp. 11–12.

40 Interview with Zohra Drif (11 June 2005).

41 *Jours de France* (11 August 1956).

42 The satirical journal *Le Canard enchaîné*, published in metropolitan

France, also claimed that the three women were Egyptian, in a mocking article denounced by Tunisian daily newspaper *L'Action* (6 August 1956).

43 Interview with Fadéla Mesli (20 December 2005).
44 Interview with Fadila Attia (19 June 2005).
45 Interview with Chérifa Akache (21 June 2005).
46 Interview with Yamina Salem (1 June 2005).
47 Interview with Djamila Boupacha (11 June 2005).
48 Interview with Djamila Bouazza (3 and 9 June 2005).
49 M. Harbi, 'Les Révoltes logiques', *Cahier du Centre de recherches sur les idéologies de la révolte*, 11 (1979–80), 78–93, p. 80.
50 Meynier, *Histoire intérieure du FLN*, p. 231.
51 SHD, 1H1564.
52 R. Seferdjeli, 'Rethinking the history of the mujahidat during the Algerian War', *Interventions: International Journal of Postcolonial Studies*, 14:2 (2012), 238–55.
53 SHD, 1H1623/1.
54 SHD, 1H2878/D1.
55 Benyahia, *La Conjuration au pouvoir*, p. 169.
56 SHD, 1H1564. None of these scandals seems to have affected the postwar career of 'H'Mimi' (a *nom de guerre*) – he occupied various posts within the FLN and was a deputy in the National Assembly. He died in 2003.
57 SHD, 1H1623/1.
58 Ighilahriz, *Algérienne*, p. 88.
59 Interview with Fadéla Mesli (20 December 2005).
60 Interview with Khadjidja Belguembour (14 June 2005).
61 Interview with Yamina Salem (1 June 2005).
62 Ighilahriz, *Algérienne*, p. 72. This masculinisation of female fighters is a common theme in narratives of war by and about women. See, for example, Schmidt, '"Emancipate your husbands!"' and Summerfield, *Reconstructing Women's Lives*, pp. 82–3.
63 Interview with Ferroudja Amarouche (10 December 2005).
64 Interview with Chérifa Akache (21 June 2005).
65 R. Seferdjeli, 'Les Femmes dans l'Armée de libération nationale: le marriage et/ou l'action?', *Pour une histoire critique et citoyenne: le cas de l'histoire francoalgérienne* (2007), http://ens-web3.ens-lsh.fr/colloques/france-algerie/communication.php3?id_article=261 (accessed 19 May 2014).
66 Interview with Khadjidja Belguembour (14 June 2005).
67 Interview with Fadila Attia (19 June 2005).
68 Interview with Fadéla Mesli (20 December 2005).
69 Interview with Ferroudja Amarouche (10 December 2005).

3

1962:
Continuities and discontinuities

Tents and villas

Lucette Hadj Ali spent six years of the War of Independence living in clandestinity, as a member of Combattants de la Libération (Combatants of Liberation, CDL), a network within the PCA which allied with the FLN in 1956. Obliged to change safe house constantly to avoid arrest, at one point in 1962 she was living with communist leaders Bachir Hadj Ali (whom she would marry in 1963) and Sadek Hadjeres on a road leading from the centre of Algiers up to the heights of El Biar, a favoured residential location amongst the European population. From the vantage point of the balcony of her rented apartment, she caught a glimpse of many of the key events which would mark the end of French rule and the birth of independent Algeria. She saw members of the OAS, the right-wing paramilitary group composed of renegade army officers and settlers who refused to accept the loss of French Algeria, murder an Algerian man who had stopped to fill up his car at the petrol station across the road. She saw the first soldiers from the *wilaya* IV (the region around Algiers) arrive in the capital straight from the *maquis*: 'They went down [what is today] the Boulevard Bougara,[1] totally ragged and with their uniform in shreds, it was really something, just before the declaration of independence'. Lucette vividly remembers the declaration of independence on 5 July 1962:

> LHA: Bachir [Hadj Ali] and Sadek [Hadjeres] had left [the apartment] beforehand to go into the Algerian districts [of Algiers]. We didn't know what the OAS was going to unleash, so it was better to be protected. I was with Eliette Loup [a fellow communist activist and wife of Hadjeres]; we ran the last copy of our newspaper

[*Al Houriyya*] and wound everything up. We needed to go to an area with more Algerians.

NV: To protect yourselves from the OAS?

LHA: Yes, and also to protect ourselves from certain elements in the FLN, we didn't really know what the impact would be on the party [PCA]. So 5 July – it was extraordinary. We found ourselves at the Ruisseau junction [an area in the centre of Algiers], we were meant to be heading up towards [the district of] Kouba. I saw the last French cop leave, there were crowds of people streaming out, we couldn't go any further. I was banging on the side of our car [chanting] 'Algerian Algeria, Algerian Algeria'. Algerians were passing by, they were heading towards the Grande Poste [main post office] in the centre of town, and they smiled at us, two European women who were chanting 'Algerian Algeria'. No one confronted us. It was joy everywhere. Those are memories which are unforgettable, unforgettable, unforgettable.[2]

In rural Kabylia, Chérifa Akache describes similar scenes of elation:

After independence, I went back to Kabylia [she had sought refuge with her parents in Algiers in the last years of the war], we paraded, we climbed up on to lorries, we said 'Long live Algeria, *tahya al-jaza'ir*', there were lots of drums, we danced for nights and nights, we spent the night outside. The *mujahidin* called us 'our mothers, our sisters'; they said to us 'Nothing will happen to you, you're safe'.[3]

The accounts of Lucette Hadj Ali and Chérifa Akache not only capture the enthusiasm and delight of the days which followed independence, they also depict a revolutionary moment, encapsulated by the disintegration of the boundaries separating 'male' space from 'female' space, 'European' districts from 'Muslim' districts, rural *maquisards* and urban areas. Women occupied public space in ways that would have been unthinkable before – dancing alongside men and staying out all night. The Algerian inhabitants of towns with significant European populations both literally and symbolically appropriated the urban geography. They marched and partied through districts which were previously almost exclusively European; they moved into the houses of departing European families, most of whom fled, fearing rightly or wrongly their only choice was between 'the suitcase or the coffin'. Ferroudja Amarouche migrated from her village of Bouzeguene to Algiers at the end of the war and acquired the former apartment of a European family. She explains: 'We took the house of some French people at Champ de manoeuvres [today Place du 1er mai], and my mother-in-law said to me, '*Al-hamdulillah* [Thanks to God], they smashed up our homes, now we live in theirs'.[4] Not everyone, however, got a new home, as Chérifa Akache explains:

> CA: Those who sorted themselves out, they took the villas, they took the houses, and people like us didn't take anything. We were given tents.
> NV: Who got the villas?
> CA: The smart ones, they gave them to their brothers and sisters. Those who really sacrificed themselves, they never came back so they couldn't do anything. The *mujahidin* who came back, they helped their fathers, their mothers and their brothers. Those who really sacrificed are dead and their families didn't get anything.[5]

Chérifa Akache's husband was one of those who never came back.

The undercurrent to all this joy was political uncertainty, infighting and internecine violence and the beginning of arguments about the 'winners' and 'losers' of independence. Moreover, whilst there was a feeling of jubilant recklessness at the usual order being turned upside down, there was also an intense yearning for a semblance of normality and order, which Chérifa Akache underlines when she talks about the *mujahidin* reassuring civil populations that they were now 'safe'.

As independence approached, the FLN–ALN imploded. At a basic level, this implosion was the public combustion of a conflict which had long been simmering behind closed doors, pitching the negotiators of the March 1962 Evian Accords – that is to say, the GPRA, presided over in Tunis by Benyoucef Ben Khedda from August 1961 onwards – against the army generals of the EMG, led by Colonel Boumediene, with strongholds in the border towns of Ghardimaou (Tunisia) and Oujda (Morocco). After his release from prison in France in March 1962, the founding FLN member Ben Bella made a strategic alliance with the EMG, bringing his popular legitimacy to their military manpower and firepower, although the relationship was not without tensions. Within Algerian territory, Ben Bella and Boumediene could count on the support of the *wilayat* of the Aurès (*wilaya* I), some officers in North Constantine (*wilaya* II) and Oran (*wilaya* V) and some dissenting groups, organised by emissaries of the EMG, within the

Fédération de France (*wilaya* VII). The *wilayat* of Kabylia (III), Algiers (IV), the head of the *wilaya* I (Colonel Salah Boubnider), the Federal Committee of the Fédération de France and the founding FLN leaders Boudiaf, Aït Ahmed and Krim Belkacem opposed the EMG but were not necessarily united.

This was a confused and complicated situation, far from a straightforward confrontation between politicians and military men, supporters of democracy and advocates of authoritarianism, or between soldiers of the interior against those of the exterior. As Amar Mohand Amer argues, the FLN was 'more an agglomeration of leaders than the expression of a party with democratic mechanisms to take power'.[6] The choice between the EMG or the GPRA – or, as alliances developed in the summer of 1962, between the 'Tlemcen group' (where Ben Bella set up his base in July and created a Political Bureau to replace the GPRA) and the 'Tizi Ouzou group' (the headquarters of his opponents) – was in many cases a strategic one for key FLN–ALN figures, aimed at strengthening their positions in preparation for the post-independence order.

These divisions meant little to the vast majority of the Algerian population. The inhabitants of Algiers were perplexed to see fighting break out between supporters of the Ben Bella–Boumediene alliance and *maquisards* of the interior, notably from the *wilaya* IV. They took to the streets to shout 'seven years, that's enough'. It would be the Ben Bella–EMG alliance and their superior military might which would win out, and their factions of the FLN would metamorphose from a wartime front into a state apparatus which has maintained its hold on power to the present day.

In this context, Lucette Hadj Ali's reference to the dishevelled soldiers she saw arriving in Algiers from the *wilaya* IV is not just a description: it is also a coded political statement. Their ragged appearance and shredded uniforms are both the physical evidence of their real participation in the war, fighting on Algerian soil to free Algeria, and the explanation for why these men and their allies and supporters failed to outmanoeuvre the Tlemcen group in summer 1962. By September 1962, Ben Bella was installed in Algiers as president. At the start of December 1962, he dissolved the briefly reformed PCA and Lucette and her fellow communists were forced back into a clandestine, or semi-clandestine, existence. Key figures of the Tizi Ouzou group such as Aït Ahmed and Boudiaf would soon be exiled.

This chapter examines 1962 through two approaches. The first approach is that of social history. The chapter seeks to evoke a revolutionary moment, challenging the vision of women going 'back into the kitchen' in 1962 after the 'parenthesis' of the war, whilst at the same time exploring how continuities between the colonial and post-colonial periods – and women's levels of education and socio-economic status – determined to what extent independence would offer them new opportunities. In women's testimonies, 1962 is neither a cut-off point nor a year zero, but a whole new world in which many things stayed the same. Precisely because we are working with oral history, the second approach engages with the highly politicised historiography of Algeria. The chapter explores the symbolic significance which 1962 has acquired in accounts of independent Algeria, as the watershed moment when either independence was consolidated or the revolution betrayed. It seeks to unpick how women's narratives of where they were and what they were doing in 1962 are entwined with anxieties about their own political legitimacy and relationship to power in Algeria then and now. We begin with this second approach.

Narratives of political legitimacy: Where were you in 1962? Who were you with and what were you doing?

Unlike Lucette Hadj Ali and Chérifa Akache, Khadjidja Belguembour did not celebrate independence on 5 July 1962. When I interviewed her, Khadjidja Belguembour lived in a working-class district of Algiers, but her origins are in a small village, Douar Ben Yeftah, in what is today the *wilaya* of Jijel. She had little access to formal education and says that she had never seen a settler or a Frenchman before the War of Independence. A *maquisarde* in the east of Algeria (*wilaya* II), Khadjidja describes the period between March and July 1962 as one of very limited communication, in which infighting between different factions of the FLN–ALN manifested itself in assassinations and violence which baffled most *maquisards*. Indeed, her *maquis* unit did not initially know that a ceasefire had come into place with the signing of the Evian Accords in March 1962 – they had no radio. In the months that followed, the head of Khadjidja's *wilaya*, Colonel Boubnider, tactically allied with the GPRA, whilst one of his commanders, Larbi Berredjem, sided with the EMG. But Khadjidja did not know this at the time: 'I was apolitical so I didn't even know there was an interior [army] or an exterior [army]. I didn't know.'

Following her marriage in the *maquis*, in May 1962 Khadjidja left her rural guerrilla unit to join her new husband in the city of Constantine. She saw him twice before he disappeared, kidnapped, she says 'by the army of Tunis, the army of Ben Bella'. She then thinks the brothers of her husband – who were also *mujahidin* – managed to get him released, and he was in Morocco, or maybe even France: 'Independence for me, it wasn't joyous. We didn't have a home, we didn't have anywhere to go, and we didn't have any money. Our lives were threatened every second of the day, there was a price on our heads, all those who were in the *maquis*, who were in the interior.'

In mid-June, Khadjidja Belguembour returned to her parents in Mila, a town fifty kilometres from Constantine, but a few days later she says that she too was kidnapped by supporters of the Ben Bella–EMG alliance:

> KB: The women, they stuck us in barracks, we were three hundred girls. Three hundred *mujahidat* stuck in the Beni H'Miden barracks, a kilometre outside Constantine. You needed to see in what conditions! They housed us in tents, it was a former French army barracks, and the conditions were appalling. The leaders, the *maquisards* with whom I carried out the revolution, I never saw them again. Other people came – it was strange, we asked the question, 'where are our brothers from the *maquis*?' These people, we don't know them, they don't look like soldiers. First off, the night before we saw them in civilian clothes. They are rude, vulgar; they are there to get revenge on us. They don't know how to carry their weapons, they don't look right in their uniforms.
> NV: Why did they put all these *mujahidat* in the barracks?
> KB: Because we were a threat, some men had stayed in the *maquis* – those who had understood. But we hadn't [...] [In the barracks] we didn't eat properly, our lives were in danger, we were not safe, they swore at us instead of respecting us. Out of disrespect, at night they came and pissed on our tents.

According to Khadjidja Belguembour, these women were being held to stop them joining the men who had remained in the *maquis* and to serve the new soldiers who had taken control of the city, by cooking and cleaning. These women were also a pool of potential marriageable young women:

One day, I can't remember the exact date because it was horrible, they brought around a group of men. They made the girls come out, they asked them to take a shower beforehand, and they chose brides. They sold them like sheep, because there were some girls with us who had no family left. So they said: 'You can marry this one, you can marry that one.' Like sheep.

Khadjidja describes terrified *mujahidat* stealing guns and sleeping with them under their pillows at night as 'we were scared we were going to be raped'. 'Even after 5 July, we weren't freed, they brought us along [to an independence day celebration], they made us put the uniform on, they told us it was "5 July". We were made to do it.' This independence day 'celebration' nevertheless provided Khadjidja with the opportunity to meet some injured *maquisards*, who were still in hospital and who wanted to be nursed by women who had been in the *maquis* – and who spoke Arabic – rather than French doctors. Khadjidja was allowed to go and work at the hospital, but she was picked up and returned to the barracks every evening. 'Even if I had been allowed to go out, I didn't have any money [...] I saw young women in town with nice haircuts, fashionably dressed, I was wearing a filthy uniform and shoes one size too big which hurt my feet.' Eventually, in late July 1962, her former leaders – 'those that negotiated so they wouldn't be killed' – and the 'Tunis leaders' – by whom she means the Ben Bella–EMG alliance – came to a deal. The women were released, albeit 'into the wild, we had no housing, no care, no money'.[7]

Khadjidja Belguembour's detailed account of her experiences in the months just before and after independence is difficult to cross-reference. The broad brushstrokes of her story fit with what was happening in her *wilaya* at the time. Some elements of her story might seem vague, or even unclear. Not least, it is difficult to locate the myriad of anonymous 'theys' and occasional names she uses within the already complex political factions outlined in the existing literature. Although she states that she never again saw the *maquisards* with whom she had carried out the revolution, suggesting the liquidation of genuine veterans, she did actually meet a number of them: some came to the barracks where she was imprisoned, seemingly as visitors; she describes another officer whom she had fought alongside being well placed enough after independence to be able to help former *maquisardes* such as herself acquire employment in hospitals. All of this is symptomatic of the highly confused situation at the time, in which individuals switched sides, rivals were assassinated and compromises negotiated.

The significance of Khadjidja Belguembour's account lies not so much in the detail but in her (re)reading of 1962, which is deeply impregnated with a post-hoc vocabulary of revolution betrayed. Her moral division between those who are the rightful – and righteous – children of the revolution and those who are opportunistic impostors is unequivocal and presented in the most vivid terms. Legitimacy is expressed in morality and dress. The army of the exterior do not look right. The uniform sits uncomfortably on their shoulders, it is suspiciously new; their weapons are props rather than the instruments of the revolution. The *maquisards* of the interior have the war impregnated in their worn-out uniforms and ill-fitting boots, in their wounds, even in their grime. Khadjidja and her fellow *maquisardes* got put in tents, whilst presumably these outsiders received better accommodation. Worse, the exterior army imprisoned the *mujahidat* in the barracks of the former colonial enemy.

These new arrivals are depicted as not only politically illegitimate but also morally bankrupt. Khadjidja's description of the fears of the *mujahidat* about being raped or forced into marriage is in sharp contrast with her depiction of her experience in the *maquis* as a very young teenager. The rough-and-ready *maquis*, was, she says, a milieu that was 'healthy' and 'pure'. She immediately felt 'safe' with her 'brothers', even though of course she was in the most dangerous of situations. In her words, the post-independence FLN single-party state, and its new army, the ANP, 'weren't clean'. She concludes: 'Since 1962, since I left the army [the ALN], I have never felt safe'.[8]

Political illegitimacy expressed through moral corruption, misogyny and box-fresh uniforms is a common theme in a number of women's accounts of post-independence Algeria. Interviewed for the newspaper *El Watan* in March 2005, the former member of the Algiers bomb network Zhor Zerari described how, on 3 July 1962, she went to attend a political meeting about independence at Sidi Fredj, a coastal town on the western outskirts of Algiers. 'At one point, a young man in a brand new military uniform came up to me and said in an authoritarian and aggressive tone, "Go with the women"'.[9] When Zhor protested, he threatened to shoot her and she was forced to leave the meeting. This meeting, and what happened at it, are loaded with symbolism: on 3 July 1962, Algerians reappropriated Sidi Fredj, almost 132 years to the day after French forces had used this coastal town as their beachhead for the invasion of Algiers. At the same moment, an eleventh-hour *mujahid* sought to assert his authority by imposing a separation of men and women at the meeting, thereby excluding a woman who had fought alongside men during the 1956–7 'Battle of Algiers', and who, in her own words, was brought up 'like a boy' and lived alongside women for the first time when imprisoned for her anti-colonial activism aged twenty.[10] As Algerians reclaimed public space, Algerian women seemed to be excluded from it.

Yet whilst there was certainly a moral backlash in the first years of independence, as Chapter 4 explores, those fuelling it were not all false *mujahidin* or men of dubious wartime credentials. Moreover, when I interviewed Zhor Zerari a few months after the publication of this *El Watan* interview and I asked her about this incident at Sidi Fredj, she seemed to minimise its importance: 'It was little jokers trying to be zealous'.[11] Should we interpret this episode as an ominous presaging of independent Algeria and the marginalisation of women, or an annoying, but ultimately insignificant, incident in a period of major upheaval? Zhor Zerari's two interpretations of her own story point to the near impossibility of separating the event from its subsequent politicised interpretations.

The different ways in which Lucette Hadj Ali, Chérifa Akache, Khadjidja Belguembour and Zhor Zerari depict 'old' and 'new' soldiers echo a broader counter-narrative to the top-down official discourse on independence, one that cuts across gender, geography, age and social class in Algerian society. This is a narrative of revolution confiscated that puts into play a set of dichotomies familiar to all Algerians – true/false *mujahidin*, insiders/outsiders, authentic/foreign rulers and legitimate/illegitimate power. In its most politicised form, the term 'Oujda clan' – taking its name from the Moroccan town ten kilometres from the Algerian border where the EMG was based – evokes a powerful politico-military faction within the FLN, including the current president Abdelaziz Bouteflika, which snatched power and prosperity for themselves in 1962. At the very least, passing part of the war in Morocco or Tunisia – even if it was only the last few months – seems to suggest that an individual was not doing much for the war effort.

This is a noticeable theme in fiction about this period. Assia Djebar, who worked for the FLN's wartime journal *El Moudjahid* in Tunis during the war, published *Les Alouettes naïves* in 1957. Set in Tunisia, the novel's central characters are nationalist militants who seem to while away the time in cafés, pursuing aimless political discussions and falling in love, as much as they work in refugee camps with Algerians fleeing the conflict.[12] In *La Grotte éclatée* (1979), a semi-fictionalised account of the experiences of a *maquisarde* working in the Aurès mountains and then on the Algerian–Tunisian border, trying to save wounded and dying *maquisards*, the author Yamina Mechakra fustigates those who in Tunis 'told me to have a rest, and spoke to me about my country without knowing anything about my country'.[13]

Even if this version of the uninformed, unengaged, opportunistic 'men on the borders' would be vigorously denied by those targeted, few would proudly foreground that they spent much of the war in Morocco or Tunisia. In a nation-state built on the sacrifice of one and a half million martyrs – and this is not just an official slogan, it is widely held to be true – not spending the war on Algerian soil suggests you did not give much up. Indeed, taken to its logical conclusion, having *anything* left at the end of the war might be seen as suspicious: as Chérifa Akache puts it, 'those who really sacrificed are dead'.[14] This celebration of sacrifice, a cult of the dispossessed, serves as a critique not only of the EMG but also, by ricochet, of the GPRA, marginalising the role of political action and international campaigning in winning the independence struggle. Thus, rather than a confrontation between 'official' and 'counter' history in Algeria with clear demarcation lines, it is more useful to think about the relationship between 'official' and 'counter' history in terms of a Venn diagram, sharing at the centre a dominant history which is widely held to be true, although it might be put to different political ends.

The impact on women's narratives of both this popular rejection of what the Ben Bella–EMG–Tlemcen group–Oujda clan is seen to represent and the lionisation of an anonymous, authentic Algerian interior is illustrated by the way in which Salima Bouaziz describes how the war ended for her. Between 1961 and August 1962, Salima and her husband Rabah Bouaziz – a senior figure on the Federal Committee of the FF–FLN – played a leading role in creating a Section des Femmes (Women's Section) within the Algerian migrant community. This Section sought to place women's rights at the heart of the programme for the soon-to-be independent state.[15] Salima Bouaziz has a clear position on what should have happened in 1962 – the GPRA should have taken power and organised free elections:

> I returned [to Algeria] upon independence, but not straightaway because there was the coup d'état. Independence didn't take place as it should have done. We had the president of the GPRA, Ben Khedda, and Ben Bella came to take his place. In the Fédération de France, we were legalist, legitimist [...] We were against this coup d'état and so we only went back three months later in September, via Paris. The factions who were fighting it out in Algiers sent envoys [to Paris] to try and convince us to side with this camp or that camp.

In the first months following the March 1962 ceasefire, Salima describes organising political and professional seminars for Algerian women living in France, preparing to send them back to rebuild a country that had been destroyed. After the official declaration of independence on 5 July 1962, a seminar was held to identify women from the migrant community who could be potential candidates for elections to the Constituent Assembly:

> We hadn't yet chosen the camp we were going to follow [...] Amongst the women who participated in this seminar, five were chosen – I was one of them – as a candidate for the National Assembly. Unfortunately, none of us were ultimately selected, because there was a problem between those who were in the immigrant community and those who were here [in Algeria]. We weren't living the same situation. In France we were more politicised, in Algeria they were in the action.

Salima Bouaziz is very assured in explaining that she was firmly against the EMG's 'coup d'état' – an unequivocal word choice. Her actions once this coup took place are more ambiguous, and reflect the desire to move on and find a way forward despite, or perhaps because of, the confusion that reigned. Whilst she fundamentally disagreed with the marginalisation of the GPRA, she nevertheless considered becoming a candidate for the Constituent Assembly, even when it was becoming quite clear that the Tlemcen group would win the internal power struggle. When her candidacy for the Constituent Assembly failed to materialise for political reasons, she still returned to Algeria to make her contribution to society.

The distinction that Salima makes between those who suffered in Algeria and those who had a greater margin of manoeuvre for political activity in France is telling. This could be a coded critique of the failure of the wartime FLN–ALN to effectively accompany armed action with a programme to educate the masses politically. But a second explanation is more likely. Being in Algeria, spending the war in Algeria trumps everything in terms of legitimacy. 'I wish I had gone to the *maquis*,' Salima tells me.[16]

The contemporary resonance of spending part of the war on the borders presents a potentially uncomfortable subject for interviewees who did. The three *maquisardes* I interviewed who were in the *wilaya* V (Oran) were evacuated in late 1957 to the Moroccan border, where they worked in refugee camps. Fadila Attia had made her way to Morocco on a clandestine mission in summer 1957. Fadéla Mesli, arrested in the *maquis*, and many members of the Algiers bomb network who were also arrested, were in prisons in metropolitan France when the Evian Accords paved the way for their release in March 1962. Given the ongoing violence in Algeria, many did not, or could not, return straightaway, and were thus repatriated to ALN bases in Tunisia and Morocco.

Interviewees who today clearly express their political affiliation with the current political system quickly insist on the utility of their presence on the borders. Saliha Djeffal is a former member of the FF–FLN and at the time of the interview was a senior figure within the FLN. She explains that she was working as a nurse for military personnel in the EMG and for Algerian refugees on the Algeria–Tunisia border near Souk Ahras from early 1960 to the end of the war. The fact that Saliha was working with refugees – and she provides a lengthy description of this – is also her way of underlining to the listener that, whatever one thinks of the 'side' that she appears to have been working for, she was doing something worthwhile.[17]

Some of the *mujahidat* who had become well-known figures during the war were housed in the luxurious homes of senior Moroccan or Tunisian dignitaries upon their release from prison. This materially comfortable situation did not always sit well morally with the individuals concerned: as one woman put it, under the cover of anonymity: 'we were full of idealism [...] this really bourgeois milieu was not at all our ideals'. Zhor Zerari, released from prison in France after the ceasefire in March 1962, and taken to Tunisia to protect her from OAS revenge attacks, explains:

'I went to Tunisia, in a big villa, very nice, I hung around there. [But] I wanted to go home. I wanted to vote for the referendum [on independence, held on 1 July 1962].'[18] The opposition between those who got tents and those who got villas is once again foregrounded, with women such as Zhor Zerari keen to underline that they did not belong to the group that got the villas, i.e. those who profited – and profiteered – from independence.

Fadéla Mesli arrived in Morocco in late 1961, having been released from prison in France in 1960. She explains that her departure from France was precipitated by a threatening letter that she received from the OAS: '"Terrorist of [GPRA President] Ben Khedda, you kill the innocent and you steal from the poor. The OAS is here, it will strike when it wants, how it wants and where it wants."' The fact that Fadéla could still recite this letter word-for-word forty-five years later underlines to the listener that staying in France was not an option. Yet Morocco, she says, was not 'easy'. When I asked her what she meant by this, she initially evoked the very concrete difficulty of returning to Algeria, because of the electrified fence built by the French army during the war to prevent ALN movement across the Algerian border with Morocco. However, as the discussion continued, it also became clear that Fadéla wanted to be back in her country, doing something she considered to be useful. In the meantime, and with great difficulty – because she was an Algerian in Morocco, who had recently been released from prison – she managed to get permission to work as a volunteer in a Moroccan hospital:

> I worked there for a few months, and when I learnt that there was a plane which was returning [to Algeria], I begged, I said to them, 'I'm going back, I know I will be useful'. They let me go back, I was the only woman on the plane. I was so moved to be going home, to go back to Algeria, I was crying so much I became breathless. In the end, it was Mr Akbi, a former ambassador who at the time was an officer in the ALN, who came over to speak to me just before I got on the plane: [he said] 'You're crying so hard you can't breathe, have they made you go back? I am a commander, and I can get you back to Morocco.' I said, 'No, I'm crying because I'm so happy to go back to my country.'[19]

These were perhaps also tears of relief. If Fadéla Mesli was relieved to physically arrive back in Algeria in 1962, in my 2005 interview with her she also seemed much more at ease when her story got back on to Algerian soil. She explains that she went straight to the seat of the Provisional Executive at Rocher Noir (today Boumerdes), forty kilometres outside Algiers. The Provisional Executive, composed of Muslims and Europeans under the presidency of the moderate nationalist Abderrahmane Farès, was created as a result of the Evian Accords to organise the transition of power. Although the Provisional Executive was in theory an independent body, Farès recognised the GPRA as the legal representative of the FLN and anticipated transferring power to it. In addition to the presence of the Provisional Executive in the Algiers region, Commander Azzedine (Rabah Zerari, uncle of Zhor Zerari) had been sent by the GPRA to fight the OAS but also to re-exert the GPRA's authority over the FLN–ALN's Zone Autonome d'Alger (Algiers Autonomous Zone, ZAA). In summer 1962, the former ZAA head Yacef Saadi, freshly released from French prison, would succeed in taking control of Algiers and would offer up the capital to the Tlemcen group after allying with Ben Bella and the EMG against the GPRA and the rural guerrillas in the area surrounding Algiers (the *wilaya* IV).

This struggle for power, which at a number of moments spilled over into violent clashes on the streets of Algiers, is not part of Fadéla Mesli's account of this period. Instead, she describes joining the ZAA's sanitary services team, working to open medical facilities safe for Algerians to be treated in during a period when the OAS could finish off in hospitals those whom they had injured in street attacks, and when the OAS was also implementing a scorched-earth policy, seeking to leave as little working infrastructure behind for the nascent Algerian state. Her story is one of the OAS against all Algerians rather than one of internecine violence. When Fadéla Mesli began working in Algiers, the ZAA appears to have been at least partly under the control of Commander Azzedine – at one point in summer 1962, she was briefly detained at an OAS road block, and she describes Azzedine's threats to 'unleash carnage' ensuring her rapid release. After a birthing clinic was requisitioned in the Clos-Salembier district of Algiers (today El Madania), Fadéla Mesli worked twenty-four hours a day – 'I know it is difficult to believe', she says – alongside two doctors who had come from metropolitan France: 'The shootings started at six o'clock in morning, the OAS was completely out of control by that point. They started at six o'clock in the morning and they went on into the evening. We

were constantly receiving injured people.' Fadéla then helped nego-
tiate the requisitioning of a Red Cross hospital in Algiers, where she
had carried out work placements as a student before the war.

Even though they lived in Algiers, Fadéla Mesli did not have time
to go and see her parents and she missed the independence celebrations: 'Unfortunately, I didn't even see all the population [out to
celebrate independence], I've seen it on television, but I didn't see
the ultimate happiness of the people. Women, even without the
hayk, abandoned their husbands, their children, they came out to
dance in the street. But at least I was useful.'[20] Once again, we see
the importance of being, and being seen to be, in the right place, at
the right time, doing the right thing and being useful. At the end of
summer 1962, the Provisional Executive transferred power to the
Constituent Algerian Assembly dominated by the Tlemcen group.
Fadéla Mesli became a deputy in the Assembly.

Interviewees' desire to put physical distance between themselves
and Tunisia and Morocco, not just literally at the time, but also –
and especially – in subsequent retellings of their story – is also a way
to distance themselves from the political crisis of summer 1962. To
a certain extent, women's lack of discussion of infighting in interviews makes sense. Women were not key figures in power struggles
because they were not in senior positions. This was a period of significant confusion with few, if any, actors in possession of a global
view, particularly those only recently released from prison where
the circulation of information was limited and where stories about
infighting were dismissed, not without reasonable cause, as French
propaganda. Yet women's reticence might more convincingly be
explained not so much by a lack of first-hand, detailed knowledge
of the political and personal conflicts of 1962, but more as the result
of acute sensitivity to the post-hoc frames through which Morocco
and Tunisia in 1962 have been read.

Zhor Zerari tells me: 'I saw the leaders coming and going.' When
I ask her if the various camps tried to convince her to take a particular side she says that they did not. The men spoke to her 'like
brothers'. She adds, 'After imprisonment, exhaustion, we were lost.
It was after the events that we realised': suggesting that physical and
mental fatigue made it hard to engage with the unfolding political
situation. For Zhor, this feeling of being disconnected from events
continued after her return to Algiers: 'In Algiers, they were partying day and night. But for me too many people were dead. I could

neither sing nor dance.'[21] She looked in vain for her father, who had disappeared after his arrest and torture by parachutists.[22]

Zhor Zerari also reminds us that the political confusion needs to be located within the widely documented phenomenon of the difficultly of adapting to postwar life, for both soldiers and civilians.[23] Amongst the twenty-seven *mujahidat* I interviewed, such difficulties often express themselves through references to their post-war marriages. Ten women were already married before the war began (including all five rural women) and seventeen were unmarried. Sixteen of these unmarried women got married either just before the end of the war, or straight after. Nearly all of these women married a fellow *mujahid*. As one interviewee put it, under the cover of anonymity, at the end of the war, she wanted to socialise only with men who had also been involved in armed combat. She felt that they had a different language because they had shared a similar life. She said that her status as a former combatant frightened some men off, and that for women like her a 'civilian' was not considered a worthy match. After the war she went out on a date with a student who had been in the FF–FLN, and he spent the whole time talking about the revolution. She describes herself sitting in silence, thinking 'you don't know who I am'. Not disheartened, the young man persisted, and, in the end, they got married and were happy: 'He brought me something else. Between *maquisards* we were all a bit not right […] we had kind of lost touch with reality.' Zohra Drif, who married Rabah Bitat, a founding member of the FLN, also touches on the idea that young, educated *mujahidat* perhaps had a distorted view of how a *mujahid* might be different from an 'ordinary' man: 'Coming back to everyday, daily reality, you take a while to understand that the *mujahidin* were not different, it was the situation that prompted different behaviour'.[24] Personal relationships begun in the intense conditions of the anti-colonial struggle could fail in the cold light of the postwar period when veterans realised that apart from the war they might not have much in common at all. One interviewee, a devout Muslim, realised with horror that the man she had married – a key figure in the FLN during the war – was a communist and an atheist. They rapidly divorced.

As well as the continual references to being lost and exhausted, the vagueness of women's language when talking about the leaders around them in 1962 – i.e. military and political figures within the FLN and ALN – is striking. The vocabulary is one of 'those in charge' [*responsables*], 'brothers', 'they' and the impersonal French pronoun 'on' (variously translatable as 'we' or 'they'). Bahia Ben Ali, a former *maquisarde* in the *wilaya* IV (Algiers region), uses similar language to talk about infighting: 'I didn't want to have anything to with it, I said, "Now we're independent, there is no need to be against this one or that one."'[25] Mimi Maziz, a member of the FF–FLN, talks about the efforts made to recruit her by supporters of the Ben Bella–EMG faction:

> They came to get me and they said 'Come and join the Tlemcen group'. I said 'I am joining neither the Tlemcen group [*nor, her sentence implies, any other group*], I am free and independent, I am for Algeria, and now you don't know me, and I don't know you. I am joining no one; I am going back to Algeria and my family. I've had enough.'[26]

At this point in the interview, Mimi's friend Salima Bouaziz – they were interviewed together – joined in. As we have seen, Salima has a very clear narrative of stolen independence. Yet she simply adds: 'It was very difficult, that period'.[27] Mimi then continues: 'When independence came we were split between wanting to go back to our childhood and becoming adults'.[28] This sentence has more than one layer of meaning: on one level, young women who had joined the FLN–ALN as teenagers had lost out on their adolescence: they had left their parents as children and they were coming back as women. However, the context in which Mimi expresses this view hints that this end of the 'age of innocence' is also political.

Interviewees' expressions of exhaustion, of confusion, of feeling disconnected or indeed depressed at the end of the war thus have a dual meaning. Through the lens of 1962, interviewees evoke what it felt like to win independence but lose loved ones, the sense of being emptied of everything they had to give, of seeking out a normality which had been irrevocably transformed, yearning for a return which was impossible. At the same time, their narratives are constructed in the post-hoc knowledge of the existence of discourses which have developed since independence about 'the interior' and 'the exterior', the 'Oujda clan' and 'stolen independences'. In this context, personal narratives of being tired, fed up and homesick become a political necessity. They simultaneously bear an unspoken or semi-spoken narrative of (personal) legitimacy and integrity: 'I was not part of a clan which benefited politically or economically from independence and I am a real *mujahida* who fought on Algerian soil'. This narrative is necessarily unspoken. To say these words aloud would be a powerful and potentially dangerous act, because one would have to assume its political and social implications – excluding 'others' and menacing the idea of the war as kind of social glue, the foundation of Algerian society. Few are prepared to make such a full frontal attack on this dominant history – Belguembour is the exception rather than the rule, and she does so safe in the knowledge that she is a *maquisarde* who was still in the interior in spring and summer 1962, in a *wilaya* opposed to the EMG.

New opportunities, old continuities

Amidst this internecine conflict and post-hoc political sensitivities, there were also more mundane, but essential, questions. On a national level, how could a functioning state be built? On an individual level, how could men and women start to make a living? The trajectory of Mimi Maziz helps us to begin to explore these questions.

Mimi Maziz's entry into the FLN came through the activities of a cousin, who built bombs for the FLN. The teenage Mimi helped him to transport materials. Arrested in 1957 and imprisoned without trial, she was released a year later. She spent the rest of the war as a member of the FF–FLN, moving between France, Germany, Switzerland and refugee camps on the Moroccan border where she worked to prepare Algerian refugees for the return to Algeria by undertaking censuses, delivering vaccinations and detecting cases of contagious diseases such as tuberculosis. Briefly returning home in October 1962, Mimi soon left again, as she felt that, politically speaking, 'the heat was still on, it wasn't yet safe' for her: 'So I said to myself, I'm going back to Switzerland. I had wonderful parents who trusted me. They said "Go, my girl, let God protect you." I left hoping to start my studies up again.'

Yet Mimi was unable to make the right contacts to recommence her studies and she was unemployed. One day in 1963, sitting on a Swiss café terrace drinking a coffee with the last coins in her pocket, she began to talk to a French-speaking African man sitting next to her. He asked her if she was French. Mimi enigmatically replied, 'I used to be, now I'm not. Guess.' After a while he gave up guessing: 'When I said that I was Algerian, he stood up, kissed me on the head and on the shoulders'.[29] It emerged that this fellow customer was a Madagascan ambassador. Thanks to this chance encounter and a self-taught crash course in typing, Mimi found herself in a lucrative job working for the United Nations in Geneva. Mimi's story is full of revolutionary role reversals. In terms of generational change, Mimi's parents happily let her leave the family home alone to go abroad, something unthinkable a generation previously.[30] In terms of upsetting hierarchies of gender and social class, as an unemployed, female student, she was shown the ultimate mark of respect by a male ambassador kissing her on the forehead, his gesture an expression of the enthusiasm which Algeria generated as a model for anti-colonialists in these heady first years of independence. And perhaps in the most striking demonstration of the reversal of fortunes between coloniser and colonised, Mimi even had a Swiss cleaner to polish her floors at home, a radical inversion of colonial 'European' and 'Muslim' roles.

Yet Mimi's veiled mother and grandmother were unwilling to visit her in Switzerland as neither wished to unveil or walk around in the *hayk* in a European country. Homesick, Mimi resigned, went to Paris and sought out the Amicale d'Algérie, the organisation created by the post-independence Algerian state to control and organise the Algerian migrant community in France:

> I told the head [of the Amicale], 'I want to return to Algeria'. 'Yes', he said. I said to him, 'Will you pay for the ticket?' 'Yes', he said. I said to him, 'I want to be a journalist', 'Oh!' he said, 'A journalist?!' I said, 'Yes, a journalist'. Because it was [the Amicale] which had got me to leave the UN. They said, 'Come and work with us', and I said yes, on the condition that I could get work experience on a newspaper, but afterwards they put me answering the phones. They didn't keep their promise. I got angry, and I said, 'I'm going back, call a newspaper called *Le Peuple* [which existed 1962–65], once I've got my ticket, tell the director the day and time when he's going to pick up a journalist. Don't say who it is. Otherwise, I swear, I will smash this place up.' He said, 'OK, don't get angry'. And who came to the airport? Tayeb Belloula [director of the paper, a lawyer by training], thinking that the journalist was a foreign woman. We said hello to each other and I said, 'What are you doing here?' He said, 'I'm waiting for a journalist'. I said, 'No need to wait any longer, it's me'. He said, 'It's you?!' I said 'Yes, it's me, and yourself, have you got experience in journalism? And now you're chief editor? Well, I'm a journalist too.' He was disappointed, disappointed. He said to himself, damn, another useless one.

When Mimi arrived at the newspaper, she met another familiar face from the Fédération de France, Salah Louanchi, who founded *Le Peuple* in 1962, having worked in the 1950s on the review *Consciences maghribines* and wartime publication *Résistance algérienne*. Louanchi also asked where 'the journalist' was, and then, his disappointment put to one side, sent Mimi out to cover the next day's presidential activities. When Mimi arrived home to her family, she proudly announced her new employment. Her mother was less than impressed.

I said to my mother, 'I've found a job, I'm going to work on a newspaper'. She said, 'Well yes, what can you do my girl, we the indigenous' – her thinking was still in the French era – 'we're newspaper sellers and shoe shiners'. I said 'No, I'm not going to sell newspapers, I'm going to be a journalist.' She said 'Whatever, it's the same thing.'[31]

The story of Mimi and her mother tells us much about the opportunities open to some women in the immediate post-independence period. For Fadéla M'Rabet, student activist in the Fédération de France and radio presenter in post-independence Algeria until her exile in 1971, 'Algeria was going to be the model for the world! At the radio there was a revolutionary spirit.'[32] Algeria had been devastated by seven and a half years of war. The economy had ground to a halt. The countryside had been bombarded, including with napalm. The vast majority of the settler population, which had dominated public administration, institutions and the majority of private enterprise, had fled Algeria, meaning state employees – civil servants, the judiciary, police and teachers – disappeared overnight. As the *pieds noirs* (settlers) were leaving, many people were arriving: nationalist leaders and refugees who had been exiled in Europe, Tunisia and Morocco, Algerian émigré workers from France hoping to rebuild their lives back in the newly independent state as well as tens of thousands of *coopérants* and *pieds rouges*. *Coopérants* were technical advisers and specialists, sent by the French state within the framework of co-operation agreements with Algeria. *Pieds rouges*, a wordplay on *pieds noirs*, was the term coined to describe the international revolutionaries and left-wing sympathisers who flocked to Algeria after independence, seeking to create a Third Worldist utopia which would eschew both capitalist exploitation and the repressive aspects of communist regimes.[33] There was an immense desire to make it work.

And yet post-independence Algeria was not really being built from nothing. The kinds of roles that women and men would play in (re)construction would depend on their skills and level of education as well as their political allegiances. The kinds of roles women would be able to play would also depend on attitudes towards what was permissible. Interviewed in 1968, the *Révolution africaine* journalist, and future Mrs Ben Bella, Zohra Sellami declared that independence had changed nothing for Algerian women: 'It is very simple and it is to be expected because social structures cannot be changed in one year, or five years, or ten years unless there is a real revolution'.[34] On this 'blank slate' of 1962, engrained conceptions of gender roles persisted, although they were also constantly challenged. The simple fact of desperately needing men and women who could read and write – a small minority of the largely illiterate Algerian population – meant that independence potentially provided a wealth of professional opportunities for the tiny minority of women who possessed such skills, particularly young women without family responsibilities.

The story of Mimi and her mother shows that Fadéla M'Rabet's sense of a 'revolutionary spirit' and Zohra Sellami's vision of social inertia could co-exist. Part of the tiny, educated minority with a useful set of wartime contacts, Mimi was able to make a place for herself within the professional sphere, contributing to the creation of Algerian journalism as a sector. For her mother, the horizons that this had opened for her daughter were so far out of reach that they were impossible to imagine. The career of 'journalist' was meaningless to this older, informally educated woman. Mimi's mother's vocabulary reflects the idea of continuity rather than change between the colonial and post-colonial periods; her worldview continued to be structured around a socio-ethnic class of the 'indigenous' poor ruled by a distant elite.

Opportunities?

Describing her childhood memories of summer 1962, the left-wing politician Louisa Hanoune says: 'I still remember the men from the prefecture who took to the streets to ask all the families where there were girls who knew how to read and write, or type, to free them up to come and work'.[35] A publicity pamphlet prepared for the Afro-Asian congress – the 'Second Bandung' – which was due to begin in Algiers on 29 June 1965 (it was postponed indefinitely when Boumediene overthrew Ben Bella in a bloodless coup on 19 June 1965, but also because of Chinese–Soviet rivalry) depicted July 1962 as 'a black month in Algeria':

> Not enough doctors for the mutilated victims of the last bombs. Not enough typists, civil servants, or secretaries; one lone telephone operator lost in the vast Oran exchange to answer calls and replace, if possible, her two hundred European colleagues who had fled. A single preciously guarded typist in the cabinet of President Ben Bella. In the office of the newly appointed minister of education, not a file, not a folder, not even a telephone was left. The departing French officials had left nothing but emptiness behind them. There would be no bread, perhaps no water... Alarming rumours spread through the back streets.[36]

Many of the 'missing' roles described here were ones often filled by women – secretaries, nurses, typists and telephonists. 'Women', states the former member of the FF–FLN Akila Ouared, 'did a monumental job because it was them who replaced the former French employees and who participated in the construction [*édification*] of the country in exactly the same way as men'.[37]

Amongst the twenty-two *fida'iyat*, *maquisardes* and FF–FLN activists whom I have interviewed, who lived in Algeria in the 1960s, all exercised a professional activity after independence. Five went into the medical profession: Salima Bouaziz and Akila Ouared became doctors, Fadéla Mesli was an anaesthetist, Yamina Salem was a pharmacist and, after some difficulties, Khadjidja Belguembour obtained a job as a nurse. Five women worked in various state agencies, or in the civil service: Fadila Attia was a presidential secretary, Djamila Boupacha worked for the Bureau de Main d'Oeuvre Féminine (Office for Women's Employment) and also participated in Algerian official visits, Annie Steiner was a judicial adviser, Jacqueline Guerroudj prepared the *Journal officiel* (the official gazette publishing key legislation) and El Hora Kerkeb worked as a social worker in the police. Zhor Zerari and Mimi Maziz worked in print journalism, Fadéla M'Rabet was a radio presenter and Djamila Bouazza worked for the state press agency. Zohra Drif became a lawyer, Lucette Hadj Ali a teacher, Malika Koriche a telephonist and Bahia Ben Ali helped run the family business. Louisette Ighilahriz and Habiba Chami were in the UNFA, Saliha Djeffal was in the Jeunesse FLN (Youth FLN, JFLN) and

Fettouma Ouzegane concentrated on her oppositional political activities.

Indeed many women who had professional careers were also involved in political life: Fadéla Mesli and Zohra Drif were in the Constituent Assembly in 1962, Akila Ouared was in the UNFA in the 1960s and 1970s, Jacqueline Guerroudj was an activist in the Union Générale des Travailleurs Algériens (National Union of Algerian Workers, UGTA) and Malika Koriche was a local FLN councillor. Lucette Hadj Ali was in the PAGS, an underground communist movement created in 1966.[38]

The social ascent and political engagement of these women embody the moment. They most certainly did not 'go back into the kitchen'. And yet, the profiles of these individuals demonstrate that they were able to take on the roles that they did in the public sphere because they already had significant social and educational capital, dating from before independence. With the exception of the three women of European origin, who were all married with children and in employment, and with the exception of Bahia Ben Ali (a housewife married with one child), Malika Koriche (divorced after a brief marriage aged fifteen following only three years at school) and Khadjidja Belguembour (from a small village in the mountains with limited formal education) and Fettouma Ouzegane (married, five children), all of these women, at the point of their engagement in the nationalist movement, were single, educated young women. Some were still at high school; a few were even university students. They were a tiny minority in colonial Algeria – less than five per cent of the female population was literate – and their access to education had been determined by the social class of their family or their geographical location: that is to say, if they were fortunate enough to live near a school which would give places to 'French Muslim' girls.

In the first years of independence these women, who had the educational background to capitalise upon the opportunities that independence created, notably the urgent need for a literate workforce, were still a tiny minority. In 1966, only 1.82 per cent of women in Algeria were recorded as being in paid employment.[39] This statistic needs to be taken with significant caution: it is highly likely that it omits rural women working on family farms, urban women working from home in cottage industries such as weaving, and widespread undeclared employment. However, it is likely that this figure of 1.82 per cent does include all the women working in the public sector: doctors, teachers, nurses and government employees – that is to say, the kinds of roles which urban, educated interviewees filled.

For women who did not have the same social and cultural capital, such opportunities were further from their reach. With her husband, Bahia Ben Ali established a furniture business in Algiers after independence, but she says that in her home town of Blida this would have been a tricky endeavour: 'Blida was strict, the women were veiled and they didn't work [outside the home]'.[40] Having learnt nursing skills on the job in the *maquis*, Khadjidja Belguembour struggled to find work after 1962. Alongside other *maquisardes*, she was initially given a placement in a hospital as an auxiliary, but when a doctor encouraged her to take the exams for a nursing diploma she ran into difficulty: 'The placement opened my eyes a bit. I failed the exam because my writing was poor. I carried on working, as an auxiliary, without the CAP [*Certificat d'aptitude professionelle*, i.e. a professional qualification]. And then the husband appeared after a year and a half.'

At this point in the interview, Khadjidja pauses and lights a cigarette before continuing. Her husband – she describes him as 'an intellectual' – had interrupted his studies to participate in the war, so he wanted to finish his degree. They moved to Algiers and scraped by a living, and then her husband went to Egypt to continue his education: 'I couldn't follow my husband abroad, he was in a country where I didn't speak the language, well, I was a bit in Egypt, I liked it but it didn't last longer than four months, I lived here.'[41] The slip Khadjidja makes, before she corrects herself, is telling: Egypt is of course an Arabophone country, but for a speaker of Algerian dialect (*derja*) who, moreover, has never studied classical Arabic (*fusha*), 'Egyptian' might well seem a foreign language. Eventually, an officer whom Khadjidja knew from the *maquis* campaigned for a number of former *maquisardes* to be automatically attributed the status of professional nurses in recognition of their contribution in the *maquis*, and these women began to receive a small salary. The ability of female – and male – veterans to use their wartime contacts to find employment was hampered by a lack of overall strategy. Chronic material shortages and practical problems, especially illiteracy, meant that, in this period of great change, there were also many continuities from the colonial period.

The continuities in the kinds of roles available for uneducated women were seen as a troubling situation in 1960s Algeria. This was not just a gendered problem: Ben Bella was equally keen to take shoeshine boys, who under French rule were a daily reminder of colonial humiliation, off the streets and into education and training.[42] In a similar way, women toiling in menial and domestic labour seemed starkly at odds with the revolutionary fervour so enthusiastically repeated in official speeches and on the world stage. Describing her job as an employee of the Office for Women's Employment after independence, Djamila Boupacha, a former member of the Algiers bomb network, suggests that she was uncomfortable sending women looking for work into that old colonial role for 'indigenous' women, *femme de ménage* (domestic cleaner): 'There were illiterate women who wanted to be cleaners, I sent them to learn a trade, such as seamstress, which doesn't need a lot of schooling. Those who had a good level [of education], they went into accounting, into secretarial roles.'[43] A photograph published in 1967 in *Algérie actualité* shows a female cleaner in a school, standing in front of a blackboard upon which is inscribed a Third Worldist ode to African unity, written in classical Arabic. The cleaner is not looking at the words, but wringing out her floor cloth. There is no accompanying text, the caption simply reads: 'Ah, if only I had been educated'.[44]

In January 1965, the journalist and war veteran Zhor Zerari produced a series of reports for the newspaper *Alger ce soir* on the issue of women cleaners. She interviewed Aïcha Hamdaoui, a fifty-three-year-old school cleaner, and revealed that independence had brought Aïcha few material benefits: '[Aïcha] asks me if I understand Kabyle. I say yes, and the ice is broken. In a roundabout way, she tells her story.' Before independence Aïcha had been regularly and relatively well paid. But since independence, when teaching became universal and free, pupils had been obliged to club together to pay her wages as the head teacher had no funds.[45] Zhor's approach in this text is rather subversive: it makes unfavourable comparisons between the colonial and post-colonial periods, and her interview is pointedly conducted in Kabyle (Berber/Tamazight) as the political drive to 'rediscover' Algeria's Arabo-Islamic identity was gathering pace.

In March 1963, journalists from *El Moudjahid* visited Le Centre des Trois Martyrs (The Three Martyrs Centre) in the working-class district of Bab el Oued in Algiers. This was a weaving workshop created by the state to provide paid employment for the wives and daughters of men killed in action. Its director, Madame Allouache, had already run textile workshops during the war, making ALN uniforms on the Tunisian border. To the journalists, she insisted that women's employment was empowering: 'You know, I'm not a theorist of the emancipation of women. But I know some simple things. The war left us with thousands of orphans and widows, all breadwinners. To give aid is good, but I think it's better to teach a trade.'[46]

The *pied rouge* Catherine Lévy, who worked as a secondary-school teacher and UGTA activist in Bab el Oued, has a very different perspective on such workshops. She describes women working ten hours a day making hospital sheets and army and police uniforms, doing unpaid overtime and being fobbed off with till receipts rather than given proper pay slips.[47] Newspapers from the 1960s refer to a number of cases of women struggling to make ends meet. In Mme Allouache's workshop is Keltouma, a twenty-three-year-old war widow whose husband died in the mountains of Kabylia during the anti-colonial struggle, leaving her the only breadwinner for her four children and mother-in-law. It was the Ministry of Mujahidin which had sent her to the workshop. A fellow employee, Fatma Boussat, another war widow with an eight-year-old son, is described as having arrived in the capital at the end of the war, but obtaining a job in the workshop via the Ministry of Mujahidin only after waiting for a year with no income whatsoever.[48] Moreover, it seems unlikely that many of these female employees would have framed working outside the home in the language of 'emancipation', even in less exploitative working conditions. When I asked the war widow Chérifa Akache if she 'worked' after her arrival in Algiers she did not immediately understand what I meant. The interpreter gave her the hint 'weaving frame' and she replied: 'I wove, I sold, I did knitting too, jumpers'.[49]

For educated men and women, independence offered new opportunities. For the majority, who had not received a formal education (according to the 1966 census, 63.3 per cent of Algerian men and 85.9 per cent of women were illiterate),[50] and despite mass literacy campaigns (80 per cent of adult women were still illiterate in the mid-1970s),[51] it was likely that they would take up an occupation with a similar socio-economic status to that which they had occupied in the colonial period. For illiterate women, working outside the home was likely to be a low-paid, low-status job which would be accomplished for reasons of financial necessity in the absence of a sufficient male wage.

Returns?

When I ask Chérifa Akache whether relations between men and women remained as open as they had been during the war, when she mixed with men who were not family members, she is amused: 'Just after the war it was finished. We had a good time, we said *"tahya al-jaza'ir* [Long live Algeria]" and everyone went back to where they were before, the relations weren't the same.'[52] Fatma Yermeche gives a similar account of her post-independence life: 'On independence each woman returned to her place. What can I do? I never went to school, I can't do anything! I didn't have a choice.'[53] Yet despite Chérifa Akache's and Fatma Yermeche's claims that they did nothing after the war and everything went back to how it was before, this was a period in which women were adapting to significant change. Two of the key themes which emerge in rural women's accounts of their postwar lives are the return (or not) of male members of their family and whether or not they feel that their contribution to Algerian independence was recognised. This latter debate is tied up very much with war pensions and war widows' pensions. Both these themes raise key questions about changes in the position of these women within family structures and the relationship these women have with the state.

A 'return' to how things were before was not really possible. Many 'rural women' were not even 'rural' any more. The war had led to massive displacement, including the forcible removal by the French army of more than half of the 6,900,000-strong rural population into temporary camps and alternative villages.[54] Villagers had also fled to Algerian towns and refugee camps on the Tunisian and Moroccan borders. Aerial bombardment had destroyed homes and livelihoods, making much rural to urban migration permanent. By 1966, when the first postwar census took place, 16.9 per cent of the population of the *wilaya* of Tizi Ouzou, where these rural interviewees' villages of origin are located, had migrated to towns both within and beyond the borders of Algeria.[55]

The village of Agraradj had been flattened by French bombs, bulldozers and arson, reducing to rubble the homes of Fatima Berci, Fatma Yermeche and Fatima Benmohand Berci. In the village of Aït Abderrahmane, Chérifa Akache's house was smashed to pieces, as was the home of Ferroudja Amarouche in Bouzeguene. In 1962, all five of these women were living in other villages in the region or in Algiers. According to Fatma Yermeche: 'Everyone had gone. After the bombing, people were reluctant and they didn't want to come back. They returned little by little.'[56] Chérifa Akache and Ferroudja Amarouche chose to migrate permanently to Algiers in the first years of independence.

With many men dead, missing or pushed to migrate to France to find work,[57] women outnumbered men. In a breakdown of the 1977 census of the population according to age and sex, statistics from the *wilaya* of Tizi Ouzou reveal that below the age of twenty-four, males and females were equal in number. This age group constituted 64.12 per cent of the population. It was in the category 35–9 that the gender differences became dramatic: there were 11,644 men in this age group in Tizi Ouzou, compared to 21,185 women. The oldest men in this category would have been seventeen when the war began and twenty-four when it ended. In 1977, these men would also have still been young enough to be migrant workers in France. There were around twice as many women for the number of men up until the age of fifty-five, when the difference began to decline, although women still outnumbered men.[58] In the 1970s, the anthropologist Camille Lacoste-Dujardin reported that some families in Kabylia had been obliged to break with the custom of exclusively male inheritance and pass land on to women because there were no surviving male relatives, although the author believed that this would be a temporary phenomenon.[59]

In August 1963, the former member of the Algiers bomb network and deputy in the Constituent Assembly Zohra Drif was quoted in the newspaper *Le Peuple* as saying that she had heard reports that in Kabylia men back from prison, exile or the *maquis* had repudiated their wives because these women had taken over the household responsibilities.[60] In her study of ten women in the Aurès, Zoubida Haddab states that one of her interviewees experienced great difficulty being accepted by her parents-in-law when she married after independence simply because she had mixed with men in the course of her wartime activities.[61] This was not an issue for the five women whom I interviewed, nor did a radical reorganisation of gender roles within their families take place. As Chapter 2 shows, new relations during the war had been framed in a familiar and familial language of brothers and sisters, mothers and sons; women had not necessarily experienced their demanding wartime responsibilities as heads of household in a time of shortage, want and suffering as a taste of liberation; and demographic domination by women does not automatically lead to a renegotiation of gender roles.

When I asked rural interviewees what their hopes had been in 1962 for independent Algeria, one of the most common responses was that the men would return from the war. For Fatma Yermeche: 'I was waiting, hoping that the children, the husbands, those who had left [would return]. My husband was imprisoned in France, and he was only freed after Independence.'[62] Ferroudja Amarouche describes her joy at seeing her *maquisard* husband for the first time after four years' absence: 'I was very happy, he had come back from the dead, and what's more he was the only son of his mother, he didn't have a brother'. She adds: 'When he came back, there was a relative of mine who asked him: "Has Ferroudja done her hair?" because I hadn't done my hair since my husband had gone [*she laughs*]. Of course, I did my hair for my husband!'[63]

Chérifa Akache's husband did not return. As the mother of two children, she had already fulfilled the procreative purpose of marriage in the eyes of her community, and was not expected to remarry. Now that her husband was dead, custom dictated that she live with her parents-in-law. Indeed, Fatima Berci's sister, whose husband died in combat when she was eighteen, was married to the deceased's brother, her former brother-in-law – a way of keeping the children of the first marriage within the paternal family whilst also providing for the widow. In the end, Chérifa Akache preferred to stay with her own parents, and, after two years in Kabylia, she came to Algiers and bought a house where she lived with her father and mother. She also entered into paid employment, and applied for a war widow's pension.

The creation of a pension for war widows in the months following the end of the war meant that many women acquired an independent source of income for the first time. In many cases, this source of income was essential to the subsistence of their family and/or community. In her study of the commune of Iflissen (*wilaya* of Tizi Ouzou), Camille Lacoste-Dujardin found that, in 1962, only ten *maquisards* from Iflissen were still alive. In 1970, the total population of the commune was 6,700, with 900 women holding widows' pensions. Women outnumbered men three to one, partly as a result of the economically active male population migrating to Algerian cities or to France, but also as a consequence of the war dead.[64]

Acquiring a war widow's pension was not a straightforward process. For a start, it required filling in forms, a task which was impossible without help for those who could not read or write. The process also required a workforce to process claims and the Ministry of Mujahidin was initially reliant on recruiting student volunteers to do this: in June 1964, *Alger républicain* reported that high-school students who had volunteered to work every Thursday at the Ministry of Mujahidin were getting through 1,500 to 2,000 files a day, and had already completed 54,000 applications.[65] There were delays, as the journalist Albert Paul Lentin discovered when he set off for Kabylia in autumn 1963 to try to find out why there had been such a low voter turnout in the region in the elections to ratify the first constitution. He cites the case of a war widow who had been waiting six months for her claim to be processed: 'In Algiers, those who are victims of these delays when they happen at least get some aid from the town hall or charitable organisations. Here there is nothing.'[66] This financial explanation masks a far deeper political problem – Lentin goes to Kabylia in the middle of the FFS revolt, an armed rebellion against the seizure of power by Ben Bella and his allies – but the journalist's choice of example highlights what is, in the accounts of rural women I have interviewed, a major bone of contention between them and the state.

'Those who sorted themselves out' – i.e. were quick off the mark and had the necessary skills at their disposal – 'they got their pensions,' says Fatma Yermeche.[67] She is talking about pensions for veterans, rather than those for war widows, but Fatma Yermeche's experiences, and those of rural women like her, reveal the general difficulties these women faced when seeking to access state benefits. Fatima Berci and Ferroudja Amarouche have only recently – i.e. in the 2000s – begun to receive a pension for their own actions. Fatima Benmohand Berci and Fatma Yermeche do not have a pension of their own, but as wives of *mujahidin* benefit from their husbands' pensions, as do the other two women. Fatima Benmohand Berci says she had her application prepared but that the paperwork was stolen from her house: 'When I went to redo the dossier they refused'.[68] Fatma Yermeche says her husband did not sort her paperwork out for her in time. Ferroudja Amarouche's husband did not want his wife to have a pension on principle: 'He said, "Look, you did that for our country. Me, if I had come back [from the *maquis*] with my health I wouldn't have asked [for a pension]."[69] It was the son of a colonel who knew Ferroudja from the war who finally organised her application for her.

For Chérifa Akache, who today has a pension both as a war widow and in her own right, the fact that she did not get a pension immediately after the war was not just an unfortunate combination of practical difficulties and slow-moving bureaucracy:

> Once the war had finished I hurried to get my papers. In the office where I was supposed to do my application I found a *harki* who told me, 'We don't recognise you'. This *harki* discouraged me. I'm angry with him to this very day. But I still did my application, I got my papers, and some people say to me 'You should have been amongst the first to get your papers'. As well as the pension, I know that some *mujahidin* got property, money, I didn't get that.[70]

Here we return to one of the key themes in many interviewees' accounts when they talk about 1962 and after: they explain their disappointments in the post-independence period as the result of betrayal from within. The figure of the fraternal *mujahid* is replaced by that of the *harki*. Algerians who fought in the French army are depicted as opportunistically sneaking into positions of power to the detriment of genuine veterans who sacrificed all to free the motherland. Whether or not this man in the office actually was a *harki* is perhaps less significant than the way in which Chérifa Akache explains exclusion and injustice by stigmatising post-independence enemies in the same way as foes from the anti-colonial struggle. Fatima Berci makes similar criticisms to those of Chérifa Akache: 'I'm seventy-two years old. It's only in the last ten years that they give me a very small pension, all the rest is lost, what they should have given me since independence.' And whose fault is this? Again the outsider is accused: 'Algeria is not in the hands of its children',[71] she explains. Fatima Benmohand Berci declares: '*Al-hamdulillah* [Thanks to God], the war is over. We make do with what we have. We wanted it to be over. France has gone. Apart from some of them, the *mujahidin* have betrayed us.' Later on in the interview, she repeats: 'They forgot us. They betrayed us.'[72]

The war pension is not understood by these rural interviewees as a source of independent financial income or a means to renegotiate their position within their family. Indeed, as a recipient of a war widow's pension, a woman could become the target of 'pension chasers'. This term referred to men who would marry war widows in religious ceremonies, but avoid officially registered civil marriages, because the war widow's pension ceased to be paid if its recipient remarried. These unscrupulous men would acquire financial control of the pension, and then abandon the widow, often leaving her with illegitimate children. The post-independence state considered 'pension chasers' a significant social problem, and women who found themselves duped were subject to a mixture of condescending compassion and moral condemnation. A 1973 UNFA investigation into 'The condition of widows of *shuhada* ten years on' exhorted these women to protect the memory of their heroic first husbands and to set a better example for their children, who were, after all, the children of martyrs.[73]

The rural women whom I interviewed do think that women's position within their communities has changed, but they do not necessarily make a connection between these changes and the war. Fatma Yermeche states: 'Before there was no way women would go to France, never', implying that this is not the case today.[74] Female members of her family belonging to younger generations have gone to school and university and have professional careers. Fatma Yermeche would situate this as part of an evolution in morals, customs and access to education over time rather than linked to the historically specific moment of women's participation in the War of Independence. Indeed, the fact that she sees such changes in attitudes and opportunities as being logical developments with the passage of time, rather than triggered by specific events or policies, is clear from her next sentence: 'When France was here [i.e. under colonial rule] we had to go and search for wood to make a fire. Now we're independent and we cook with gas. Before there was all the smoke, it made us cry.'[75]

In the decade following independence, and subsequently, younger women with access to formal education seized upon 'women's participation in the war' as one of the key factors in explaining transformative change in 'the condition of women'. This is reflected in a major survey into attitudes of and towards women, carried out in the early 1970s in the Constantine region. Hélène Vandevelde-Dallière and a team of researchers from the University of Constantine interviewed 925 women and 367 men of different ages and social backgrounds, from urban and rural areas. In response to a question about whether women's attitudes towards men had changed since the revolution, 90 per cent of female high school students responded that women were 'less oppressed' since the war. Uneducated rural women who had not been to school had very different responses: only 32 per cent said that women were less oppressed, 50 per cent said attitudes had not changed and 18 per cent said women were more oppressed.[76] Clearly young, urban, educated women had very different opportunities in the post-independence period from older (or at least married), rural women without formal education. Yet these responses reflect not only their lived experiences but also, and perhaps more interestingly, the importance of examining how these lived experiences were perceived and explained.

Another question in Hélène Vandevelde-Dallière's survey was about women's interest in political life. She calculated that only 15 per cent of all women questioned were interested in politics compared to 50 per cent of men. To measure informants' engagement with political life, they were asked to state what names of government ministers they knew, what Algeria's political institutions were and who their local councillors were. One woman in the forty to forty-nine age group with an unemployed husband was recorded as stating: 'Since independence, our lives have been miserable. All the efforts we made during the war have not been rewarded.'[77] This is presented by the researchers as a reason why women were *not* 'interested in politics' – yet such a declaration is in fact profoundly political. The rural women whom I interviewed do not refer to institutions, politics and parties, but when they talk about the pension they are most definitely making a political statement. The pension is a bond which creates a direct link between rural female veterans and a state which they might otherwise have little contact with. As Chapter 6 explores further, they consider that they have done their duty for Algeria and that the Algerian state has a 'blood debt' towards them.

Conclusion

Describing women who got involved in planting trees on national reforestation day, the cover photograph of the newspaper *Révolution africaine* on 7 December 1963 was of a woman in a *hayk* holding a pick. The accompanying slogan read: 'In December [19]60 Algerian women were at the forefront of demonstrations. For the day of the tree last Sunday, they also got involved.' Comparing the mass anti-colonial demonstrations of December 1960 associated with the FLN's greatest diplomatic success – United Nations Resolution 1573 in favour of the right of Algerian people to self-determination – with symbolic tree planting involving a select few in 1963 might seem a rather incongruous juxtaposition. The hyperbole nevertheless captures the revolutionary fervour of the first years of independence.

When we seek to cross the colonial/post-colonial divide, we uncover a history of continuity and change that has been buried under fifty years of self-justification by the Algerian state and the rankling resentment of many Algerians who consider the revolution betrayed. The conflictual and potentially problematic nature of 1962 as both symbol of political (il)legitimacy and signpost signalling one's relationship to power then and now is expressed by interviewees in a number of ways: through an emphasis on their apoliticism, through the metaphor of moral corruption, through their insistence on being useful citizens, despite everything.

The extent to which independence offered new opportunities for female veterans would depend on their socio-economic circumstances, level of education, family status and geographical location. For the minority of women who had begun to acquire educational capital in the colonial period, the blank slate of Algerian infrastructure in year zero could present significant opportunities. For the majority of women who were without this capital, family structures and social expectations of women's roles proved resistant to change, even in the context of the major wartime upheaval. For these women, 1962 barely registered as a tremor on their daily lives because it had an imperceptible effect on engrained conceptions of their place within family and society. Yet at the same time, 1962 indicated a seismic shift in shaping the way in which all these women, literate or illiterate, rural or urban, would view their relationship to the state. From the colonial power to which nothing was owed and of which nothing was expected, the post-independence state was meant to fulfil its citizens' hopes, and, at the same time, citizens now had a moral obligation to contribute to state-building. This was a shifting and unwritten social contract, but a social contract nevertheless.

Notes

1 Colonel Si M'hamed (Ahmed Bougara) was head of the *wilaya* IV (region around Algiers) between 1958 and 1959. He died on 5 May 1959, officially killed in action by the French, although the circumstances of his death have not been fully elucidated and there are rumours he was victim of an internal settling of scores.
2 Interview with Lucette Hadj Ali (18 December 2005).
3 Interview with Chérifa Akache (21 June 2005).
4 Interview with Ferroudja Amarouche (10 December 2005).
5 Interview with Chérifa Akache (21 June 2005).
6 Amer, 'La Crise du Front de libération nationale de l'été 1962', p. 68.
7 Interview with Khadjidja Belguembour (14 June 2005).
8 *Ibid.*
9 *El Watan* (24 March 2005).
10 Interview with Zhor Zerari (21 December 2005).
11 *Ibid.*
12 A. Djebar, *Les Alouettes naïves* (Paris: Juillard, 1967).
13 Y. Mechakra, *La Grotte éclatée* (Algiers: SNED, 1979).
14 Interview with Chérifa Akache (21 June 2005).
15 For more on this Section des femmes, see Macmaster, 'Des Révolutionnaires invisibles'.
16 Interview with Salima Bouaziz (18 December 2005). This is a view Salima Bouaziz repeats in an account published in *El Watan* in 2009. 'Autour du 8 mars, contribution au souvenir des sportives et sportifs algériens', *El Watan* (26 March 2009).
17 Interview with Saliha Djeffal (21 June 2005).
18 Interview with Zhor Zerari (21 December 2005).
19 Interview with Fadéla Mesli (20 December 2005).
20 *Ibid.*
21 Interview with Zhor Zerari (21 December 2005).
22 The loss of her father is a major theme in Zhor Zerari's book of poetry, *Poèmes de prison* (Algiers: Bouchène, 1988). The last lines of the book are: 'Que importe le retour / Si mon père / N'est pas sur les quais / De la gare [What does the return matter / If my father / Is not on the platform / Of the station]'. The difficulty of postwar re-adaption is also a theme which she explored in a series of short stories, which became a series of film shorts, *Faits divers* (c. 1981–2).
23 The difficulty of returning to civilian life after armed conflict first began to be documented in post-First World War literature, by authors such as E. M. Remarque, *Drei Kameraden* (Amsterdam: Querido, 1938 [1936]), and Colette, *Chéri* (Paris: Fayard, 1920) and *La Fin de Chéri* (Paris: Flammarion, 1926).

24 Interview with Zohra Drif (11 June 2005).
25 Interview with Bahia Ben Ali (19 December 2005).
26 Interview with Mimi Maziz (18 December 2005).
27 Interview with Salima Bouaziz (18 December 2005).
28 Interview with Mimi Maziz (18 December 2005).
29 *Ibid.*
30 Fadéla M'Rabet underlines how exceptional it was that her father, an erudite, open-minded man, allowed her to go and study abroad in the 1950s: 'I went to France because my brother was there; otherwise my father wouldn't have let me. If there hadn't have been my brother, I wouldn't even have been able to have studied in Algiers. My father kind of delegated the power to my brother.' Interview with Fadéla M'Rabet (1 November 2005).
31 Interview with Mimi Maziz (18 December 2005).
32 Interview with Fadéla M'Rabet (1 November 2005).
33 At the end of summer 1962, the French Embassy in Algiers registered 200,000 French citizens in Algeria, compared to 900,000 the previous year. A non-official census on 1 April 1963 identified 13,800 French civil servants working in Algeria within the framework of *coopération*, C. Simon, *Algérie, les années pieds-rouges: des rêves de l'indépendance au désenchantement (1962–1969)* (Paris: La Découverte, 2011), p. 12; p. 34.
34 Interviewed for the documentary *Les Filles de la révolution* (André Harris and Alain de Sedouy, Office national de radiodiffusion télévision française, 16 January 1968).
35 L. Hanoune with G. Mouffok, *Une autre voix pour l'Algérie* (Paris: La Découverte, 1996), p. 43.
36 *Algeria on the Move* (Algerian National Centre of Documentation and Information, 1965). Quoted in D. Ottoway and M. Ottaway, *Algeria: The Politics of a Socialist Revolution* (Berkeley: University of California Press, 1970), p. 9. Note that Ben Bella was not actually president until September 1962, despite what this pamphlet suggests.
37 Interview with Akila Ouared (13 June 2005).
38 These figures for the *mujahidat*'s subsequent employment are largely confirmed by Amrane's work. Amrane interviewed fifty-one women who fell into the categories of *fida'iyat*, *maquidardes*, members of the FF–FLN or women of European origin. The annexe to her book states each interviewee's post-1962 socio-economic situation. These fifty-one women included seven who went into the medical profession, five who became teachers, three who became lawyers and three telephonists. Amrane describes only fifteen of these fifty-one women as housewives or without a profession. Therefore, even though Amrane argues that after independence women withdrew from public life, her own research

suggests that for a certain group of women this was not true. Amrane, *Les Femmes algériennes dans la guerre*, pp. 286–92.

39 A. Lippert, 'Algerian women's access to power: 1962–1985', in I. L. Markovitz (ed.), *Studies in Power and Class in Africa* (New York: Oxford University Press, 1987), p. 222.

40 Interview with Bahia Ben Ali (19 December 2005).

41 Interview with Khadjidja Belguembour (14 June 2005).

42 R. Merle, *Ben Bella*, trans. C. Sykes (London: Michael Joseph, 1967), pp. 30–1.

43 Interview with Djamila Boupacha (11 June 2005).

44 *Algérie actualité* (27 April 1967).

45 *Alger ce soir* (30 December 1964 and 1 January 1965).

46 *El Moudjahid* (30 March 1963).

47 C. Lévy, 'La journée du 8 mars 1965 à Alger', *Clio: histoire, femmes et société*, 5 (1997), www.clio.revues.org/pdf/415 (accessed 19 May 2014).

48 *Révolution africaine* (18–24 November 1966).

49 Interview with Chérifa Akache (21 June 2005).

50 Mazouni, *Culture et enseignement en Algérie et au Maghreb*, p. 213.

51 J. Minces, *L'Algérie de Boumediene* (Paris: Presses de la cité, 1978), p. 74

52 Interview with Chérifa Akache (21 June 2005).

53 Interview with Fatma Yermeche (16 June 2005).

54 A third of the 6,900,000 rural inhabitants in Algeria were 'regrouped' into French *camps de regroupement*, and a further 1,175,000 'displaced' into *villages de recasement*, neighbouring villages which the French army considered less threatening because geographically more exposed. A. Mahé, *Histoire de la Grande Kabylie: anthropologie historique du lien social dans les communautés villageoises* (Paris: Bouchène, 2001), p. 418.

55 Adjusting this figure to include a very young population and family migration, this represents sixty to seventy per cent of the active male population. Mahé, *Histoire de la Grande Kabylie*, p. 449.

56 Interview with Fatma Yermeche (16 June 2005).

57 Abdelmalek Sayad is widely recognised as one of the finest sociologists of Algerian migration to France. See *The Suffering of the Immigrant* [La Double absence], trans. D. Macey (Cambridge: Polity, 2004).

58 'Répartition de la population selon sexe et âge de 1977, Direction de la planification et de l'aménagement du territoire (DPAT)', in M. Dahmani, *Atlas économique et social de la Grande Kabylie* (Algiers: Office des publications universitaires, 1990).

59 See Lacoste-Dujardin, *Un village algérien*.

60 *Le Peuple* (22 August 1963).

61 Z. Haddab, 'Les femmes, la guerre de libération et la politique en

Algérie', in iMed Institut Méditerranéen, *Les Algériennes, citoyennes en devenir* (Oran: MM Editions, 2000).
62 Interview with Fatma Yermeche (16 June 2005).
63 Interview with Ferroudja Amarouche (10 December 2005).
64 C. Lacoste-Dujardin, *Opération Oiseau bleu: des kabyles, des ethnologues et la guerre d'Algérie* (Paris: La Découverte, 1997), p. 145.
65 *Alger républicain* (27 June 1964).
66 *Révolution africaine* (21 September 1963).
67 Interview with Fatma Yermeche (16 June 2005).
68 Interview with Fatima Benmohand Berci (17 June 2005).
69 Interview with Ferroudja Amarouche (10 December 2005).
70 Interview with Chérifa Akache (21 June 2005).
71 Interview with Fatima Berci (16 June 2005).
72 Interview with Fatima Benmohand Berci (17 June 2005).
73 *El Djazaïria*, 22 (1972).
74 Interview with Fatma Yermeche (16 June 2005). Whilst it may have been the case in Fatma's village that women did not migrate to France, the work of Amelia Lyons challenges the long-held view of Algerian migration in the 1950s as a phenomenon involving young, single men. See 'Invisible immigrants: Algerian families and the French welfare state in the era of decolonization (1947–74)' (PhD thesis, University of California at Irvine, 2004).
75 Interview with Fatma Yermeche (16 June 2005)
76 Vandevelde-Dallière, *Femmes algériennes*, p. 216.
77 *Ibid.*, p. 234. The choice of the Constantine region was, according to the author, based on its typicality: in addition to high levels of illiteracy, unemployment and low levels of industrialisation, it was more homogeneous with less 'Western influence' (i.e. there had been fewer settlers) than the Algiers or Oran regions, there was a local, inward-looking economy of cereal production, and thus 'Arabo-Islamic culture' and 'properly Algerian traditions' had been best maintained. The categories of analysis of the study very much fit with official ethno-cultural definitions of Algerianness of the time, although the fact that the study considers attitudes to gender roles as a valid field of enquiry and seeks to explain the marginalisation of women goes against the dominant line that there was not a 'woman problem'. This wide-ranging study, covering topics from the war and politics to marriage and social life, provides a fascinating insight into how educated urban women in the 1970s conceptualised the 'woman problem' and how the researchers' questions, informed by this gendered framework, were understood by women of different social classes and geographical locations.

4

Embodying the nation

Women, walls and the boundaries of the nation

Zhor Zerari was one of the first female journalists in independent Algeria. Having honed her writing talents composing poetry in prison, the former member of the Algiers bomb network wrote for the daily *Al Chaab / Le Peuple* from its creation in 1962, later contributing to *Alger ce soir* and the weekly *Algérie actualité*. In summer 1962, delegates were meeting in Algiers to discuss cleaning the walls of the capital city, which were covered with wartime graffiti. Whilst hastily painted expressions of support for Algerian independence were politically correct if unsightly, there was a keen desire to rapidly scrub away pro-OAS slogans and indeed pro-GPRA messages warning the population against building a 'personality cult' around soon-to-be-president Ben Bella. Armed with her notebook, Zhor Zerari attended the meeting.

Attending in the gender-neutral capacity of journalist, blending into a sphere dominated by men, Zhor Zerari embodied one of the claims made in the FLN's June 1962 Tripoli programme, the supposed blueprint for independent Algeria, hastily put together in the middle of the internal power struggle:[1] 'The participation of women in the fight for liberation has created favourable conditions to break the centuries-old yoke which weighs upon her in order to associate her fully and totally in the running of public affairs and the development of the country'.[2] The meeting took an unexpected turn, however, when one male delegate, filled with self-satisfaction at his sense of humour, dropped into the debate the phrase 'lemra ['woman' in dialectical Arabic] hachak'. 'Hachak' is a colloquial expression, an apology for mentioning something that it is not usually considered polite to refer to in public: for example, shoes, toilets or dirt in general. 'Lemra hachak' is also sometimes used

Figure 3 Women walking through the Algiers Casbah, 1969

when men talk to other men about the women in their family, supposedly as a mark of respect for the private sphere, in the sense, 'My wife, although I shouldn't speak her name publicly ...'. At best, this delegate was verbally denying women their place in the public sphere, at worst – and much more likely, given that this was a debate about scrubbing off the physical traces of conflict from the streets of Algiers – he was suggesting that the postwar women of Algiers needed cleaning up too.

This latter interpretation is how Zhor Zerari understood the comment, and she was outraged. She says she was held back from physically attacking the delegate by some of her former brothers-in-arms. Early the next morning, however, she tracked him down to his workplace and demanded to know whether his view of women extended to thinking that his wife, his daughter and his mother also needed 'cleaning up'.[3]

This story of walls and women is indicative of a wider moral panic which swept through Algeria in the immediate postwar period. The early years of independence saw a demographic explosion which would continue into the 1970s. Already by the mid-1960s, a new generation, too young to have actively participated in the war, was coming of age. These teenagers appeared to be disconnected from the war and, in urban areas at least, looking towards a global youth culture. Newspaper editorials and National Assembly debates reveal the degree of anxiety. In December 1963, *El Moudjahid* ran the results of an investigation about youth in Algiers. It depicted self-centred and materialistic teenagers, interested only in dancing the twist, and, in the case of young men, multiplying their sexual conquests.[4] In February 1964, a similar investigation by *Alger républicain*, the former PCA newspaper, revealed the fear amongst its informants that mixing between the sexes would lead to debauchery, drinking, miniskirts and, once again, dancing the twist.[5] From Oran, reports came in of young men and women being arrested 'in flagrante delicto'.[6] In the same month, National Assembly deputy Abbas M'hamed presented a bill to prohibit slot machines, deploring the sight of 'scruffy, turbulent youths, who spend their whole day glued to slot machines or sat down listening to hysterical music'.[7] In December 1967, a police-led 'Anti-Womaniser Operation' (*Opération anti-dragueurs*) took place in Algiers. Thirteen young men were arrested for harassing women in the street. Their photographs were printed on the front page of *El Moudjahid*, alongside their names, ages and occupations.[8]

As similarly anxious debates in 1960s Europe demonstrate, fears about moral decline and the threat which youth culture was seen to pose to social order were not particular to Algeria.[9] Yet a very specific set of historical references framed this Algerian moral panic. Young couples walking in the street were not only subject to checks on whether they were married or not, women considered to be too 'Westernised' in their behaviour were insulted as 'girls of 13 May'[10] – a reference to women who unveiled at the behest of settlers following the attempted coup led by *pieds noirs* and some army generals in Algiers in 1958. In 1963, *El Moudjahid* interviewed a young male veteran who expressed his despair at this new generation, in his words, 'mummy's boys' contaminated by the twist. They complain about everything, he said, but neither fought in the war nor work to rebuild Algeria, and, moreover, they 'don't respect our sisters'.[11] *Révolution africaine* expressed the fear that, whilst French colonialism had been kicked out, cultural neo-colonialism might have found its way in through these 'new *pieds noirs*' – carefree young men with flashy cars and (some) girls who wore too little and came home too late. The model, this left-wing weekly newspaper dedicated to international revolution declared, should be Cuba where 'singing together, girls and boys construct their future'.[12]

At the heart of all these stories is a debate about how to regulate the public and private spheres in a way that would enable the newly independent nation to (re)define the boundaries of the imagined community. If in the colonial period it was considered necessary for nationalists to imagine women as the repositories of an unchanging culture, impervious to and hidden from colonial attempts to subvert their collective identity, the very fact of independence implied that this bulwark was no longer needed. This reimagining of the nation intersected with the very concrete, practical problems which Chapter 3 evokes: the need for a workforce to rebuild the state after seven and a half years of war and the collapse of the economy and infrastructure. Indeed, the revolution was potentially in danger if women did not play an active part in economic reconstruction. Speaking to trainee typists in March 1963, Ben Bella declared: 'The march [towards socialism] cannot take place without [the Algerian woman]. Out of twelve million Algerians, seven million and maybe more are women.'[13]

The intertwining of utilitarian and ideological arguments in favour of women's entry en masse into the public sphere can be traced also in a speech made by Ben Bella in 1963, at the first May Day demonstration since independence. 'Let the woman problem be posed once and for all', he insisted. 'Liberate your women so they can take up their responsibilities; by leaving women prisoners, it is half of our people, half of our country which is paralysed. Don't think that the veil will protect them. The Revolution will protect them.'[14] This speech, aimed at encouraging men to allow female family members to come out to work, insisted that there was no longer the need to hide women from the colonial gaze, but equally sought to reassure men that the moral purity of 'their' women was safe in the hands of the revolutionary state and society. Two weeks later, speaking in Oran, Ben Bella insisted that 'It is not the wearing of the veil which makes us respect women, but the pure sentiments which we have in our hearts'.[15] The president implied that the proclaimed socialist society would simultaneously defend women from losing their collective identity through neo-colonial mimicry and protect them from the potentially lascivious gaze of male co-workers because they would be devoted to the nobler task of national construction.

It is worth underlining that references to the veil in the 1960s were references to the *hayk* worn by many women in urban areas. Given that the *hayk* is a loose white (or in Constantine, black) cloth which has to be held around the body with one hand, from a practical point of view this would make it difficult to accomplish workplace tasks such as typing or weaving. This is not to say that arguments against veiling in the 1960s were purely practical, but they were not only ideological, and they tended to be presented in terms of 'the veil gets in the way of work' both literally and psychologically.[16]

Algeria's second president, Boumediene, who overthrew Ben Bella in a bloodless coup on 19 June 1965, is commonly depicted as more socially conservative than Ben Bella, seeking to pair the development of a modern, industrialised nation with a greater commitment to 'rediscovering' Algeria's 'Arab Islamic' roots.[17] Speaking at the 1966 UNFA congress, Boumediene declared that:

> The Algerian woman has, in effect, imposed herself in our society thanks to her efficient action, her sacrifices and the many martyrs which she has given to the cause of a free, modern and socialist Algeria [...] All the same, it is absolutely necessary that this evolution takes place in a natural way and within the framework of the Muslim religion, since our society is at the same time Arab, Muslim and socialist and it has foundations and traditions which we must respect.[18]

Boumediene urged women not to concern themselves with what he considered to be superficial problems: polygamy, he argued, was effectively forbidden by the Qur'an because scripture stated that a man could not take more than one wife unless he was able to treat them all equally. The veil, he insisted, was not worthy of the attention that it had garnered in other Muslim societies: instead, women needed to go beyond this trivial issue and challenge outdated customs which were a deviation from Islam. In doing so, Boumediene argued, they would participate in the construction of Algerian society.[19]

The kinds of arguments used by Boumediene to state his position on 'the woman question' are thus similar to those of Ben Bella. Neither sought to question the ways in which some of the causes of women's exclusion from the public sphere might result from practices and beliefs from within autochthonous society rather than simply being conditioned by external factors. The end of colonial rule was presented in a very straightforward way as the beginning of a new era. As Boumediene put it in a speech in 1972: 'It is time for the Algerian woman to seriously and actively take up her positive role in the construction [*édification*] of our country, which only yesterday was exposed to multiple infernal attempts seeking her deformation, alienation and loss of collective identity [*dépersonnalisation*].'[20]

As Zhor Zerari's experience as a journalist in a public meeting reveals, discussions about the place of women were not just abstract formulations in grandstanding presidential speeches or in a state-controlled press that most of the population could not read. These debates also translated into a series of burning, concrete questions about interactions between men and women in everyday life. Where do 'our' women belong? How can social change be managed? Will women be safe, both physically and morally, if they mix with men? Will the revolutionary woman be able to defend herself in a male-dominated world? As during the war, in the post-independence period women were publicly told that there was no need to fear the intentions of 'our' men, whilst at the same time there was a deep anxiety about what these intentions might actually be.

Setting out the terms of the debate: A crisis of identity or a battle to appropriate authenticity?

These questions have been interpreted both at the time and subsequently as part of a conflict between 'tradition' and 'modernity'. Since 1962, Algeria has frequently been diagnosed as suffering from an 'identity crisis'. In the words of the psychiatrist Khaled Benmiloud, writing in 1964: 'We are no longer what we were, we're something else. We don't yet have a full and clear idea of what this is.'[21] Yet Algerians did have a sense of self in 1962, be it based on family allegiances, local identities, class or religious belonging, or identification with potent symbols of the new nation such as flags and the slogans 'long live Algeria' and 'Algerian Algeria'. Whilst public debate might have been couched in terms of 'who are we?', evoking a kind of psycho-anthropological journey of (re)discovery, the question really was 'who do we want to be'? – and this was a profoundly political question. Would the revolution which began in 1954 be completed by cultural renaissance (i.e. the revival of Islam and Arabic, no longer bastions of withdrawal but the foundation of dominant national identity) or agrarian and industrial transformation (i.e. socialism)?

The fact that the debate was couched in terms of 'who are we?', apparently open to a single factual definition, rather than 'who do we want to be?', an expression of multiple dreams and desires, alerts us to the fact that the language of the debate was one of absolutes. Following similar strategies of legitimisation and delegitimisation to those Chapter 3 explores in relation to true and false veterans, the army of the interior and the exterior and the revolution fulfilled or betrayed, debates about Algerian identity played out in the black-and-white vocabulary of true and false interpretations of Islam, correct and erroneous understandings of socialism, authentic and foreign versions of the Algerian 'personality' (*personnalité* in French; *shakhsiyya* in Arabic). 'Personality' was a collective rather than individual identity, with the political connotations of national character. Representations of (un)acceptable moral behaviour followed a similar binary pattern: the wartime *maquisard* was depicted as a virile egalitarian, the non-combatant was a pseudo-macho sexual predator; loose women were colonial pawns and materialistic men wannabe colonisers. Each side in the debate claimed to hold the definitive answer, which in turn was presented as the panacea to all problems.

Yet whilst these dichotomies were presented as obvious and opposing views stigmatised as self-evidently misguided, none of these claims should be taken at face value. Since independence, political actors in Algeria of all ideological tendencies have sought to appropriate authenticity as the unanswerable argument to silence opponents. It is a rhetorical device and not necessarily a historically meaningful description. 'Conservatives' accused 'progressives' of abusing the purity of the Algerian collective identity through innovation which they considered heretical Westernisation, whilst 'progressives' argued that colonialism had distorted Islam and that the true face of the Muslim faith, freed of colonial attempts to subvert its identity (*dépersonnalisation*), was one of progress, challenging established social, racial and gendered orders. This fight to claim the monopoly on authenticity was not unique to Algeria. In newly independent Tunisia in 1956, as President Habib Bourguiba pushed through the new Personal Status Code, outlawing polygamy and repudiation and recognising right of mothers to pass Tunisian nationality on to their children, he justified each innovation with a quotation from the Qur'an, arguing that this was a 'return' to the pre-colonial religious reformism which had flourished in Tunis.[22] In Algeria, as in Tunisia and elsewhere, this was not a conflict between 'tradition' and 'modernity', instead this was a struggle between a series of visions of the modern nation-state to appropriate 'tradition' and impose a specific definition of authenticity.

In a public sphere where there were limited opportunities for political discussion, debating the 'woman question' provided a forum for coded ideological confrontations through the language of culture. Algeria after independence rapidly became a single-party state under the banner of the party of the FLN, and therefore ideological debates did not take place between competing political parties. Marxist sympathisers and Muslim theologians existed as different tendencies and factions within the party of the FLN and the state apparatus, with shifting levels of influence. There were also small, clandestine political movements such as the PAGS, formed in 1966 by members of the banned PCA, and Al-Qiyam al-Islamiyya (Islamic values), established in 1963 by some former members of the Association des 'Ulama Musulmans Algériens (Association of Algerian Muslim 'Ulama, AUMA), and officially banned in 1966. For Marxists, Algerian socialism was not radical enough – this was, as Eastern bloc observers in Algiers joked, socialism without socialists,[23] and can best be described as a redistributative statism, through nationalisation, *autogestion* (the occupation and collective management of nationalised land and factories), industrialisation, mass education and universal healthcare. For religious conservatives, re-Islamisation was not thorough enough and socialism was heretical.[24]

Socialist and (Arabo-)Islamic tendencies provided the most significant sources of both contestation and social, economic and cultural policy inspiration for the single-party state during the 1960s and 1970s. Whilst individual political rivals and underground movements were suppressed through arrest and imprisonment, the ideas of these rivals – and indeed sometimes individuals themselves – were often co-opted. Under both Ben Bella and Boumediene, the values of equality, freedom and justice were felicitously depicted as the true basis of both socialism and Islam.[25]

In terms of imposing a cultural vision, as James McDougall underlines, the *'ulama* and their descendants had a major advantage in that since the 1930s they had mastered the language of the national culture, the national past and 'personality'.[26] This did not mean that political leaders were prepared to allow the *'ulama* to exert a monopoly on these concepts. In March 1963, Ben Bella declared: 'We will block the road to false doctrines and we will break the back of false preachers of Islam and Arabism'.[27] This was an attempt by Ben Bella to wrest the language of Islam and Arabity from the *'ulama*, rather than challenge an Arabo-Islamic definition of 'authentic' Algerianness. After all, arriving in Tunis in spring 1962 after his release from prison in France, Ben Bella famously declared: 'We are Arabs! We are Arabs!! We are Arabs!!!', apparently prompting an Algerian minister in his entourage to mutter ironically, 'That will end up coming true'.[28] The Tripoli programme promised that 'Muslim civilisation' would provide the social structure of Algerian society: according to Harbi, the reference to Islam was at the request of Ben Bella, who challenged the idea of a secular state.[29] Ben Bella's 'false preachers' speech was nevertheless used in an article published in *Le Peuple* in July 1963 as the basis of an argument in favour of women's integration into the workplace. The author insisted that, if this integration was to happen, certain traditions – such as the veil and the separation of the sexes – would have to be dropped: 'Young women cannot be left on the sidelines. Their work means that they will have to be integrated into groups of men.'[30]

Examining how the 'woman question' was debated in the 1960s enables us to question both convenient claims of the harmonious synergies between Islam and socialism made at the time and subsequent insistence on their inherent incompatibility. Common to both Marxist sympathisers and Muslim theologians in the immediate post-independence years was the anxiety that the revolution was in danger. Where they diverged is in defining what this danger was. Was it sex, alcohol, short skirts, partying and pop music? Or was it disrespect for women, the failure to let them take their place in society, materialism and a general lack of revolutionary seriousness? On closer examination, puritan desire to curtail 'debauched' cultural practices and revolutionary zeal to construct a new state and society were not so diametrically opposed. The yearning for order was not just a conservative reflex, there was a general agreement that a state needed to be created and boundaries put in place in society to avoid chaos. Social change was not necessarily seen as the enemy of morality, as long as it was carefully controlled, and the onus was put on women to demonstrate the required degree of political and social respectability.

In March 1965, at a conference of the UGTA, Halima Belarbi, a member of the executive commission and an auxiliary nurse, complained that in Oran there were cases of women 'with a loose past' who had been sacked from the administration. Whilst she argued that 'this attitude is not really fair', Halima Belarbi did not approve of the women's behaviour. In her words, they needed to 'correct' themselves.[31] Reaping the collective benefits of economic growth left no place for any sexual distractions, comrades were depicted as being as asexual as wartime 'brothers' and 'sisters'. Sexual revolution was not a part of the socialist revolution, despite the best attempts of twist-dancing teenagers.

Official speeches and the state-controlled press in the 1960s and 1970s were full of opinions about women's place in the public sphere, how women should dress, whom they should marry, what their names should be and which individuals and organisations should represent women. Rather than simply reproduce these debates, the following section seeks to locate moments when discourses about women intersected with the lived experiences of interviewees, exploring if and how they responded to 'embodying' the nation.

Are you Algerian enough?
The nation in ethno-cultural-political terms

One of the most controversial pieces of legislation in the first years of independence was the 1963 Nationality Law. Elections in September 1962 brought men and women on single lists of candidates into the Constituent Assembly. At this point in time, the members of this assembly were of fairly mixed political allegiances – many of its members would later withdraw from political life, or else enter into underground opposition or exile, and the National Assembly would be much more closely affiliated to presidential power. Ten out of 196 deputies in the Constituent National Assembly were women, all were war veterans. These included the first three women arrested in the *maquis*, Safia Baazi (deputy for Algiers), Meriem Belmihoub (Algiers) and Fadéla Mesli (Médéa), as well as Zohra Drif (Tiaret) and Samia Salah Bey née Lakhdari (Médéa), both key figures in the 'Battle of Algiers'. Other female deputies included Eveline Lavalette (Algiers), an FLN wartime activist of European origin, and Fatima Mechiche-Khemisti (Tlemcen). This was a small minority – 5 per cent – but it was a significant percentage for the time: prior to 1987, women had never made up more than 5 per cent of MPs in the British House of Commons. The Nationality Law, which was eventually adopted on 27 March 1963, provoked the most heated debates in the assembly's seven-month history. The final version of the text defined 'Algerian' as 'any person who has at least two ascendants in the paternal line who were born in Algeria and who possessed Muslim personal status'.[32] That is to say, it defined being Algerian in similar terms to how the colonial law of 1865 defined not being a full French citizen: the dividing line was whether or not the individual was ruled by Muslim family law. Article five of the 1963 Nationality Law gave Algerian nationality by filiation to a child born of an Algerian father, as defined above, or born of an Algerian mother, whose father was unknown. In a euphemistically worded – or perhaps euphemistically reported – critique, the deputy Eveline Lavalette stated that article five left little doubt about what constituted Algerian nationality.[33] It was being Muslim, defined as an ethno-cultural identity inherited through the paternal line. Non-Algerian women who married Algerian men acquired Algerian nationality; Algerian women who married non-Algerian men lost it.

At the same time, the 1963 Nationality Law also had to pay lip service to the March 1962 Evian Accords, which set out the possibility for the European population of Algeria to choose Algerian nationality within three years of the date of self-determination, as long as they could demonstrate that they had been resident in Algeria for a period of at least ten years (if the individual was born in Algeria) or twenty years (if the individual was not born in Algeria but his or her parents were). Whilst reproducing this provision, the 1963 Nationality Law put in a clause to exclude anyone considered to have committed 'crimes against the Nation' after the date of the Evian Accords.[34] Fear of the 'enemy within' appears as a major concern in much of the debate in the National Assembly, with lengthy discussions about how to effectively exclude members of the OAS and *harkis* – the latter group in particular could potentially be included in an ethno-cultural definition of Algerianness.[35]

Much of the National Assembly debate also centred on how an ethno-cultural definition of being Algerian would exclude those

Europeans who had supported the independence struggle, but who could not demonstrate the lengthy residency required. This was a particular concern for deputies Meriem Belmihoub, a former *maquisarde*, and Abdelkader Guerroudj, a wartime communist activist. Guerroudj's wife was Jacqueline Guerroudj, who was born in France and moved to Algeria in 1948, joining the FLN before being captured and condemned to death. Belmihoub and Guerroudj successfully brought forward an amendment to enable the acquisition of Algerian nationality for any current resident of Algeria who could prove that he or she had participated in the independence struggle.[36] In order to benefit from this clause, a specific demand needed to be made on an individual basis to the Ministry of Justice in the six months following the promulgation of the law.

The final vote on the Nationality Bill, held on 13 March 1963, attracted the largest number of voters in the assembly's history thus far. The only woman who voted in favour of the bill was Fatima Mechiche-Khemisti. Ironically enough, Mechiche-Khemisti was also the deputy who made the first 'feminist' speech in the Constituent Assembly in December 1962, demanding that the Algerian woman be 'defended' and her problems considered by the assembly.[37] She was also behind the Khemisti Law, which raised the minimum age for marriage to sixteen for girls and eighteen for boys. Meriem Belmihoub, Eveline Lavalette, Fadéla Mesli and Safia Baazi, as well as men including Krim Belkacem and Abdelkader Guerroudj, all voted against the Nationality Bill. Eveline Lavalette is reported to have protested, even as the bill went to a vote.[38] Obliged to submit to the new law, on 4 July 1963, she officially acquired Algerian nationality.

There was a significant decrease in the proportion of women deputies in the 1964 National Assembly: of 138 representatives, only two – Lavalette and Mechiche-Khemisti – were women, meaning that the percentage of women dropped to 1.5 per cent. Only a fifth of the female deputies from the 1962 Constituent Assembly kept their seats in the 1964 Assembly, compared to around a third of the male deputies. The reasons for the reduction in the number of female representatives remain unclear. Fadéla Mesli told me that she resigned. When I asked her why, she replied, after a long hesitation, 'for personal reasons'.[39] Given the small numbers, we cannot definitively conclude from the statistics that a gender bias was at work. Instead, the reduction in the number of women in the National Assembly is mostly likely a combination of, on the one hand, marginalising individuals who did not unquestioningly follow the single-party line and, on the other hand, individuals who refused to follow the single-party line resigning. Ferhat Abbas resigned from his role as President of the National Assembly in August 1963, in protest against the new constitution. This constitution was written outside of the Assembly, by FLN delegates gathered by Ben Bella at the Majestic cinema, and centred power in the hands of the president. As it became increasingly clear that Algeria was going to become a single-party regime, the National Assembly may well have appeared a moribund body for deputies – such as Fadéla Mesli – keen to 'do something useful' for their country. That said, Mesli returned to the assembly in 1977, along with fellow *mujahidat* Baya Hocine and Saliha Djeffal, as one of ten female deputies out of a total of 273 (3.7 per cent).

As the provisions of the nationality law made clear, a marriage between an Algerian man and a non-Algerian woman and a marriage between an Algerian woman and a non-Algerian man (with 'Algerian' defined in the above terms, i.e. as a Muslim – the conflation was intentional) were not perceived to be equally problematic by lawmakers. Indeed, plenty of leading figures in the history of Algerian nationalism, including the father of Algerian nationalism, Messali Hadj, had French wives. Algerian women married to non-Algerian men were seen as more troubling, even if these men converted to Islam – as both religious precepts and, from the mid-1960s, Algerian law, required – and even if these men had Algerian nationality and the political credibility of having participated in the War of Independence.[40] Zhor Ounissi, a member of the wartime FLN (and Minister for Education, 1985–88) from a Constantine *'ulama* background passionately critiqued mixed marriages in 1965. Writing in the newspaper of the Algerian army, *El Djeïch*, she asked: 'What will become of virility, Algerian glory, the Arabo-Islamic national character of our vigorous youth? In what state will our young men be when they see their sisters in the arms of foreigners who are their enemies and the enemies of all the Arab nation?'[41]

Although mixed marriages were a relatively small social phenomenon, the fact that they were a cause for concern for law makers, the press and the UNFA indicates that there were young men and women with little interest in defending 'Arabo-Islamic' culture through endogenous unions. Amongst my interviewees,

Abdelkader Guerroudj was the second husband of Jacqueline Guerroudj (Netter-Minne) and Bachir Hadj Ali was the second husband of Lucette Hadj Ali. Fadéla M'Rabet married Maurice 'Tarik' Maschino shortly after independence and together they presented a programme on state radio. Non-Muslim men acquired Muslim names as part of religious conversions, motivated by piety or and/or social (and legal) conformity. Some non-Muslim women also acquired an 'Algerian' name. Acquiring an Algerian or Muslim name provided the most obvious exterior sign of belonging. Some of these names were aliases dating from the War of Independence – this is how Lucette Hadj Ali acquired the name Safia, for example. During the independence struggle, and notably in prison, when constantly under the gaze of the colonial enemy, taking on a Muslim name and participating in Muslim rituals, such as fasting during Ramadan, when you were not Muslim were considered acts of solidarity. It was a form of identification with a people whose ethno-religious identity relegated them to second-class citizenship, whose mother tongue, or at least the mother tongue for many, Arabic, had been demoted to the rank of foreign language. Some Muslim families in which children had French first names changed their names 'back' to Muslim ones during the war as a symbol of their rejection of colonialism and its failed promises of assimilation.[42] In the colonial period, Islam and Arabic were the religion and language of the dispossessed. To adopt them, therefore, might first and foremost be interpreted as a political challenge to the colonial status quo, rather than a religious act.

In post-1962 Algeria, switching (or not) to an Algerian-Muslim name if you were not from a Muslim background came to acquire a different significance. From being a subversive political statement under French rule, taking on a Muslim-Algerian name when you were of a different cultural background became an affirmation of belonging, conforming even, to the new post-independence nation. Later still, it would metamorphose into a necessary means of protection against exclusion for one's 'otherness'. Lucette Hadj Ali explains that, after her husband Bachir was imprisoned in 1965 for his opposition to Boumediene's coup, when he was eventually allowed to write to her he always used her Algerian name, Safia. This is also the name she used professionally in the high school where she taught. In her preface to *Lettres à Lucette*, a 2002 publication of the letters sent to her by Bachir during his incarceration, Lucette suggests that her husband was 'no doubt desiring to affirm and underline to the security forces and political leaders my "Algerianness"'[43] – although Lucette reclaimed her first name of birth in the title of the book. From a legal perspective, the 1975 civil code stated that 'First names must be Algerian-sounding: alternatives are possible if a child is born to parents who are not Muslim'[44] – a rule which underlined the semantic equivalence made between 'Algerian' and 'Muslim', and which also excluded a lot of pre-Islamic Berber first names.

One former FLN militant and ex-Barberousse detainee who did not change her name was Annie Steiner. Upon returning to Algeria in 1962, Annie was nominated to the central administration. Right up until her retirement, and through a series of major political changes, she worked as Director of the Secretariat of the Government, responsible for producing the *Journal officiel*. She was the only woman on her team and although she chose to take Algerian nationality she never changed her European name. She remarks that, 'despite this', she was still promoted under Boumediene, on the basis of her competence. The only concession Annie Steiner made as a woman was not smoking during meetings, even though all the men around her smoked: 'I wanted my colleagues to listen to me, I didn't want to shock them. A feminist acquaintance criticised me for that. I said to her that she was missing the point, after all, it was me who was running the meetings.'[45]

Keeping one's European name could be seen as an act of resistance to an 'Arabo-Islamic' vision of Algeria, although both Lucette Hadj Ali and Annie Steiner are very careful to underline that they feel they have no automatic right to 'Algerianness'. 'This country, I earned it,' says Annie Steiner.[46] Lucette Hadj Ali also underlines her desire to be recognised as a citizen who has earned her right to be considered Algerian by making sacrifices for the nation:

> I've had Algerian nationality since 1964. All the same, it took a while. After they'd done the first nationality law, I asked for nationality and they wanted to give it to me as the wife of an Algerian. I refused, because there was article eight which gave those who had participated in the liberation struggle the possibility to obtain nationality. They gave it to me through article eight. It was good of them because afterwards they changed the law and they stopped [nationality] for Europeans, even the wives of Algerians.[47]

Such expressions of gratitude for being allowed to belong come from a political desire to firmly oppose a certain settler vision of Algeria as a 'blank space' before colonialism that belonged to no one and which was constructed through the act of colonisation and French *mise en valeur* (development and 'improvement'). The fact that these two women, whose families had been established in Algeria since the nineteenth century, insist that they have no automatic right to be considered Algerian nevertheless might be interpreted as an unspoken recognition of an ethno-cultural (i.e. 'Arabo-Islamic') definition of Algerianness. Both these women of European origin were confronted with a series of situations in which they had to decide what they were willing to concede in order to belong, without losing their sense of self as individuals. Each of these negotiations was very personal. This was not just a set of negotiations facing Algerian women of European origin, but women of European origin were perhaps more sensitive to them as they were most exposed to accusations of alterity.

The 'Arabo-Islamic collective identity' was open to a wide variety of interpretations. But, owing to the exclusionary system based on language and religion which characterised the colonial system, the margins of manoeuvre for imagining an Algerian collective identity outside of this broadly defined framework were narrow. This is revealed by the unlikely figure of Fadéla M'Rabet. In 1962, this former student in the FF–FLN began to present a controversial radio programme dealing with problems faced by young Algerian women, such as forced marriage, sexual harassment and suicide. On the basis of her observations, Fadéla M'Rabet wrote two critiques of retrograde and discriminatory treatment of Algerian women in post-independence society, *La Femme algérienne* (1964) and *Les Algériennes* (1967). Both books caused a scandal and were banned. In 1971, she and her husband were forced into exile in France. She received little support from other women:

> FM'R: I was the only one to fight in conferences, on the international stage, right up until the 1980s. Do you know what they said to me when I was lynched in the [Algerian] media? When I met them [other women] in the street they said to me 'Oh you give us shivers down the spine, they [the authorities] want to kill you, you need to leave!' [*She laughs*] That's how they encouraged me! They told me that it was too soon.
> NV: Who said this?

FM'R: Everyone, intellectuals, women, they said it was too soon. And that we had our Arabo-Islamic values. They [women] idealised these Arabo-Islamic values, these same values brandished today by girls who wear the veil, because they think that they have some kind of particularity!

And yet, despite her radical position compared to other interviewees, even Fadéla M'Rabet recognises why this 'Arabo-Islamic collective identity' might be considered central to definitions of Algerianness. Her father was a close friend and collaborator of Ben Badis in the *'ulama* movement. In the 1930s, she argues, they were radicals for their time: 'In Skikda, my father and [Ben Badis] put on plays in theatres, all the families brought along their wives and children. These plays were real educational tools which attacked obscurantism and sorcery.' Fadéla M'Rabet studied in France to become a biologist, and sees her political and professional trajectory as the result of her father's investment in her education. Today, she argues that Algeria 'started badly' by making Islam the religion of state, for her, 'that means they didn't want a democratic state'. And yet, she says that at the time:

> We thought that it was a way to show our gratitude towards Islam, because Islam was the common denominator, insurance against the death of the Algerian collective identity [*personnalité*] during colonisation. We didn't think that [...] it was going to be a literal reading of Islam, but a historical one. The prophet was a revolutionary in his time. He gave [women] a legal personality, he placed us under the authority of God, rather than the father. Only he didn't know that by giving us to God, he was giving us to his representatives! Despotic Caliphates, pathological emirs and neurotic little chiefs ...[48]

In a discussion of the much-maligned concept of Arabism, James McDougall argues that the real and imaginary worlds and networks that the notion evoked provided a key set of 'symbolic resources' for Algerians in the second half of the twentieth century, capable of 'expressing belonging and aspiration beyond [the] predictable parameters' of fossilised official discourse and subversive political reappropriation.[49] Fadéla M'Rabet's statement similarly reflects the power of Islam – in this context, in the 1960s – to provide a meaningful framework to express nationalist aspirations. The 'Arabo-Islamic collective identity' was not just a romantic trope produced by, and confined to, a conservative elite of religious scholars, it could also resonate with French-educated, Marxist, secular feminists such as Fadéla M'Rabet, as it could with Algerians of European origin.

Representing ourselves to the world

It is therefore less paradoxical than it might initially seem that the most famous symbol of Algeria in the first few years of independence was Djamila Bouhired. A former member of the Algiers bomb network, Bouhired married her Franco-Vietnamese wartime lawyer Jacques Vergès shortly after the end of the conflict and had two children with him.

After independence, Djamila Bouhired and Djamila Boupacha – another member of the Algiers bomb network, whose public denunciation of the torture she was subjected to by the French army turned her into a cause célèbre – became official envoys for the nascent Algerian state. They were living symbols of the fusion between forward-looking youthful courageousness and historical integrity, the harmonious coming together of pan-Arabism and socialism. In November 1962, Djamila Bouhired went on an official tour of the Middle East with the aim of collecting funds for the Algerian war orphans' organisation Al-Jil al-Jadid (The New Generation), which she presided over jointly with the Constituent Assembly deputy and fellow veteran Zohra Drif. The Algerian daily *Al Chaab* celebrated the enthusiasm of 'our Arab brothers' in welcoming Bouhired in Kuwait, Egypt, Syria, Morocco and Tunisia: 'our sister has been celebrated everywhere she goes and a range of events have been organised in her honour',[50] 'No other woman in the Kuwait Emirate has ever received the official reception that Djamila Bouhired was given'.[51] Four months later, in March 1963, Djamila Bouhired left on a two-week trip to China with Jacques Vergès. Chairman Mao, the Communist Party, the education system, the army, the position of women in China and the religious freedom accorded to Chinese Muslims were reported on at length by the couple in a series of articles in *Révolution africaine*. One of the many accompanying photographs shows Bouhired taking tea with Mao, the communist leader grinning jovially whilst Bouhired and Vergès sit alongside him smiling.[52]

Nor did post-independence Algeria forget the capitalist ex-colonial powers in spreading its diplomatic net. In March 1963, as Djamila Bouhired was travelling through China, Djamila

Boupacha was one of four members of the first official delegation to Britain since Algerian independence, the guests of Queen
Elizabeth. According to *Alger républicain*, 'Mrs Djamila Boupacha
is particularly interested in women's organisations, whilst the men
participating in this delegation have expressed a particular interest
in visiting the different industrial sectors in Britain'.[53]

Considering how women responded to the roles that they were
asked to play enables us to go beyond simply writing off these
foreign visits and meet-and-greets as another example of first ladies
acquiescing in a window-dressing role, shaking hands and kissing
babies. When I asked Djamila Boupacha how she came to participate in the official delegation to the UK, she replied: 'They chose
me as a woman, just like that. They needed a woman.'[54] Djamila
Boupacha's phrase 'they needed a woman' clearly indicates that
she was being asked to fulfil a gendered role: the image of Algeria
needed some gender balance in its delegation, she was called upon
and she felt that she had a responsibility to serve.

Djamila Bouhired, however, seems to have been more interested in using her symbolic value to make political statements,
both abroad and at home. During the 1973 Arab–Israeli War,
Bouhired and Drif – both women were married mothers at this
point – sent an open letter to President Hafez al-Assad, offering to
join the Syrian army. Previously, Bouhired had attempted to get
Boumediene to send her to Vietnam.[55] Such displays of pan-Arab
and anti-imperial solidarity were in the spirit of the times and
consolidated Algeria's self-image as a leader of the Third World.
Less likely to attract the support of the Algerian state, however,
were Drif's and Bouhired's complaints about the difficulties they
encountered in effectively running Al-Jil al-Jadid. On 1 March
1963, the two women invited national and international journalists to a press conference, during which they complained that
neither the Arab states nor the Algerian government had lived up
to their donation promises.[56]

After the first few years of independence, Djamila Bouhired
withdrew from public life, which might be interpreted as a form of
resistance to political manipulation. She refused to participate in
any more diplomatic visits, ceremonies or interviews.[57] She participated in campaigns against the Family Code in the early 1980s, but
has only really begun to re-emerge as a public figure since 2009, to
criticise the lack of healthcare available to her, to join campaigns in

Algiers against rampant urbanisation and to express her opposition to President Bouteflika running for a fourth term. Embodying the nation can leave individuals no longer recognising themselves. Whilst Djamila Boupacha seems to accept being a symbol of Algeria as part of her contribution to the nationalist struggle, she also makes it clear that she feels – and felt – uncomfortable with this role. This unease expresses itself in a number of ways. Sometimes it is a humorous anecdote. Around the same time as her visit to the UK, an intimidated Djamila Boupacha describes trying to hide from Nasser at an official reception for the Egyptian president in Algeria. Her attempts failed when Ben Bella expressedly came to seek her out and insisted on presenting her to Nasser, who in turn promptly insisted that Boupacha visit his country. Djamila Boupacha also describes knowingly playing on other people's failure to recognise the real woman behind the symbol-laden image. In the mid-1990s, the original painting of her by Picasso, produced as part of the wartime campaign to publicise her brutal torture, was brought to the Musée de Beaux Arts (Fine Arts Museum) in Algiers. At the exhibition opening, a visitor who did not recognise her asked her if it was the painting of Djamila Boupacha. She says that she replied: 'No, it's the woman at war'. Djamila Boupacha seeks to minimise the place of the war in her life story. If the war had not have taken place, she says, she would have got married and had children, 'but [instead] I was able to participate a bit in the liberation of my country'.[58]

In 1984, Bouhired gave a rare interview to a journalist working on an Arabic-language magazine, in which she discussed the international impact of – and unwelcome interest in – her marriage to her wartime lawyer. Djamila Bouhired asserted that she would not have married Vergès, from whom she was separated by that point, if he had not converted to Islam, but this did not stem the flow of critical comments addressed to her at the time: 'I received a huge amount of letters from all over the Muslim world, even from Pakistan, and in their letters people treated me like public property'.[59] The symbol had consumed the individual, limiting her choices to a politically and socially acceptable path.

Representing women: The UNFA

The organisation which, in theory, embodied 'the Algerian woman' abroad, represented her interests and needs at home, and prepared her to participate in the running of the state was the Union Nationale des Femmes Algériennes. The UNFA was the newest, the least organised, the least influential and the least autonomous branch of the FLN's mass organisation apparatus. After the creation of the Algerian students' union (UGEMA, later UNEA) in 1955, the Algerian workers' union (UGTA) in 1956 and the Algerian youth movement (JFLN) in summer 1962, a 'Union des Femmes Algériennes' (Union of Algerian Women, UFA) was mentioned for the first time in October 1962. In November 1962, *Alger républicain* published the UFA's statutes,[60] and, after a two-day founding congress in January 1963, the UFA became the UNFA, changing name perhaps not least because UFA was also the acronym for the communist Union des Femmes d'Algérie in the pre-independence period.

The UFA/UNFA leadership was constantly changing, with numerous 'first congresses' taking place. Press reports continually present different women at the head of the organisation, including former members of the prewar UFMA Fatima Benosmane, Mamia Chentouf and Nefissa Lalliam, war veteran Djamila Bouhired (as president of honour) and National Assembly deputy Samia Salah Bey, as well as Farida Khadir, Nadra Saïm, Mme Ghani and Fatima Zohra Arabdiou, amongst others.[61] In 1966, a year after Boumediene's coup, yet another 'first congress' took place. The official declarations of the UNFA at this 1966 congress promised to promote women's work whilst ensuring that female workers could also be mothers, to extend family planning whilst excluding abortion as a means of contraception, and to strengthen women's voices in both the political and personal spheres whilst expressing anxiety about the growth in the number of mixed marriages between Algerian men and non-Algerian women and Algerian women and non-Algerian men. This latter phenomenon, one resolution declared, 'gravely upsets the equilibrium of the family' by failing to be 'in keeping with the Algerian collective identity and its Arabo-Islamic culture'.[62]

In January 1963, Samia Salah Bey declared: 'All the sisters here participated in the Revolution. Today they must participate in the consolidation of independence and the construction of a socialist state. The UNFA is not a charitable organisation.'[63] Yet most of its activities fit comfortably into the category of good works carried out by ladies belonging to a social elite rather than tasks of state construction. The UNFA was involved in organising fundraising meetings and collective circumcisions for the children of war martyrs, giving hospitalised children presents for Eid, running housekeeping and sewing workshops and getting 'Keep Algiers Tidy' cleaning sessions under way as well as some literacy campaigns. The other major UNFA activity was meeting foreign delegations and forming delegations for overseas visits. Official visits took UNFA representatives to Eastern Europe, Africa, Russia, Cuba, China, Vietnam and the Middle East. A photograph in June 1963 published in *Alger républicain* shows a UNFA delegation which had just completed a tour of China, Vietnam and Russia descending on to the Algerian tarmac in particularly good spirits – all dressed up in Chinese peasant hats.[64] In the angry words of an anonymous letter writer to the UNFA magazine *El Djazaïria* in 1980: '*El Djazaïria* magazine is just for show. Mrs X is going to welcome Mrs Y at the airport: this is of no importance to us.'[65]

That *El Djazaïria* published this letter is perhaps not as surprising as it might initially seem. Public criticism of the UNFA appears to have been unproblematic in the single-party state, especially when these criticisms came from within the system. In autumn 1964, Mohand Said Mazouzi, a member of the FLN Central Committee, described the UNFA as 'inefficient and inoperative',[66] and in his 1966 International Women's Day speech Boumediene declared that 'the UNFA has played no role since independence and cannot play an effective role in the liberation of women unless its action extends to the countryside'.[67] None of the rural women whom I interviewed had heard of the UNFA.

Eleven interviewees, all from urban areas, were associated with the UNFA in the early years of independence. A few stayed on, and felt that, at a micro-level at least, they were doing something useful. More left. Women who were opponents, or critical, of the single-party regime in public, or, more frequently, in private, were unlikely to join the UNFA: it was seen as totally subservient to the party of the FLN. The former PCA member Lucette Hadj Ali says that she had some friends who initially joined 'to try and orientate it, but they were rapidly weeded out'.[68] Whilst other state organisations such as the UGTA and JFLN managed, despite their official status, to generate some degree of debate, however limited, about the political direction of the country, the UNFA struggled to form any distinct voice. At the same time, the UNFA lacked autonomy to such a degree that it did not even work as an effective satellite for the FLN, and its lack of power and influence meant it was a little valued organisation for the single-party state.

Perhaps most important in explaining why the UNFA remained small and weak is the fact that many women rejected the fact that the UNFA was 'for women': they found this reductive. This is despite a history of women's sections within political movements between 1943 and 1962, albeit on a relatively small scale: there was the PCA's UFA, the PPA–MTLD's UFMA, and the Section de Femmes of the FF–FLN. Documents captured by the French army upon the arrest of Yacef Saadi and Zohra Drif in October 1957 suggest that Drif was planning a women's organisation for the wartime ZAA. It was envisaged that the majority of women in this network would distribute food supplies to needy families, provide intelligence and participate in demonstrations, with 'those women who were capable and needed' transferred into the politico-military organisation.[69] It is telling that, in these plans, it was envisaged that Drif would organise other women to provide logistical support and propaganda, but her own role, and that of women with the same profile as her, was considered to be in the mixed-sex underground bomb network.

This wartime experience of having challenged a male-dominated public sphere, and the feeling of having been accepted into it, in part explains the reluctance of many women with the requisite educational, social and historical capital to take a leading role in the UNFA. Saliha Djeffal states that she did not join the UNFA: 'Because I believe in one struggle without a split between men and women, I never wanted to join a feminine organisation'. Instead, she enjoyed a rapid ascent from local to national politics within the JFLN. Saliha argues, 'The JFLN was an avant-garde organisa- tion. There was no difference between male and female militants. There was no separation'. This was also true, she insists, of the Scout movement and the UGTA 'where there were always male and female workers'.[70] Jacqueline Guerroudj joined the UGTA because, she states, she was in favour of mixing between the sexes.[71]

Between 1974 and 1978, Louisette Ighilahriz says that she visited eighteen different countries on behalf of the UNFA, ostensibly with the task of looking at socio-economic models which might work in Algeria.[72] Her biggest regret about joining the UNFA seems to have been less its lack of ambition, inefficiency and clientelism (she even describes '*harki*' women, who, in her words, were 'more malleable' being brought into the UNFA), although these were factors, than the UNFA's very essence as a single-sex organisation:

> When I had finished my university studies, I don't know what happened, I was contacted and I was caught out and I found myself in the Secretariat of the UNFA. Almost without thinking, and I'm angry with myself. I cannot accept single-sex activism. And I had lots of problems, even though I got to travel. It was not my orientation, it wasn't my ideology. This man–woman dichotomy, I accepted it and I don't know how I found myself caught up in it.[73]

Creating a women's organisation was not seen by these educated female veterans as a positive step towards gender equality; rather they saw it as a regression into female difference, and, by inference, inferiority.

The one moment when there is a glimpse that the UNFA could have been an effective mass movement for women, appealing to a broad social base, was at the International Women's Day demonstration of 8 March 1965. One of the organisers of this march was Zhor Zerari, who earlier that year had been asked to organise the UNFA congress, and who had agreed to do so on the condition that she would remain outside of its formal structures.[74] In press interviews that she gave in the weeks leading up to the demonstration, Zerari sought to explicitly link 8 March with the rights of women as workers – the date, fortuitously, was also the eve of the UGTA congress.[75] The event was also pitched as a prelude to the Afro-Asian women's conference planned in Algiers for that summer.

The International Women's Day demonstration of 8 March 1965 was successful beyond any of the organisers' expectations. Thousands of women – estimates range from three thousand to twelve thousand – massed at the Place du 1er mai and marched in front of all the government ministries along the seafront, down to the working-class district of Bab el Oued. Wives of ambassadors of countries still fighting for their liberation attended alongside high-profile politicians such as Zohra Drif, followed by women from all social backgrounds. Whilst official banners declared their solidarity with 'our Angolan sisters', spontaneous chants suggested that men 'go and do the cooking, we'll take care of politics' and 'stay at home and look after the children, we'll look after ourselves'. Barricades of women blocked cars and buses, terrified men fled their vehicles and some women threw their *hayk* into the sea.[76] For the first –

and, until the early 1980s, the last – time, women were making demands for improvements in their working and social conditions, as women. The meeting ended with crowds of women seeking to enter the Majestic cinema in Bab el Oued, to hear Ben Bella make a series of increasingly radical promises to the angry crowd. In the words of Zhor Zerari: 'He said, "You have rights, seize them!" The next day he wanted to see me. He said that he was going to give us all the help that we needed. He saw that this was a force that needed organising.'[77]

On 20 August 1965, freshly designated as National Mujahidin Day following the 19 June coup, Boumediene made an uncompromising criticism of the 8 March demonstration. He stated that his image of Algerian women was of sisters who had fought alongside their brothers in the mountains, and emphatically not the women of the 'Majestic meeting hall and the Place des Martyrs, launching *you yous* [cries of joy]'.[78] In 1966, Zhor Zerari says that the UNFA organised activities for 8 March requiring participants to hold invitation cards. Newspapers report a hushed recital of *al-Fatiha* (the first verse of the Qur'an) at the grave of the war martyr Hassiba Ben Bouali at 8.30 in the morning on 8 March 1966. These graveyard ceremonies would continue to mark International Women's Day throughout the 1970s.

The demonstration of 8 March 1965 was not a spontaneous event, but the march took on a dynamic of its own. The enthusiasm it generated and the presidential reaction which it provoked surpassed the expectations of its organisers. Whether there was real political will to push through the promises which Ben Bella made on the day is a moot point, as he was overthrown a few months later. Women such as Zhor Zerari remained resistant to organising specifically as women. The social resistance to such change was made very clear the day after the demonstration, when around fifty participants came to the Bab el Oued UGTA office, beaten and repudiated by their husbands. Neither the UGTA, nor the FLN, nor the UNFA wished to take responsibility for these women: they were left to fend for themselves.[79]

Your dowry for the nation

The UNFA was a small, urban, and – apart from on 8 March 1965 – largely elite organisation. The only national programme which explicitly reached out to rural women to bring them into nation- and state-building was the Fonds de Solidarité Nationale (National Solidarity Fund, FSN). The FSN was launched on 16 April 1963 and lasted for a number of months. Algerian women were called upon to donate their jewellery to boost the meagre Algerian gold reserves and in turn combat unemployment, poverty and inadequate housing. In practice, this was asking most women to give to the state the only capital that they possessed. Nearly all Algerian women would have owned some jewellery. Notably at the moment of marriage, the family of the groom often gave a *mehazma*, a belt usually made in gold, sometimes in gold coins. Such jewellery was rarely worn apart from on festive occasions such as weddings and circumcisions, but in practical terms it provided a financial buffer if a women's husband died or the couple divorced.

The slogans surrounding the FSN campaign suggested that such stockpiling was no longer necessary. Slogans included: 'a piece of jewellery for Algeria is a treasure for the country' and 'jewellery is dead capital, give it to your country to make it strong [in the catchier French version, 'un bijou est un capital mort, offre-le à ton pays pour qu'il soit fort']'.[80] Meetings, often attracting thousands of women, were held in schools and public halls, organised by the UNFA and the Union Générale des Mères, Veuves et Orphelins de Chouhada [*sic*] (General Union of Mothers, Widows and Orphans of Shuhada, UGMVOC). Local FSN teams travelled across the countryside. Women handed over gold and silver, rings, bracelets and necklaces, marriage gifts and family heirlooms. Soundless arms stripped of clanking bracelets were waved in the air and women let out *you yous*, as Ben Bella exhorted women to physically show him that they were no longer wearing any jewellery: 'The exhibition of jewellery is incompatible with the objectives of our revolution', he declared.[81] Women were told that getting rid of 'frivolous' objects was both an act of solidarity with the socialist revolution and a step towards liberating themselves. According to Fatiha Maziri, giving a speech on behalf of the UNFA, women needed to get rid of their chains – of the mental and eighteen-carat varieties. She called on women to hand over their jewellery, 'the sign of a class': 'This is the only way, dear brothers and sisters', she punned, 'to show that the Algerian woman is free and that no chain holds her back'.[82] Traditional ideas about modesty and unnecessary adornment thus found their expression in the modern utilitarian discourse, at the same time as feminist declarations of emancipation were expressed in a language of anti-materialism and anti-capitalism.

Unlike much state discourse which was aimed at foreign audiences or reproduced in newspapers which most women (and men) could not read, the way in which the FSN sought to reach out to as wide an audience as possible means that ordinary women, including those in rural areas, can remember the campaigns. At the mention of Ben Bella's name, Fatima Benmohand Berci immediately says: 'Ben Bella, he took the jewellery and he left!' This is a reference to the FSN, although she does not use the official campaign title. She says fundraisers did not come to her village of Agraradj, but they did go to other villages in Kabylia, where many women gave all their jewellery. Fatima Benmohand Berci also saw an FSN campaign in Algiers in 1963: 'I saw with my own eyes Ben Bella at the Place des Martyrs, an old woman came and she had brought a sheep and a gold necklace. She brought it in front of us just like that.'[83]

Sheep were definitely not part of the list of items requested to restock the gold reserves, but this well-meaning participant was perhaps under the impression that Ben Bella was hungry, after all solidarity amongst neighbours generally meant food gifts. Or perhaps the offering of a sheep was in keeping with the custom of making a practical contribution to the cost of festive occasions. The interaction between 'old' and 'new' was striking in the different components which made up FSN rallies: with a mixture of political speeches, female-only sociability, *you yous* of joy and sacrificial sheep, these were public gatherings borrowing from the codes of a family wedding.

The socialist–feminist discourse was not necessarily understood in the way that it was intended. Indeed, it is worth underlining that Fatima Benmohand Berci would not have understood the speeches in French and Arabic at the Algiers rally which she attended, as she is a Tamazight speaker. Moreover, despite the moral pressure exerted on women to participate as a demonstration of their patriotism, and the collective euphoria at large FSN events, not everyone was convinced. Fatima Benmohand Berci saw the campaign in very straightforward terms: the state asked her to do something and she neither had the desire nor felt duty-bound to comply: 'It suited me not to give,' she says, 'I don't want to flatter those in power'.[84] The prevailing view amongst these rural women that Ben Bella 'left with the jewellery' implies they feel that they got little return on their investment during his short presidency.

I'm not a woman, I'm an Algerian: Insisting on gender-neutral citizenship

In the 1960s and 1970s, debates about the political direction and cultural identity of Algeria were expressed through a series of opinions on every aspect of women's public and private lives: whom they should marry, what their name should be, whether they should work, how many children they should have, which customs they should maintain and which they should get rid of. For rural interviewees, this discourse remained, for the majority of the time, distant and fairly meaningless. But for urban interviewees, who read the newspapers and who were employed by the state and/or were involved in politics, these exhortations were the sound of their everyday lives. Djamila Bouhired and Djamila Boupacha sought out anonymity to try to escape the confines of being living symbols of Algeria. Female veterans who might have otherwise been quite interested in creating a women's mass movement avoided it. The main technique which urban, educated interviewees adopted to avoid being saturated by their gender was insisting on being not women but rather gender-neutral citizens.

In the 1970s, Fadéla Mesli was involved in local politics as member of the *qasma* (section) of Ben Aknoun in Algiers. She describes Ben Aknoun at the time as a working-class area (it has since become much more middle-class), and most of the members of the *qasma* were older, illiterate men, accustomed to a public sphere where there were only men. Fadéla was the only woman until fellow *mujahida* Baya Hocine came to join her. One day the university halls of residence at Ben Aknoun came up on the agenda. The young women who lived there had been accused of 'looseness': '[The men] said, hesitantly, "It's a problem of morality, so we're going to ask sister Fadéla Mesli to leave the room".' Fadéla Mesli says that she promptly replied:

> 'I come here to debate all the problems, whatever they are. As I am here with you, you must not consider me a woman. I am a citizen of this country and all its problems are of interest to me. I don't see you as men' – imagine saying that to men! – 'For me you are Algerians,

full stop. There is no sex.' Afterwards, I said to myself, I'm going
to get lynched on the way out, but [the men] were – [*sentence left
unfinished*] – it's the husband of Djamila [Boupacha] who told me,
'That day, your popularity rating reached its summit!' – which just
goes to show, that when you have a certain confidence, a sincerity,
you transmit that, and everything can be accepted.

For Fadéla, getting her voice heard involved taking on the role of
the universal, abstract citizen ('citizen' being used very loosely, this
was after all, a single-party state). She uses a nationalist argument –
we are all Algerians – to circumvent the gendered boundaries of
the public sphere. Moreover, although acutely aware that she was
challenging social hierarchies and taboos about what is talked
about where and with whom, Fadéla underlines the importance
of 'self-help emancipation' – each woman needed to fight her own
battles. In Fadéla's account, how the women's halls of residence
issue was resolved is not mentioned: this is a story of one woman
making herself heard, not women challenging conceptions of what
constitutes women's 'loose behaviour'. Indeed, Fadéla may well
have considered that these young women should in any case have
been prioritising their studies over more frivolous pursuits. She
argues: 'It's not laws which make women counted; women have to
assert themselves on the ground. We need laws, but you can make
yourself heard by work, by a serious attitude, by your behaviour.'[85]
Fadéla both believes in the moralising rhetoric of revolutionary
seriousness (with all the accompanying synonyms that 'sérieux' has
in French – modest, restrained, composed, dignified and austere)
and uses this rhetoric strategically to leapfrog over constraining
gendered categories.

Fadéla Mesli's insistence that rights are fought for, not handed
over on a plate – a mythologised wartime 'spirit' which echoes
official discourse – is a subtext of many other educated women's
accounts of their post-1962 trajectories. Fadila Attia insists that
'liberty is seized, it is not given'.[86] For Habiba Chami, 'If [women]
don't seize their rights like they seized independence alongside men,
it's not men who are going to give rights to them!'[87] Whilst the
Neo-Destour newspaper *L'Action* patronisingly informed Tunisian
women in 1956 that 'We have done nothing to obtain [emancipa-
tion], alas! Accustomed to leaving men to decide for us, we left it to
them',[88] Algerian women were exhorted and exhorted themselves to

exert the rights which they had ostensibly already obtained through the wartime struggle.

In August 1963, *Le Peuple* ran a series of articles in which Zohra Drif and Meriem Belmihoub were asked to respond to the question 'Is there an Algerian woman problem?' Neither woman thought that there was. Instead, both insisted that the condition of women needed to be placed within the wider context of economic development and education, thus reinforcing the dominant discourse which subsumed gender issues to the wider political and economic project. Belmihoub underlined: 'We must not talk about the emancipation of women in terms of the veil and traditions, but by giving [women] employment'. Drif insisted: 'The liberation of men and women comes down to the question of education'. Although Belmihoub critiqued the enduring Muslim personal status laws governing the family, her solution to this was to address much broader socio-economic issues: 'This status was possible in a certain context. It is no longer possible today. We need to ensure the equality of rights and duties and notably equal pay. This can only take place in a socialist context.' Even though Drif cautiously referred to retrograde attitudes amongst some former brothers-in-arms, she insisted that this was a problem for men to deal with, not the collective responsibility of women to confront: 'Some of our brothers, not all of them, we need to be nuanced, used women in an instrumental way [during the war]. This is why after liberation we can see a move backwards on their part.' Drif called the 'woman problem' a 'myth' and for Belmihoub it was 'a false problem'.[89]

Resisting the concept of a 'women problem' was a means for both these women to avoid finding themselves the unwilling representatives of 'women's issues'. When I interviewed her in 2005, Zohra Drif reinforced this point: 'I never enclosed myself in women's struggles. Quite simply for reasons that strike me as obvious: in '62 we had to construct a state, a society and for me, the starting point was that we were citizens in our own right.' Speaking in 2005 as a non-elected senator appointed by the president, Drif rejects the idea that women who participated in the war struggled to find their place in post-independence Algeria:

We determine, by our behaviour, by the positions we take, the behaviour of others. This idea that the *mujahida* found herself rejected,

I think that this is a construction of the foreign gaze on Algerian society, which some of us [*mujahidat*] have adopted for political reasons [...] It's also a question of vocation. To participate in the liberation of the country is an act of citizenship, that doesn't mean you have the vocation to be a politician, that's something else. These are choices that you make on the basis of your aspirations and ambitions. There are many men who participated in the War of National Liberation who went back to the jobs they were in before. It's the same thing for women [...] Many women got married, and when you have lived through exceptional moments you are nostalgic for a normal, simple life like everyone else. [Women who remained in the home] made a choice. [90]

Drif's arguments are largely echoed, with some caveats, by Saliha Djeffal, a militant in the FF–FLN who after independence worked her way up through the ranks of the JFLN. In 2005, she was a senior figure in the party of the FLN:

During the revolution we were told: 'On independence everyone will be free, everyone can participate in reconstruction'. But in '62, it has to be said, and as a woman I say it, from some leaders, there was another discourse. They said to us: 'Women, return to your pots and pans'. And there were militants who stuck it out and others who chose, or who had the decision made for them, to start a family and have children. And it is true that having children is noble, it's also replacing the million and a half martyrs [from the war]. But having children can also stop women emerging in politics. [91]

Both Zohra Drif and Saliha Djeffal conveniently sidestep social resistance to changes in gender roles, unburdening the state from its responsibility in perpetuating them. Their emphasis on free choice after 1962 – that is to say, women choosing to be militants or mothers – suggests an unlikely liberal individualism, at odds with both the political context of the single party regime and the dominant social structures of kin networks. [92]

The responses of these two women are perhaps hardly surprising – when I interviewed them, both were establishment figures. Yet many urban, educated and politicised female veterans who have a critical view of post-independence Algeria are equally suspicious of the 'woman question'. They too argue that, in 1962, it was a sub-question of a much wider set of issues and that they did not consider it useful to campaign on a question which seemed so specific, or indeed, particularistic. Lucette Hadj Ali says that she had no interest in re-establishing a section for women within the communist movement in 1962: 'We needed to rebuild on other foundations'.[93] Women were members of the clandestine PAGS in an individual capacity. The feminist Fadéla M'Rabet, who in the mid-1960s would decide that there most definitely was a woman problem, states that in 1962 she felt that 'There was the struggle of Algerians, all citizens. I didn't distinguish between Algerian women and Algerian men.'

Fadéla M'Rabet also points out that it was not her public pronouncements about women which made her such a controversial figure:

> Why were they so furious when I published *La Femme algérienne* [in 1964]? They wanted to strip me of my Algerian nationality. It's not because I was presented as a suffragette. It's because I asked, 'By what miracle will we liberate women, when men are not free [either], when [neither men nor women are] citizens in Algeria?' That is the problem.[94]

The former urban bomber Zhor Zerari insists that the same remains true today: 'We need to fight for citizenship. Once women become citizens, many problems will disappear.'[95] In the 1960s, she refused to be pigeonholed with 'women's issues'. She rejected the offer to write the women's column in *Le Peuple* ('Chroniques féminines') and specialised in investigative journalism on industrial and agricultural issues, notably assessing the impact of Algeria's 'socialist path' on these sectors, and, in many cases, its failings. When Mimi Maziz joined the staff of the newspaper *Révolution africaine*, she point blank refused to write the newspaper's women's page, or, worse still, 'take care of the recipe section'.[96]

This doesn't mean that Zhor Zerari did not write about 'women's issues': in 1963, she took the initiative to prepare an article for *Le Peuple* on how International Women's Day was celebrated in countries in the Soviet bloc. However, when she handed the article over to her editor he bluntly dismissed the importance of the subject. According to Zhor Zerari: 'I ripped it all up, I slapped him, and I left. I came back the next day to get my things.' As Zerari rather understatedly puts it: 'I was not a timid young girl'.[97] It is significant, however, that in this anecdote she fights to have her professional integrity respected rather than the story on International Women's Day printed.

Less politicised women argue that 'acting like a man' helped them to advance in their professional careers. On returning to Algeria in 1962, Fadila Attia worked as a secretary for the provisional government, and then served on Ben Bella's staff before moving to the Ministry for Tourism in 1965:

> People think that I'm a strong woman. [*In reality, she says, she is very shy*] I worked very well in all the ministries and I made myself heard, but in the end people don't know you. But I gave a lot. A minister could leave me to it; I could run the place during his absence [...] Ben Bella used to call me to present me to the ambassadors, because you should have seen how I was elegant. I liked dressing nicely; I liked having fun [...] But I also used to get stuck into the work [...] I was a good colleague. I was hardworking. I used to go with a file and get it signed. That's how I got myself noticed.

Glamorous galas aside, it was better if your colleagues saw you first and foremost as an efficient worker. Fadila Attia sees her successful career as the result of thinking 'like a man': she describes herself as 'feminine in my behaviour, but in my head I'm masculine. I can take decisions and everything.' When I suggested to Fadila that women could also take decisions she concurred, before insisting, as did many interviewees: 'But women don't make their presence felt, women have to make their presence felt.' Fadila Attia suggests that the fact that she never married or had children also enabled her to firmly establish herself in the world of work: 'I have never had any problems with men. Maybe if I had married I would have had them. But I married Algeria. If I had thought like a married woman I would have been stuck. I was free to come and go. I didn't come home, I spent the day at the Ministry until midnight, two, three o'clock in the morning.'[98] This is a kind of extreme revolutionary morality. Fadila Attia cannot marry a man because she is married to Algeria, and, at the same time, being married to Algeria is a liberating experience.

The former *maquisarde* El Hora Kerkeb attributes to her wartime experiences this ability to make her presence felt in a male-dominated workplace. One of her roles as a social worker in the police after independence was protecting victims of domestic violence. Sometimes the perpetrators were also her colleagues and hierarchical superiors, making for politically delicate and potentially unpleasant situations: 'You feel a personal satisfaction, you say to yourself, I do my job, vis-à-vis men, I have no complex. Whether he's a minister or a general, the fact of having joined the ALN aged sixteen or seventeen, we were already mature, we were already the avant-garde, we were already ahead of many people.'[99] This at least in part explains why when Fadéla M'Rabet did decide to engage publicly with the 'women question' in the mid-1960s she received very little support from female former combatants: 'My generation felt humiliated when I said that we were oppressed women'.[100]

Conclusion

The newly independent Algerian state sought to redefine the nation through 'the Algerian woman'. The debates reproduced in presidential speeches and the state-controlled press are the visible tip, not so much of the iceberg but rather of a series of currents of opinion about the political and social direction of Algeria in the 1960s and 1970s. The absence of a clear ideological direction in 1962 proved auspicious for the spread of the ideas of the *'ulama* and their descendants and their vision of women as the defenders of a recovered cultural identity based on a conservative reading of Islam. But this reactionary trend was intertwined with the upheavals of the postwar context, the necessity of state-building, revolutionary rhetoric and dreams of a socialist utopia.

Looking at discourses about women, we see that these different tendencies were not diametrically opposed. This was not the felicitous dovetailing of Islam and socialism based on common ideas about sharing and equality as claimed in official discourse, but rather a converging of moralising views on the appropriate attitude for the individual to take in a revolutionary moment. A conservative vision of morality (don't let women mix with men!) and a revolutionary version of morality (all eyes on national construction!) could find a convenient accommodation. This is not to say that the socialist vision of Algerianness was the same as that of the *'ulama*, of course it was not. But there was remarkable symbiosis in some of the language.

As women were called upon to embody the nation, or had 'the nation' foisted upon their bodies, they reacted in different ways. Rural interviewees were largely unaware of or ignored this discourse. Urban, educated interviewees, who were depicted as representing the happy medium between 'tradition' and 'modernity', through being both workers and war veterans, refused to be labelled women or speak on behalf of women. By insisting on the gender-blind universalism of Algerian ethno-cultural-political particularism, these women fashioned a defensive weapon to impose their presence in the public space. This was a double-edged sword. Women used the wartime discourse of rights being seized, not given, to empower themselves, but at the same time this was a disempowering narrative in that it suggested that there were no automatic rights, only 'privileges' to be fought for. Moreover, as discussions of the place of gender in French universalism have demonstrated, when dominated groups, such as women, are seen to embody particular identities, it is impossible for them to become abstract citizens, however much they might aspire to this. Women are defined as 'the Other', man is the neutral.[101]

Nevertheless, urban, educated *mujahidat* shared in the puritanical language of the revolution. There was a single-minded determination at the heart of the most sincere proponents of revolution, a belief that one model could fix all. And if these women still remarked discrimination in their daily lives, it was not because the revolution had failed but because it had not finished. Indeed, this presents an interesting counterpoint to the popular view that 'it all went wrong' in 1962: when we try to uncover what women's perspectives were in the 1960s, they did not think it had all gone wrong, but rather they believed that the revolution had not yet come right.

In 1984, the official slogan of the festivities to mark thirty years since the outbreak of the War of Independence was 'work and seriousness are the guarantee of the future'. A shortened version of this slogan 'work and seriousness' (*al-'amal wa-'l-sarama*) subsequently became a joky expression amongst generations born from the 1970s onwards. It was used as an ironic comment on both rising unemployment and the banality of everyday routine. Yet for interviewees of the wartime generation who participated in state-building after 1962, work and seriousness were not banal at all – they were part of revolutionary construction.

Notes

1 The main authors of the Tripoli programme were left-leaning elements of the FLN, including Mohamed Harbi, Mostefa Lacheraf, Mohamed Benyahia and Redha Malek. Harbi describes the programme as a

hotchpotch of various Marxist, nationalist and religious influences, hastily put together in Libya in ten days and passed with little discussion as power struggles between personalities came to dominate proceedings. *FLN, mirage et réalité: des origines à la prise du pouvoir (1945–1962)* (Paris: Editions Jeune Afrique, 1980), pp. 331–7.

2 Part II, article 5, 'Liberation of Women', Tripoli Programme, Libya, June 1962, www.el-mouradia.dz/francais/symbole/textes/tripoli.htm (accessed 19 May 2014). This article was also directly quoted in the Algiers Charter, adopted by the first congress of the party of the FLN in 1964.

3 Interview with Zhor Zerari (21 December 2005).

4 *El Moudjahid* (21 December 1963).

5 Series of articles and letters to the editor on 'La jeunesse et le problème de la mixité', *Alger républicain* (14–20 February 1964).

6 *Alger républicain* (18 February 1964).

7 *Le Peuple* (21 February 1964).

8 *El Moudjahid* (26 December 1967).

9 Stanley Cohen is widely credited with popularising the term 'moral panic' in *Moral Panics and Folk Devils: The Creation of the Mods and Rockers* (London: MacGibbon and Kee, 1972).

10 Such incidents are described by eyewitnesses Marie-Aimée Helie-Lucas and Michel Martini, who both participated in the liberation struggle. The former became a feminist scholar and activist, the latter was a doctor at the Hospital Mustapha Pacha in Algiers for a number of years after independence. M.-A. Helie-Lucas, 'Women, nationalism and religion in the Algerian liberation struggle', in M. Badran and M. Cooke (eds), *Opening the Gates: An Anthology of Arab Feminist Writing* (Indianapolis: Indiana University Press, 2nd edn, 2004 [1990]), p. 110. M. Martini, *Souvenirs algériens: l'Algérie algérienne, 1962–1972* (Paris: Glyphe and Biotem Editions, 2000), p. 45.

11 *El Moudjahid* (21 December 1963).

12 *Révolution africaine* (13 June 1964).

13 *El Moudjahid* (23 March 1963).

14 *Les Discours du Président Ben Bella année 1963 au premier trimestre 1964* (Annaba: Direction de la documentation et des publications, 1964). Speech 1er mai 1963, Fête du travail, pp. 72–4. Also quoted in *Le Peuple* (3 May 1963).

15 *El Moudjahid* (18 May 1963).

16 The types of veil increasingly popular in Algeria since the 2000s, notably the *hijab* (headscarf pinned to the hair), present fewer practical constraints in the workplace, thus arguably making the decision to veil or unveil at work more about ideas and beliefs.

17 Evans and Phillips, *Algeria: Anger of the Dispossessed*, pp. 85–6.

18 'Discours du Président Houari Boumediene à l'inauguration du congrès de l'UNFA', UNFA, *Bulletin intérieur*, 4 (1966).

19 *Ibid.*

20 'Salut du frère Boumediene aux femmes algériennes', reproduced in *El Djazaïria* (1972).

21 *Révolution africaine* (1 February 1964).

22 See for example *La Presse de Tunisie* (4 August 1956) and the Arabic-language journal of the Neo-Destour party *Al Amal*, quoted in *La Presse de Tunisie* (7 August 1956).

23 Ottaway and Ottaway, *Algeria: The Politics of a Socialist Revolution*, pp. 1–2.

24 See M. Harbi, *L'Islamisme dans tous ses états* (Paris: Arcantère, 1991).

25 See B. Hardman, *Islam and the Métropole: A Case Study of Religion and Rhetoric in Algeria* (New York: Peter Lang, 2009); O. Carlier, *Entre nation et jihad: histoire sociale des radicalismes algériens* (Paris: Presses de Sciences Po, 1995).

26 See McDougall, *History and Culture of Nationalism*.

27 *El Moudjahid* (23 March 1963), also reported in *Alger républicain* (17–18 March 1963).

28 E. Mallarde, *L'Algérie depuis* (Paris: Table Ronde, 1975), p. 32, quoted in Hugh Roberts, *The Battlefield Algeria*, p. 139.

29 Harbi, *FLN, mirage et réalité*, p. 333.

30 *Le Peuple* (17 July 1963).

31 *Révolution africaine* (27 March 1965).

32 *Journal officiel de la République algérienne* (2 April 1963), p. 308.

33 *Al Chaab* (5 March 1963).

34 *Journal officiel de la République algérienne* (2 April 1963), p. 306.

35 *Al Chaab* (6 March 1963).

36 *Alger républicain* (2–4 March 1963).

37 *Alger républicain* (8 December 1962).

38 *Al Chaab* (13 March 1963). In her memoirs, Lavalette includes an image of the telegram sent to her in summer 1962 by Fadéla Mesli, Safia Baazi and Meriem Belmihoub, inviting her to present herself as a candidate for the Constituent Assembly. Lavalette does not elaborate on this invitation, or discuss her role in the assembly. She simply states that she was elected to the Constituent Assembly in 1962 and the National Assembly in 1964, and that in 1965 she was one of a dozen deputies who refused to rubber-stamp the seizure of power by Boumediene's Revolutionary Council (Conseil de la Révolution), *Juste algérienne*, p. 137.

39 Interview with Fadéla Mesli (20 December 2005).

40 The difficulties which the Paris-born surgeon Michel Martini (who

during the war was imprisoned for his support for the FLN in France
and who worked in Algerian refugee camps on the Tunisian border)
encountered when he wished to marry an Algerian medical student
Yamina 'Mina' Benkaddache in 1968 are detailed at length in his
memoirs, *Souvenirs algériens*.

41 Quoted in Claude Liauzu, 'Guerre des Sabines et tabou du métis-
sage: les mariages mixtes de l'Algérie coloniale à l'immigration en
France', *Les Cahiers du CEDREF*, 8–9 (2000), http://cedref.revues.
org/207 (accessed 19 May 2014).
42 For example, Henri Alleg describes members of the Amrani family
changing their names during the War of Independence. The Amrani
family lost fathers, sons and brothers to torture and summary execution in the hands of the French army as a result of their nationalist engagement – notably, Malika Amrani was the wife of Ali
Boumendjel, the lawyer 'suicided' by French paratroopers in 1957:
'Lucie, Georgette, André or Henri' became 'Malika, Leila and Djamal'.
H. Alleg and H. Douzon, *La Guerre d'Algérie – les occasions perdues*
(Paris: Temps actuels, 1981), pp. 514–15, quoted by M. Rahal, *Ali
Boumendjel: une affaire française, une historie algérienne* (Paris: Les
Belles Lettres, 2010), p. 245. An interview which Rahal carried out
with Malika Boumendjel revealed that this name change did not in
fact take place, but, as Rahal underlines, the veracity of the story is
less important than the power of the symbol: rapprochement between
the two communities of Algeria was no longer possible.
43 B. Hadj Ali, *Lettres à Lucette 1965–1966* (Algiers: Editions RSM,
2002), p. 3.
44 'Ordonnance no. 75–58 portant code civil, II.1, article 28', *Journal
officiel de la République algérienne* (30 September 1975).
45 Interview with Annie Steiner (22 June 2005).
46 *Ibid.*
47 Interview with Lucette Hadj Ali (18 December 2005).
48 Interview with Fadéla M'Rabet (1 November 2005).
49 J. McDougall, 'Dream of exile, promise of home: language, education
and arabism in Algeria', *International Journal of Middle East Studies*,
43 (2011), 251–70, pp. 252–3.
50 *Al Chaab* (29 November 1962).
51 *Al Chaab* (27 November 1962); *Alger républicain* (27 November
1962).
52 *Révolution africaine* (30 March, 6, 13, 20, 27 April and 4 May 1963).
53 *Alger républicain* (9 March 1963). The men participating in the
delegation were Ahmed Belaid, Rabah Mahiout and Mohamed
Gueriez.
54 Interview with Djamila Boupacha (11 June 2005).

55 According to an interview with Djamila Bouhired reproduced in *Al-Hadath al- 'arabi wa-'l-duwali*, 24 (2002), 38–42. Translation R. Benkhaled / N. Vince.

56 *Al Chaab* (2 March 1963) and *Alger républicain* (2 March 1963), *The Internationalist* [newspaper of the American Socialist Workers Party] (6 March 1963). A few weeks later, *Alger républicain* (19 March 1963) reported that the Al-Jil al-Jadid children's homes – which housed two thousand orphans in fifteen centres – had been placed under the control of the Ministry of Mujahidin. It is not clear if this decision was a coincidence of timing, a means to better fund these centres in response to criticisms or a way to remove influence from two 'ambassadors' going beyond their role and complaining to outsiders.

57 Djamila Bouhired did not wish to be interviewed when I was carrying out research for this book.

58 Interview with Djamila Boupacha (11 June 2005).

59 Interview with Djamila Bouhired reproduced in *Al-Hadath al-'arabi wa-'l-duwali*. The claim that the wine- and pork-loving Vergès converted to Islam is considered laughable by a friend of his interviewed for the documentary *L'Avocat de la terreur* (Barbet Schroeder, 2007). Djamila Bouhired refused to participate in the documentary.

60 *Alger républicain* (27 November 1962).

61 *Al Chaab* (4–5 November 1962); *Alger républicain* (21 and 22 January 1963, 24 and 29 June 1963); *Le Peuple* (5 July 1963 and 9 March, 20 August and 26 October 1964); *Alger ce soir* (20 February 1965); *Révolution africaine* (12–18 March and 20 May 1966).

62 UNFA, *Bulletin intérieur*, 4 (1966).

63 *Al Chaab* (22 January 1963).

64 *Alger républicain* (24–9 June 1963).

65 *El Djazaïria*, 82 (1980).

66 *Le Peuple* (6 November 1964); *Alger ce soir* (20 February 1965).

67 *Révolution africaine* (12 March 1966).

68 Interview with Lucette Hadj Ali (18 December 2005).

69 SHD, IH1246/D2: 'Organisation féminine de la ZAA'.

70 Interview with Saliha Djeffal (21 June 2005).

71 Interview with Jacqueline Guerroudj (15 and 18 December 2005).

72 Ighilahriz, *Algérienne*, p. 222.

73 Interview with Louisette Ighilahriz (8 June 2005).

74 Interview with Zhor Zerari (21 December 2005).

75 *Alger ce soir* (5 March 1965).

76 For eyewitness accounts of the 8 March 1965 demonstration see Simon, *Algérie, les années pieds-rouges*, pp. 155–9; Ameyar, *La Moudjahida Annie Fiorio-Steiner*, p. 115; Lévy, 'La journée du 8 mars 1965 à Alger'.

77 In the words of Zerari. The version of Ben Bella's speech published in *Alger ce soir* on 10 March 1965 is rather more sedate: 'You must take your responsibilities in this country [...] The Party [FLN] is open to you and I confirm that it is ready to help you.' Catherine Lévy confirms that Ben Bella sought to appease the crowd by making a series of promises about equality in work and the justice system, and that this was not reported in the press, 'La journée du 8 mars 1965 à Alger'.

78 'Discours du 20 août 1965', *Discours du Président Boumediene, 19 June 1965–19 June 1970* (Constantine: Ministre de l'Information et de la Culture, 1970), pp. 47–8. In *El Moudjahid* on 20 August 1965, this speech is attributed to the newly appointed Minister for Mujahidin Boualem Benhamouda.

79 Lévy, 'La journée du 8 mars 1965 à Alger'.

80 *Le Peuple* (15 May 1963).

81 *Ibid.*

82 *Ibid.*

83 Interview with Fatima Benmohand Berci (17 June 2005).

84 *Ibid.*

85 Interview with Fadéla Mesli (20 December 2005).

86 Interview with Fadila Attia (19 June 2005).

87 Interview with Habiba Chami (1 June 2005).

88 *L'Action* (3 September 1956).

89 *Le Peuple* (4–5 and 22 August 1963).

90 Interview with Zohra Drif (11 June 2005).

91 Interview with Saliha Djeffal (21 June 2005).

92 On the central role of kin networks on determining the margins of manoeuvre of states seeking to formulate family law, see Charrad, *States and Women's Rights*.

93 Interview with Lucette Hadj Ali (18 December 2005).

94 Interview with Fadéla M'Rabet (1 November 2005).

95 Interview with Zhor Zerari (21 December 2005).

96 Interview with Mimi Maziz on women in journalism, 'Spécial: 10 années de parution'. *El Djazaïria* (1980).

97 Interview with Zhor Zerari (21 December 2005).

98 Interview with Fadila Attia (19 June 2005).

99 Interview with El Hora Kerkeb (1 June 2005).

100 Interview with Fadéla M'Rabet (1 November 2005).

101 S. de Beauvoir, *Le Deuxième Sexe*, vol. 1 (Paris: Gallimard, 1949), p. 17. See also J. Wallach Scott, *Only Paradoxes to Offer: French Feminists and the Rights of Man* (Cambridge, MA: Harvard University Press, 1996).

5

From national construction to new battles

Making it work: Tasks of national construction

In the late 1960s, the Ministry of Information produced a booklet, *Les Femmes algériennes*, a richly illustrated, celebratory account of Algeria's achievements so far in the political and social promotion of women.[1] One particular photograph catches the eye. In it, we see a meeting hall full of women celebrating International Women's Day. Above the stage where the speakers are assembled there are two large banners. One carries the slogan, in French, 'American imperialism: get out of Vietnam', the other, in French and Arabic, rather disconcertingly declares 'Glory to the *shuhada* of socialism'. This is neither a subversive critique of victims of the Soviet gulag nor a commemoration of accidental deaths-by-tractor on Algerian *autogestion* farms. Instead, *shuhada* is to be understood as a reference to the war dead, rather than a religious term alluding to those who died to defend Islam, and 'socialism' is being used as a synonym for the War of Independence. Moreover, whilst 'socialisme' in the French-language slogan is a clear marker of Marxist ideology, its equivalent in the Arabic-language version is 'ishtirakiyya', meaning commonality or sharing.

This image captures two important aspects of post-1962 Algeria. Firstly, in the early years of independence, there was a generalised-fear of chaos, social disorder and political strife. This is reflected in the insistence on unity and collective purpose through loose definitions and flexible meanings about ideologically loaded – and therefore potentially divisive – terminology. There was a powerful desire to seek out consensus, even if this involved selective understanding, negotiation and compromise. Secondly, the references in this photograph to the international context are a reminder that we cannot understand how Algeria was seen from within without an appreciation of how Algeria was seen from without. Post-independence Algeria sought to define itself as the homeland of liberation movements and Third World radicalism. Algeria played host to Nelson Mandela, Che Guevara and the Black Panthers. The Pan-African Cultural Festival took place in Algiers in 1969. Djamila Bouhired took tea with Mao; Djamila Boupacha met President Nasser and Annie Steiner rushed out of her office one day to seize the opportunity to shake the hand of Vietnamese General Vo Nguyen Giap of Dien Bien Phu fame. There was immense enthusiasm to participate in state-building and 'make it work' in Algeria.

Enthusiasm and compromise are key themes in Salima Bouaziz's account of her post-1962 trajectory. A former activist in the FF–FLN, she says that she was opposed to the seizure of power by the Ben Bella–EMG alliance in summer 1962. She was disappointed to have been excluded as a candidate to the Constituent Assembly in September 1962, although her husband, Rabah Bouaziz, a senior figure in the Federal Committee of the FF–FLN, was elected and served 1962–64. When she and her husband tried to establish an olive oil co-operative in Kabylia in 1963, based on what Salima describes as their 'Marxist-Leninist-Socialist' principles, it was burnt down by Aït Ahmed's short-lived oppositional *maquis*, the FFS, because they were seen as pro-regime. This, Salima argues, was a simplification of the couple's position: 'My husband agreed with Aït Ahmed personally, but in political terms he did not agree that in '63 we should start the war up again'. The couple returned to Algiers and Rabah Bouaziz was nominated prefect of Algiers by Ben Bella. Salima spent a short time on the national council of the UNFA, but she left when she judged that the organisation existed only to follow orders from men in the FLN:

I was disappointed by the UNFA, disappointed by the co-operative; I saw that we couldn't put good ideas into practice. The political game took precedence over industrial, economic and social projects. It was politics and power. Who was going to take power and who was going to keep it. [I said to myself] I'm not doing anything of relevance, I'm going to study medicine, the country needs doctors [...] After a year, there was Boumediene's coup d'état [19 June 1965]. They came to arrest my husband. We fled and hid for a time with French friends who lived in Algeria. Then we went to France for a while, for a month, a month and a half. We came back, things had calmed down and the administration was back in place.

Back once again in Algeria, Salima Bouaziz returned to her medical studies and, after a stretch of unemployment, Rabah Bouaziz went into the leather-making industry and also trained as a lawyer. In Algeria from the 1920s onwards, law and medicine had been the professions of choice for educated Algerians who wanted to keep the colonial administration at arm's length. At the same time, the couple chose to come back to the single-party state after Boumediene's coup, when they could plausibly have stayed in France, as a number of post-independence dissidents did. When I asked Salima why she nevertheless opted to remain in a country whose political system she says that she was opposed to, she replied: 'You don't care as long as the job gets done. The country was completely destroyed.'[2]

This idea of getting the job done, or, to use the terminology of the time, tasks of national construction (*tâches d'édification nationale*), has a strong imprint on the language of women from a similar urban, educated background to that of Salima Bouaziz. In the 1960s and 1970s, the language of tasks of national construction tended to be associated with economic development and the establishment of infrastructure: five-year plans, strengthening the Algerian role in the hydrocarbons industry, constructing factories, modernising agriculture, building dams to improve access to water, setting up free universal education and improving access to healthcare.

Yet tasks of national construction can be understood as nation- as well as state-building: *édification* in French can also convey the idea of moral improvement and enlightenment contained in the English 'edification'. At a basic level, this was a fairly consensual message of Algerian economic self-sufficiency as the best form of resistance against neo-colonial foreign domination. When Boumediene unilaterally nationalised Algerian petrol exploitation on 24 February 1971, he described the move as part of 'the historical logic of the Revolution'.[3] Other aspects of national construction were more controversial. Whilst the Algerian state was actively promoting a pro-natalist policy to replace the 'one and a half million martyrs', some of the women I interviewed saw this booming birth rate as a threat to Algeria's capacity to develop a functioning state, efficient economy and harmonious society. The former *maquisarde* El Hora

Kerkeb describes her post-independence role as a social worker in the police, talking to women about their children's education, vaccinations and family planning, as a continuation of her wartime duties.[4] Fadéla Mesli made passionate speeches in the National Assembly and at FLN congresses in the 1960s and 1970s in favour of family planning:

> FM: I told them, we can find a solution to everything. If we are behind, we can put everything we have into catching up. [For example,] if we are behind in hydraulics we can throw everything at it and sort the problem out. But if we have lots of young people, a very big population, if we don't have the means to educate them, to provide medical care, to give them jobs, to house them – there is no point. We can't do anything unless we throw them into the sea.
>
> NV: Were you listened to?
>
> FM [*sighing*]: A little.[5]

The most obvious example of the ideological dimension of tasks of national construction was Arabisation, begun under Ben Bella and accelerated by Boumediene. Setting up the Algerian education system was not just responding to a desperate need to improve literacy. It was also about ensuring that, through this education, increasingly numerous new generations were impregnated with the official narrative of the nation – the 132 years of resistance to French rule, the importance of Islam to the struggle – and, above all, seeking to make sure that the nation would narrate itself in Arabic. The motivation, means and rapidity of Arabisation have made it one of the most politically explosive issues in independent Algeria.[6]

Participation in state construction was thus a political act. At the same time, in an undemocratic system where nearly everything was nationalised, there were few possibilities for public dissent, and for educated men and women the state provided most of the professional opportunities available. Both men and women had to face the question of whether or not it was possible to dissociate being a 'useful' citizen from being an ideologically complicit one. This question was arguably of heightened importance for women because, as Chapter 4 demonstrates, female veterans who were teachers, journalists, civil servants and medical professionals were already insisting on being gender-neutral, abstract citizens in order to resist state attempts to 'embody' them as women. Could these women also claim to be apolitical participants in national construction in the context of a single-party state?

Individual trajectories, day-to-day negotiations

For Habiba Chami, who had been a nurse in the *maquis*, participating in state-building went hand-in-hand with her belief in the single party and ethno-cultural definitions of an Arabo-Islamic collective identity. Habiba was a senior member of the UNFA for fourteen years, rising to become a member of its National Council in 1966. She was the only woman I interviewed who expressed unreserved enthusiasm for the UNFA, which she describes as the 'natural continuation of the [wartime] FLN'. She emphasises the challenging conditions in which the UNFA was operating, thus highlighting the significance of what might seem small achievements: 'You know that in some regions, in 1962, women did not have identity cards because men did not want their wives to have their photo taken. We had to have meetings just to educate the men.' Habiba is also the only interviewee who appears to agree broadly with a patriarchal conception of the family based on scripture, a vision criticised even by female veterans close to the centre of power, such as the senator Zohra Drif and the senior FLN politician Saliha Djeffal. 'Whilst remaining modern and moderate', argues Habiba Chami, 'We cannot override what the Muslim religion demands. It's up to the principal *'ulama* to decide, to review. In France, in Spain, all men have many women. I prefer that they get married legally.'[7] There appears to be no contradiction, then or now, between official discourse and Habiba Chami's views of society and of how women's political engagement should be channelled to serve the party and state.

For other urban, educated *mujahidat*, negotiating holding down a job, living in a single-party state and maintaining their ideals and beliefs was trickier. The former member of the FF–FLN Mimi Maziz was an employee of the weekly newspaper *Révolution africaine*. She remained on the publication until her retirement. Initially staffed by Algerian and international Third Wordlist revolutionaries, *Révolution africaine* promoted anti-colonial struggles and socialist construction around the world, arguing that a radical transformation of politics, society, economics and culture was imminent. However, as Mimi Maziz explains: 'The progressive air started getting polluted. So those who were hardliners and had other means to live by left'.[8] Amongst those who left, notably after Boumediene's coup, were the editor, Malika Ouzegane, and the director, Malika's uncle Amar Ouzegane. Mimi Maziz did not leave, a decision, she says, for which she was criticised.

Fettouma Ouzegane, niece of Amar Ouzegane and sister of Malika, might well have been amongst those who took a critical view of Mimi Maziz's decision to stay. Also a wartime activist, Fettouma describes herself as lone opponent of the single-party state in the immediate aftermath of 1962: 'A few women took a stand with [a few] men and afterwards, they all got back in line with the FLN', to benefit, she says, from fancy job titles and material comforts. Fettouma's position even pitched her against her uncle Amar, who in addition to his role on *Révolution africaine* served as a government minister under Ben Bella. Fettouma describes stormy debates within her family about whether it was more effective to reform from the inside or oppose from the outside. In her view, 'As a minority within you can't do anything. We were much stronger, we could push forward more by taking things head on. Never inside with them.'[9]

Yet Mimi Maziz underlines that leaving for a liberal profession, or unemployment, let alone becoming a clandestine opponent, was not a choice for everyone: 'I was criticised – I won't hide it, I earned a living, I worked to eat and to feed my family, that's it. And that's the truth. I went into the technical part [of the newspaper].'[10] Taking a less obviously political role was a way of distancing herself from the centre of power. The former member of the Algiers bomb network Jacqueline Guerroudj transcribed debates in the National Assembly after 1962, alongside working as a librarian in the section for teaching and culture of the UGTA. She describes her postwar employment as 'the least political possible'.[11]

This is not a political cop-out, to adopt Fettouma Ouzegane's uncompromising judgement, nor is it simply an unhappy but practically necessary compromise. Instead, contributing to national construction can be seen also as a positive choice, even by those who were not unqualified supporters of the post-independence political system. After resigning from the Constituent Assembly, Fadéla Mesli continued to work as an anaesthetist at the Hospital Mustapha Pacha in Algiers. Later, she also spent some time in the UNFA, in local politics in Ben Aknoun, returning to national politics as a deputy in the National Assembly between 1977 and 1982. But she is particularly proud of her role as resident nurse at the Ecole normale (teacher training college) from 1965 onwards:

> There, I think I did a positive job. I raised awareness, I had discussions with [the young women], I tried to spark their nationalist consciousness, I explained to them ... [*She trails off*] They accepted everything because I was a living proof of ... [*She trails off and does not finish the sentence*] Where the administration failed, and I'm sorry to say that, I told them that they needed to give a bit of their youth, their time, they needed to follow the same path as us [the *mujahidat*].[12]

Fadéla Mesli implies that the political failings of the state made it even more important to participate in tasks of national construction.

Annie Steiner underlines that, in the context of the post-1962 period, we should not just look for activism in political parties and mass movements: 'After independence they started building mass movements like the Organisation Nationale des Moudjahidine (National Organisation of Mujahidin, ONM). That didn't suit me. I was no longer in the FLN. But in 1962, the *cadres* [meaning, in this context, professionals] represented activism. To exercise a profession, that was activism.' Annie Steiner participated in the creation of the General Secretariat of the government in November 1962 along with the jurist and Evian negotiator Mohamed Bedjaoui. Given the small number of personnel and the increasing amount of legislation in the first years of independence, she was initially placed in charge of legal texts for a number of ministries, including education, health, employment and the Ministry for Mujahidin. With various promotions, she stayed in the same job for twenty-nine years: that is to say, she remained in post under Ben Bella, Boumediene, Chadli and also at the start of the turbulent period marking the end of the single-party state. Yet when I asked her how she was affected by these political changes, she replied: 'Where I worked was a service on its own, it was legal work. All my colleagues stayed, it was a very stable service. We weren't known, we were obscure.'[13] Annie Steiner provides a similar response when interviewed by the Algerian journalist Hafida Ameyar about the laws on Arabisation:

HA: What is your opinion, today, on the laws of independent Algeria? Were there battles at the time around certain laws?

AS: Of course, but there, you are asking me a question which goes outside my work at the General Secretariat of the government.

HA: Today I'm asking you as an Algerian citizen ...

AS: Yes, there was a big battle of ideas, at the time of Mostefa Lacheraf who was nominated Minister of Education. It was a national debate which went beyond the General Secretariat of the government. At the time, the different forces present confronted each other. Of course, I had my ideas on this question, but the president of the Republic was weighing up these forces and decided against Mostefa Lacheraf.

HA: Did you agree, for example, with the law on Arabisation?

AS: I cannot be totally in agreement with the way in which the law on Arabisation was passed, because it was a rush job. Lacheraf said that the generalisation of Arabisation needed to take place in stages.[14] But the law was pushed through by force and it became a strictly political problem.[15]

This insistence on the apolitical and unchanging nature of her role, albeit at the heart of government, also characterises the way in which Fadila Attia talks about her role as a senior secretary in the civil service:

NV: Did Boumediene's coup in 1965 change much? [*Fadila doesn't answer, so I begin to add*] In terms of your job –

FA [*interrupts*]: No, no, everything was good in my job. I worked at the presidency for a little while, then after '65, I worked in the Ministry of Tourism, two years, then I was in Industry. And then I started to have health problems, I had to go to France for emergency treatment [...]

NV: Were you interested in politics?

FA: No, no. I wasn't at all interested in politics. It was technical. I worked for example with Belaid Abdesselam who was Minister for Industry and Energy [1965–77]. When I worked at the presidency I was in a service called the Commission for Professional Training and the Promotion of Managers – that really is professional. I wasn't into politics. If I had been I would have gone to the Ministry of Foreign Affairs. But when they needed me to type, I was there.[16]

Even though Fadila Attia appears to have been moved out of the presidency after the 1965 coup – the date is not coincidental – she insists on the continuities.

Nostalgia, useful pasts and commitment

Using oral history to analyse how women negotiated their relationship with the 1960s and 1970s state is a tricky task. Women's
responses need to be contextualised within the political sensitivities
potentially provoked in talking about this period. In 2005, I was
asking interviewees to tell me their political opinions in a country
which is neither totalitarian nor entirely democratic, even if the
single-party state officially ended in 1989. Bouteflika, president
since 1999, was the political contemporary of, and in 1978 had
been expected as a likely successor to, Boumediene. The official end
of the single-party state is doubly problematic: on the one hand, it
raises the expectation that interviewees should now talk freely – and
there is the risk that interviewees feel that they are being asked to
justify themselves and their actions, a kind of implicit 'So what did
you do under the authoritarian regime, then?' On the other hand,
but also perhaps as a result of this first point, a number of interviewees express the view that historical revisionism has gone too
far. Jacqueline Guerroudj laments that today no one talks about the
positive and effective things that happened in the 1960s.[17] A few
interviewees were also wary of giving less than edifying accounts
of the post-1962 period which would, as one interviewee put it,
provide outsiders with 'a stick to beat Algeria'. This is not unique to
Algeria. As James Mark underlines in his study of the reformulation
of the communist past in post-1989 Eastern Europe, a new political
era requires individuals to repackage their life stories within newly
dominant, politically acceptable narrative frames and language. At
the same time, individuals' ability to revisit and reframe the past
might be inhibited by their anxiety not to inadvertently provide
grist to the mill of their political rivals.[18]

However, Jacqueline Guerroudj appears to be making a pre-
emptive criticism of a historical revisionism which – unlike in
Eastern Europe – has not yet taken place in Algeria. Her statement
is not borne out by the positive stories that women tell when they
do talk about the 1960s and 1970s. Moreover, the strategic choice
not to criticise 'Algeria' applies only to selective periods: interviewees who approach the 1960s and 1970s so cautiously do not shy
away from giving critical views on more recent political and social
change. In 1988, Annie Steiner demonstrated against the torture
inflicted on Algerian youths marching and rioting against the single-

party state. She was also an active campaigner against the 1984 Family Code. Fadila Attia vigorously criticises the continuing omnipresence of *mujahidin* in Algeria, and also the level of corruption in Algerian society today – everything, she deplores, can be bought, including qualifications and driving licences. Yet when I ask her what it was like to have to work with such people, by her own definition parachuted in through money and contacts rather than merit, Fadila interprets my question as applying to a much earlier period than that which I was thinking of. I asked the question with her later career in mind, she interpreted it as a reference to the immediate postwar years. Her response was indignant: 'Me, at the start, when I began to work, people were motivated. I'm sorry, but we had to fill the offices, after all. They maybe didn't have qualifications, but some did.'[19] In her account, the goodwill and enthusiasm of the immediate post-independence years are framed as a moment of solidarity and selflessness whose memory needs to be defended.

The chronological periods which these women are willing to critique is significant. In 2005, interviewees were talking about the 1960s and 1970s in light of the events of the 1980s and 1990s, which were marked by socio-economic crisis and a decade of civil violence, during which time much of the infrastructure built in the 1960s and 1970s collapsed and Algeria's international image was severely tarnished. This perceived decline is key in shaping how women see the first decades of independence, even if they did not actively participate in tasks of national construction. Rural interviewees do not tend to talk directly about any of Algeria's political leaders. Fatima Benmohand Berci has, however, a view on Boumediene. At the mention of his name, she simply states, 'Boumediene, *Allah yarahmu* [may God accord him paradise]', before adding that Ben Bella 'took the jewellery and left' and recounting her stories of Algeria's first president and the FSN.[20] If Ben Bella took, the Boumediene years gave. The exclusionary cultural politics of uncompromising Arabisation leave little imprint on the narrative of this Tamazight-speaking woman who never went to school – instead these were the years when running water, gas and electrification came to her village. The village of Agraradj, and the rest of the eastern part of the Aghribs commune, was one of the first rural areas to be provided with a system of public fountains in the mid-1970s. For seventeen years, water flowed from them, but failure to maintain the network of pipes led to the system collapsing in 1993. By the time of my interviews, many women in the area were walking kilometres every day to fetch water, as their mothers and grandmothers had done in the colonial era.[21]

Akila Ouared states that she left the party of the FLN in 1965 'because there were no longer the same ideals'. When I ask her directly if this was following the Boumediene coup she concurs and states that she was 'very upset at that moment, I suffered a shock because I wanted the people to decide'. And yet, when she comes back to Boumediene later in the interview, his coup d'état is reduced to a sub-clause and she presents a familiar description of the international prestige of Algeria and its socio-economic achievements and egalitarianism in the 1960s and 1970s:

> What I would say is that, apart from the coup d'état, which I didn't agree with, there was still a job that was done by Boumediene. He did a lot for the country, for example in terms of economic and social development. On a political level, Algeria was respected. Countries received us as equals, saying 'This is an extraordinary revolution'. The issue of freedom was something else. There wasn't any democracy. But there were factories which were built, and all the children of the people, whether the son of a worker or the son of a peasant, or the son of a civil servant, all children had equal opportunities to study and go to university. There was the agrarian revolution. He was a leader of the Third World in terms of ideas.[22]

The War of Independence, as a symbol of solidarity and unity of purpose, is the most useful past to criticise the present. The period 1962–78 is more politically problematic, but, when compared to the 1980s and 1990s, it still serves a purpose as a form of veiled political critique. As Svetlana Boym argues in her discussion of contemporary nostalgia in post-1989 Russia, 'Nostalgia works as a double-edged sword: it seems to be an emotional antidote to politics, and thus remains the best political tool'.[23] The uses of the Boumediene era as an unfavourable mirror to hold up to the here and now are revealed by the fact that it is often women closest to the centre of power today who are most uncomfortable talking about the contemporary relevance of this period. In 2005, when I interviewed Saliha Djeffal, a senior figure in the party of the FLN, I asked her what she thought of a recent decision to no longer celebrate the anniversary of the coup on 19 June as a national day:

Figure 4 On the fifth anniversary of Boumediene's coup, a woman in Oran holds a banner comparing the president with the Emir Abdelkader, the nineteenth-century hero of the Algerian resistance, 19 June 1970

SD: I don't have an opinion. It's a decision of the President of the Republic, I have no comment.

NV: Even if you have said a lot of positive things about the Boumediene period?

SD: Yes of course. I have always said lots of [positive] things about Boumediene, and I will continue to say that he was a great statesman, and he made Algeria a nation which counted in the international context.

NV: So would you say that, of the presidents Algeria has had, Boumediene is your reference?

SD: [*pauses*] You know, we had a president, elected, we had a first president of the Algerian Republic, Ben Bella, he only exercised for three years, I think that three years is too short to judge the actions of a man. Boumediene was a great statesman. Chadli was elected a number of times, he was the choice of the population, he did what he thought was best for Algeria and it's voters who judge a president's record. For the rest, [Ali] Kafi [who presided over the Haut Comité d'Etat (High State Council, HCE) in 1992 following the assassination of Boudiaf], Boudiaf, *Allah yarahmu* [may God accord him paradise], there was a lot of hope, but in ninety days ...? [A reference to Boudiaf's short time in office] President [Liamine] Zéroual [1994–99], there was a lot of hope and the population voted massively for him, but unfortunately he didn't finish his term. The current president, I think that the population has approved his first term by voting for him a second time round. I only judge a president on the basis of voters. He is elected by universal suffrage.[24]

In a country where electoral fraud has historically been rife, many might judge Saliha Djeffal's insistence on elections and the people's choice as disingenuous. Her response is more interesting, however, as being symptomatic of many interviewees' difficulty in talking about the Boumediene era without making reference to the period before and, especially, after. Augmented by contemporary clichés of Algeria's second president embodying Algerian *nif* (pride) and *redjla* (manliness), the Boumediene era serves as a key moment in a narrative of the decline of national greatness. But beyond the metaphor, scraping back the critiques of the present which this nostalgia represents, it is important to underline that many interviewees also passionately believed in tasks of national construction. This is exemplified by the post-independent career of Lucette Hadj Ali.

After Ben Bella banned the reformed PCA at the end of 1962, its members went into what Lucette Hadj Ali describes as a semi-clandestinity. The party was banned, but individual communists were tolerated. After Boumediene's coup, there was a crackdown on left-wing opponents. In September 1965, Lucette's husband, Bachir Hadj Ali, alongside Hocine Zehouane and Mohamed Harbi, amongst others, was arrested and brutally tortured by the Algerian secret services for opposition to the coup. In *L'Arbitraire*, published in 1966 by the clandestine publisher of the Second World War French Resistance, Editions de Minuit, Bachir Hadj Ali describes how the torturers of the new Algerian state used the same techniques and justifications as Nazi and colonial torturers before them. Lucette smuggled her husband's book out of prison with scraps of text secreted inside cigarette packets. It is still painful for Lucette Hadj Ali to talk about this repression. She summarises very quickly: 'When there was this story of the coup d'état, my husband was arrested, tortured, etc. You know, it's in *L'Arbitraire*. I don't want to go over it again.' No one could accuse Lucette Hadj Ali of being nostalgic for Boumediene and that is why she is one of the most powerful examples of the belief – despite everything – in tasks of national construction.

During Bachir Hadj Ali's imprisonment, Lucette, alongside the families of the other prisoners, fought to get her husband released, or at the very least have visiting rights. At the same time, she continued to work in the Algerian education system. In 1962, she was a teacher of history and geography, and whilst history was rapidly Arabised, the Arabisation of geography was more gradual. Given the shortage of teachers in the high school where she worked, Lucette taught all the geography classes across three different year groups. In the early 1970s, whilst her husband was still banned from entering the main cities of Algeria, and accused of plotting to seize power, Lucette was appointed by the state to the Institut Pédagogique National (National Institute of Pedagogy, IPN) which oversaw the production of school textbooks. She was given the job of selecting maps for the geography textbook, whilst Arabic speakers were chosen to be responsible for writing the text.

It was symptomatic of the fact that classical Arabic (*fusha*) was a second or even third language for many Algerians that Lucette's colleagues were an Egyptian, a Syrian, a Frenchman who had sat the competitive exam to teach at university and high-school level (*agrégation*) but failed the viva, and, laughs Lucette, 'an Algerian who was really the level of final year secondary school [*troisième*, about age fourteen].' Lucette had the professional qualification (the CAPES) to teach at secondary and high-school level. When she began to look at the proposed chapters, she realised the content was seriously flawed – for example, much of the science in the physical geography section was out of date. As the most qualified Algerian in the team (indeed, there were only two Algerians), Lucette wrote a report to the directors of the IPN 'saying that we were going to be ridiculed around the world, and that it absolutely had to be changed. So the management of the IPN recognised [the problem], we made the corrections, and the following year I was nominated head of the commission.'25

Lucette Hadj Ali was not leading a double life. Rather, the importance that she attached to ensuring that Algeria did not look ridiculous on the world stage and that Algerian children had accurate materials to learn from was, for her, a logical continuation of her political commitment. This commitment remained even when her activities as a communist led her, her family and her party into direct confrontation with the state which resulted in merciless repression. We also see the pragmatism at play within the Algerian state. As a communist, French-speaking woman of European origin, whose husband was accused of being the enemy within, Lucette Hadj Ali was an unlikely choice to write school textbooks. But the IPN management did not really have a choice: she was the only competent person they had, and pragmatism won out over political considerations.

Despite dissatisfaction with the single-party regime, the Algerian state as a more abstract entity still inspired enough hope for many interviewees to believe that it was worth committing to. This is a key theme which emerges when Zhor Zerari talks about her post-independence career as a journalist. 'I am for my ideas, I am for Algeria, neither Ben Bella, nor Boumediene', she declares when I ask her about her political views in the 1960s and 1970s. Given that main role of the press in the single-party state was to promote the party message, one might expect this to be an improbable career choice for someone as reluctant to toe the party line as Zerari. Yet during the course of her career, she found ways to regularly criticise government policy when she felt that it was deviating from the national slogan 'by the people, for the people'.

Zhor Zerari describes how, in the Boumediene period, there was an investment code signed by the president to favour local production by limiting imports. One Algerian producer starting making Reynolds pens. Then, suddenly, the market was flooded with Bic pens. 'Someone had given an authorisation to import them', explains Zhor. She tried to carry out an investigation at the Ministry of Commerce, which refused to give her the authorisation numbers. She went ahead and wrote the story anyway, and in the middle of the text she reproduced a speech by Boumediene about the importance of privileging national production. Suddenly, 'all eyes turned on me' and Mohamed Seddik Benyahia, the Minister for Information (and future Minister for Foreign Affairs), demanded to see a copy of her article. He told her that it was impossible to publish it, but, according to Zhor, he assured her that he would put it on Boumediene's desk so that the president could look into it, although no action appeared to be taken subsequently.[26]

Sometimes though, interviewees did see their personal interventions having an effect. Whilst working on a major law regarding expropriation in the public interest, Annie Steiner noticed that the Arabic-language text was missing some of the wording of the French-language text which safeguarded against abuses of the law. She presented this to the Commission considering the law. She says that Boumediene was there and he was annoyed by the discrepancies. Leaving the room, he passed by Annie Steiner's chair and silently shook her hand in recognition of her attention to detail.[27]

Unsolicited criticism, whatever its constructive intentions, had to be negotiated carefully. On 19 March 1967, Zhor Zerari wrote a highly critical article about Algeria's agricultural policy, published in *Algérie actualité*. The headline was: '*Autogestion*: organised confusion?' The subheading quoted an agricultural worker interviewed by Zhor: 'It's not the *méchoui* [spit-roasted lamb] which has changed, it's just the people who gather around it'[28] – that is to say, there were still people profiteering, but those who profited were now Algerian rather than French. Decades later, Zhor laughingly explained how she managed to print such direct attacks without losing her job. When she had published an article which provoked a scandal within the government, the editor got her to write a 'light' article: 'so they'd forget about me'.[29] For example, after her article 'Messieurs les ronds de cuir' [Messrs Pen Pushers],' a humorous three-page exposé of the lazy inefficiency of the Algerian bureaucracy, whose employees she describes as spending their days arranging their pens and reading comic books,[30] the prefect wanted her to be sacked. In response, the following week, the editor asked Zerari to interview the Minister of Health, Tedjini Haddam.[31] In the edition of *Algérie actualité* which followed Zhor's article on *autogestion*, there is an interview with Ali Yahia, Minister for Agriculture and Agricultural Reform, with the edifying title 'Faithful to our principles'.[32]

The driving force behind this accommodation with the post-independence political system does not necessarily come from ideological sympathy, conformism or even fear of those holding the reins of power, but the belief in the need to build a functioning state and infrastructure. These women were not naive, and in interviews in 2005 they often demonstrated an acute awareness of the complexities and contradictions of their position. They saw compromise as inevitable for the greater good, and accepted that it would involve sacrifice and personally painful choices. At a round-table tribute to Baya Hocine in June 2002, held two years after her death, Zohra Drif, Djoher Akrour, Jacqueline Guerroudj, Malika Koriche, Louisette Ighilahriz, Annie Steiner and Akila Ouared, amongst others, shared their memories of the former combatant. Most memories related to the war period and prison. The women talked about Baya Hocine's bravery, her sense of duty and her intellectual curiosity. There were very few memories of the post-1962 period, even though Baya Hocine was only twenty-two when the war ended. One of the few post-independence memories was shared by Louisette Ighilahriz, who talked about visiting Baya Hocine in the mid-1960s to present her condolences after one of her young children died – this tragedy, all the women agree, was an event which marked her profoundly. Louisette describes arriving at Baya Hocine's house, only to be met with the following words: 'Baya said, "Why did you go out of your way? We need to work."' Louisette draws the conclusion: 'We took full responsibility for our commitment'.[33]

This belief in tasks of national construction, shared across diverse political tendencies, and sharpened by a post-1990s nostalgia for the 1960s and 1970s, helps explain some of the more puzzling aspects of the way in which women talk about the first two decades of independence. Notably, it helps explain the difficulty (unless interviewees clearly state their position) of neatly categorising individuals as 'pro-regime', neutrals, opponents or politically disengaged in this period. Interviewees' accounts also demonstrate the need to see the single-party state as a heterogeneous entity. In 1962, all rivals to the Ben Bella–EMG alliance did not suddenly cease to exist. In addition to numerically small, clandestine or semi-clandestine resistance groups (such as the FFS, the PCA–PAGS and Al Qiyam), journalists tested their margins of manoeuvre in the press, teachers went beyond the official script when talking to their students and activists within mass party organisations such as the UNEA, the UGTA and the JFLN retained varying, but sometimes considerable, degrees of autonomy.

From gender-neutral citizens to the conscience of the nation: The creation of 'the *mujahidat*'

For urban, educated women war veterans who in the 1960s and 1970s had believed in a project of economic and social development, who did not agree with opposition for opposition's sake and who did not wish to be seen 'as women', the early 1980s marked a period of change. As the newly formed feminist Association of Women of Boumerdes pointed out in the first issue of its newspaper, *Voix des femmes*, on 1 November 1989, '[Before 1980] in the context of the industrialisation of the country, the proclaimed official discourse of the participation of women in economic development had created a myth but also a reality of the liberation of women through work and education'.[34] By 1989, the gap between myth and reality was increasingly stark. In 1979, an official notification issued by the government forbade women from leaving the national territory without the authorisation or presence of a male tutor. Socialist state-building and Third Worldism ended, as President Chadli Bendjedid (1979–92) sought to open up the Algerian economy to market forces. Then, in 1984, a Family Code was voted in the National Assembly. This institutionalised gender inequality by legally obliging women to obey their husbands, fixing in law repudiation and polygamy for men, and drastically reducing women's grounds for divorce. *El Moudjahid* hailed the legislation as 'a major event in the construction [*édification*] of our society'.[35] In an increasingly conservative political climate, legislation such as the Family Code was presented as the new tasks of national construction.

The 1984 Family Code was a tipping point. It ruptured – or at least put under significant strain – the link between many urban, educated female veterans and the state. In breaking the link with the state, these urban, educated female veterans also began to renounce gender-neutral citizenship. They campaigned publicly against the code, they campaigned as women and they campaigned as female veterans. A new feminist version of the nationalist genealogy was born: they became 'the *mujahidat*'.

Rumours of an imminent rewriting of family law had periodically circulated in Algeria since 1962. In 1959, the late colonial state had introduced a new civil code, replacing the 'Muslim personal status' based on a French interpretation of Muslim law which had regulated Muslim family life and excluded Muslim men from citizenship since 1865. This legislation remained on the statute books – although it was often ignored – until 1975, when it was annulled, and judges were instructed to revert to Muslim law, or use precedent. The reluctance of the state to legislate on family law reflects the ability of conservative and progressive forces to counteract each other in the first two decades of independence, notably in 1966 and 1973, when draft bills were circulated, but their existence officially denied, and in 1979, when a bill was announced, but its contents kept secret.

Finally, in 1981, the government presented a 'personal status bill' in the National Assembly based on a conservative interpretation of Muslim family law.[36] Lobbying in the National Assembly by a small group of female war veterans, including deputies Fadéla Mesli, Baya Hocine and Saliha Djeffal, a petition of ten thousand names and demonstrations led by high-profile *mujahidat* such as Zohra Drif, Meriem Belmihoub and Fettouma Ouzegane ensured that the project was put aside for a year of reflection.[37] It is at this point that 'the *mujahidat*' emerged as a category. 'The *mujahidat*' (and not '*mujahidat*', which refers to female veterans more broadly) is a politicised identity rather than a political movement or clearly defined group of individuals. When discussing 'the *mujahidat*' in relation to the Family Code, we tend to be talking about educated women who in the 1960s and 1970s had participated in tasks of national construction, and who in the 1980s sought to use their social and historical capital to campaign against a piece of legislation that consolidated gender discrimination which hitherto had largely existed in practice rather than on the statute books.

The participation of female war veterans was seen as a significant advantage by a younger generation of women's rights campaigners, who had come of age in the 1960s and 1970s, benefited from the free and compulsory education of this period and therefore often experienced significant social mobility. The left-wing politician Louisa Hanoune (born in 1954), who in 1985, alongside Khalida Messaoudi and Aïcha Benabdelmoumen, would be one of the founding members of the Association pour l'Egalité devant la Loi entre les Femmes et les Hommes (Association for Equality before the Law and between Men and Women), declared in her 2001 memoirs that the support of the *mujahidat* against the Family Code was:

> No doubt decisive in the authorities' [initial] retreat, because they put the regime not only face-to-face with its contradictions, but especially face-to-face with the betrayal of the aspirations of independence [...] They were a living symbol of the bad conscience of a regime which uses historical legitimacy to oppress its own society.[38]

For Khalida Messaoudi (born in 1958), speaking in 1995 – she subsequently became better known as Khalida Toumi, Minister of Communication and Culture 2002–14 and Bouteflika loyalist – '[Chadli] could not claim that this was a revolt of girls on the extreme left demanding revenge on the bourgeois system, or feminists struggling against misogynistic power. The *mujahidat* are the most legitimate women in the eyes of the people.'[39]

This vision of 'the *mujahidat*' as representing the people and the true aspirations of independence against unjust and illegitimate rule is formulated around the same kind of binary construction as discourses about 1962 (true/false *mujahidin*, interior/exterior) and the political and cultural identity of Algeria (authenticity/foreign imposition, tradition/modernity). It treats 'the *mujahidat*' as a homogeneous bloc, not only throwing all female veterans in with the relatively small group of women campaigning against the Family Code but also flattening out the often significant political differences within this group of campaigners. For example, Zohra Drif was very close to the centre of power – her husband, Rabah Bitat was president of the National Assembly in the 1980s – whilst Lucette Hadj Ali was in the PAGS. Fettouma Ouzegane sought to use the Family Code debates as a platform for a root-and-branch attack on the political system, whilst for other women this was a single-issue campaign – in the words of Zhor Zerari: 'I don't have any political ambition, I'm not disciplined enough. What I'm interested in is making things work. But when there is a fire, we go to the fire, for example against the Family Code.'[40] Amongst the women I have interviewed who campaigned against the code, they often differed on the best tactics to adopt. Some argued that they should try to improve the most discriminatory aspects, whilst others insisted that total abrogation was the only way forward.

Moreover, the vicious personal attacks on war veteran deputies in the National Assembly who challenged the 1982 version of the Family Code undermines the idea of the *mujahidat* as the venerated conscience of the nation. Baya Hocine energetically condemned the conservatism of the code, only to be booed and shouted down by a group of male deputies. Deeply disillusioned, she resigned from the National Assembly and the party of the FLN.[41] Fadéla Mesli was subject to similar insults:

> We were fighting over it, and I was almost attacked by a colleague who said to me, 'You, you have sons, you are following the devils, and yet you are the daughter of an honourable family'. I said: 'When they voted for me, it wasn't to defend my family unit, to favour my sons, it was to defend a whole people'. When they reacted really badly was when I raised the problem of inheritance, amongst others. They said that I was attacking the Qur'an. I said that [religious teaching] needed to be seen in its context: before women lived in their tribe, now families are no longer the same. I thought of women who don't have an occupation, and from one day to the next it's the man who gets one part, and the woman half a part.[42]

The violent reaction to Fadéla Mesli's criticisms reveals that she was seen as neither a *mujahida* nor a deputy. Instead she was addressed by her fellow National Assembly deputies as a *bint familia* (literally, a daughter of 'good family'), and asked, how can a respectable woman like you hold such culturally unacceptable views? The public language of debates about 'the woman question' had become distinctly more reactionary compared to the 1960s. Baya Hocine, Fadéla Mesli and Saliha Djeffal were no longer deputies in the National Assembly by the time the final version of the Family Code was passed in 1984.

The way in which Messaoudi and Hanoune locate the *mujahidat* as venerated elders is thus a myth, albeit a myth which in other contexts engenders a certain reality. The development of the myth of the *mujahidat* as the conscience of the nation is significant, because it indicates the emergence of a new feminist thread within the nationalist story of the nation. Rather than the dominant narrative which depicts women as bastions of cultural resistance in the nineteenth century becoming active agents in the revolution 1954–62 before transforming into the post-independence embodiment of the Algerian nation, the feminist–nationalist genealogy which emerged in the 1980s insisted on the continuous role of women in Algerian history as fighters against colonialism *and* patriarchy. 'The *mujahidat*' were positioned as playing a pivotal role in this lineage. This narrative was not made up of new elements – on the contrary, it has a number of points of connectedness with certain aspects of the top-down discourse on women. But it was a new narrative in the sense that it was seen to be oppositional and it was associated with a specific group of women, who tended to be educated, urban and of the wartime generation.

The 1990s:
Disarray and reconvergence with the top-down narrative

In October 1988, in cities across Algeria, youths – and especially young men – angry at high unemployment, corruption and the lack of opportunities for their generation attacked the flags, buildings and symbols of the post-independence state which they felt had failed them, accelerating the move towards multipartyism. In the context of economic crisis, rejection of the party of the FLN and a global rise in the popularity of radical Islam, a newly formed political party, the Front Islamique du Salut, rapidly gained support. In December 1991, the FIS won the first round of Algeria's first democratic legislative elections, with a landslide 188 seats, compared to twenty-five seats for the FFS and eighteen for the FLN, albeit with a voter abstention rate of 42 per cent.[43] In March 1992, it was estimated that, of the FIS's two million members, 800,000 were women. The FIS was particularly successful in attracting the support of women under the age of forty, and especially students and housewives, whilst its male membership was much more varied in terms of age and socio-economic occupation.[44] In January 1992, the Algerian army prevented a second-round FIS victory by interrupting the electoral process. President Chadli was forced to step down, a state of emergency was declared and Boudiaf, a founding member of the FLN in 1954, was called upon to preside a transitional body (the HCE) and resolve the crisis.

Boudiaf had opposed the Ben Bella–EMG alliance in 1962, and since 1964 had been living in exile in Morocco, running a small brick-making business. Boudiaf had historical legitimacy but was also seen as a new face, not tarnished by post-independence politics. He was hostile to the FIS but open to pluralism and had a hard line on the corruption which increasingly riddled the Algerian state. This profile gave Boudiaf popular legitimacy but also made him powerful enemies. His presidency lasted barely six months. On 29 June 1992, he was assassinated. Officially, this was the isolated act of a member of the presidential protection team, although this thesis continues to be hotly contested. Algeria descended into an increasingly horrific cycle of violence. Armed Islamist groups took to the mountains and conducted a campaign of urban and rural terror, targeting in particular artists, intellectuals, journalists and women considered too 'Westernised'. The Algerian state fought back with torture, imprisonment without trial and assassination. Algerians of all social classes sought to flee the country, by legal and clandestine means.

The activism of the *mujahidat* diversified in the 'dark years' of the 1990s into a range of different associative activities, all of which tended to share a common theme: they were about defending women's rights. When I carried out interviews in 2005, Akila Ouared was president of the Association de Défense et Promotion des Droits des Femmes (ADPDF). Lucette Hadj Ali was involved in the Oran-based organisation Ecoute pour Femmes Victimes de la Code de Famille (Helpline for Women Victims of the Family Code, AFEPEC) and the national associative network Rassemblement Algérien des Femmes Démocrates (Algerian Rally of Women Democrats, RAFD). Salima Bouaziz, Fadila Attia and Fettouma Ouzegane were all members of SOS Femmes en Détresse (SOS Women in Distress), founded in the 1990s, which sought to help victims of domestic violence. The first president of SOS Femmes en Détresse was a veteran of the FF–FLN, Aïcha Aliouat.

Women's associations in the 1990s were split over how the Islamist challenge should be dealt with. Like many democrats who had celebrated the end of the single-party state, it increasingly seemed that they were faced with a stark choice. Either they accepted the army and military rule or they continued along the path of pluralism, taking the risk that, if the FIS won, the scenario would be 'one man, one vote, one time'. 'Eradicators' favoured physical elimination, refusing any dialogue with Islamists: the acronym RAFD, of which Khalida Messaoudi was a founding member, is also the word for refusal in Arabic. 'Reconciliators', such as Louisa Hanoune's Association pour l'Egalité and Voix de Femmes de Boumerdes (Boumerdes Women's Voices), believed that dialogue was necessary to avoid turning the Islamists into martyrs. The *mujahidat* were more likely to be in the eliminator camp. In a letter addressed to President Zéroual on 23 March 1994, leading activists in RAFD and SOS Femmes en Détresse, as well as a number of other associations, declared their attachment to the army in the face of the Islamist challenge.[45] When I interviewed her in 2005, Fadéla M'Rabet concluded a scathing critique of the lack of democracy in Algeria by stating: 'The only force in Algeria is the army. And it's thanks to this army that Algeria is still standing today. Between the Taliban and the army, I will always choose the army.'[46]

The profile of many of these urban, educated *mujahidat* made them potential assassination targets. Zhor Zerari was a journalist writing for a French language newspaper. She talks about having been 'on the list' and receiving 'a phone call'. 'I stayed', she simply says.[47] As a communist of European origin, Lucette Hadj Ali was also targeted. While in France to celebrate her granddaughter's birthday she was warned by friends in Algeria not to return. She talks of 'the impression of having deserted'.[48] This is not making a hasty parallel between the 'first' and 'second' Algerian 'wars'. Instead, such language needs to be understood as part of a language of duty towards Algeria: duty to fight for independence, duty to participate in national construction, duty to fight the Family Code in the name of the perceived values of 1954, duty to face down the Islamist challenge. Mimi Maziz did not participate in any street demonstrations until the 1990s: 'Then I came out'.[49] Her friend Salima Bouaziz adds: 'It's like [the War of Independence] was yesterday. Maybe we won't be able to do it, but it's as if we still could. You don't have to keep asking us, we come. We come.'[50]

Through the different personal pronouns she uses to narrate the three main sections in her autobiography, Eveline Lavalette makes clear that, for her, the 1990s marked the (re)emergence of a collective identity with its origins in the period of the war, reframed for an era of new challenges and threats. Lavalette uses 'elle' (she) in passages covering the war period, which she says characterises 'an identical path, a bit like a single portrait of this experience of unity where everyone was FLN'. 'Elle' becomes 'Je' (I) for the very few pages she devotes to the period 1962–90s when 'each person had to build and rebuild the dreamed-of Algeria' – although the 'Je', she adds, doesn't reflect 'the heart of my life'. In the 1990s, 'Je' becomes 'us' – men and women – 'those who refuse' to live in fear of terrorism.[51]

When I carried out my interviews with *mujahidat* in 2005, the 1990s were clearly present as a filter when these women were looking back on the 1960s and 1970s, but the 'black decade' was rarely referred to directly. When I explicitly asked questions about this period, responses were truncated, reduced to brief statements about the re-emergence of a collective stance to face down at all costs the Islamist challenge, or reinforcing the idea that the only choice to be had was between the politico-military regime or a theocratic state. A lengthier discussion which could have brought light and shade to either of these stock responses was not yet possible. The 1990s seemed too close: the decade had not been digested let alone dissected. It was sometimes at this point in the interview that an interviewee would begin asking me questions, not the usual polite enquiries about my studies and family, but the kinds of questions that an oral historian, seeking to avoid influencing the responses informants, might try to avoid as far as possible, such as 'What do you think of Louisa Hanoune's position in the 1990s [promoting a negotiated solution to the crisis]?' Because interviews were loosely in the chronological, life-story format, often these questions about the more recent past would come up in the late afternoon and early evening, as the light was beginning to fade and both myself and the interviewee would begin carefully planning how I would get home, or if I would need to stay the night: a self-imposed curfew, especially for women, was still very much the norm in Algiers in 2005.

Conclusion

In the 1960s and 1970s, urban, educated women believed in tasks of national construction. They resisted being categorised 'as women', and insisted on a gender-blind citizenship in order to jump over the gender gap. This made potential opposition to the state – in deed or word – problematic, and gendered opposition even more difficult to imagine. The way interviewees talk about the 1960s and 1970s demonstrates that this period is not just a 'useful past' to critique the present; their stories also tell us something about real-life experiences of negotiating a place within the single-party state and post-independence society. In this period, the state still represented what Hugh Roberts terms the 'moral polity', whose central components he defines as belief in a strong, just and honest leader, no citizen being above the law and the views of ordinary people taken into consideration.[52]

The 1984 Family Code was a tipping point for these women. The growing strength of more conservative political tendencies meant that they could no longer find common ground with the official version of what nation-building meant. From seeking to be citizens without gender in a state that they tried to dissociate from its authoritarian politics, these women became gendered citizens and female veterans fighting a regime. They became 'the *mujahidat*' and a new feminist–nationalist narrative of the nation was born. The distinction made between the 'good' nation and the 'bad' state in this oppositional narrative tends to ignore the many and necessary everyday interactions between the citizen and the state, and the fact that many 'ordinary' citizens are also representatives of the state, in state infrastructure, local government and administration. It is, nevertheless, a powerful rhetorical tool, embodying a rupture felt across different sections of Algerian society with 'the moral polity'.

Even rhetorically, however, the rupture between 'the *mujahidat*' and the state/system was never complete. Moreover, one impact of the 1990s was to encourage a degree of convergence between this feminist–nationalist–oppositional narrative and the state narrative. Akila Ouared, an active campaigner against the Family Code since the 1980s, presents her political genealogy in the following terms:

There is a historical reference: since Fatma N'Soumer [the nineteenth-century heroine of Algerian resistance to the French invasion], women have always demanded the liberation of their country, the construction of their country. During the resistance to terrorism, and its fundamentalist ideology, for ten years, women defended the Republic in Algeria. They were in the avant-garde; they were in the street; they defied gangs of terrorists. And they were targeted. I was targeted in my family; my family was targeted by terrorists. But that is not going to stop me from carrying on, because we knew that, if the fundamentalists took power, it would be finished for the rights of women.[53]

This is a narrative of eternal resistance to outside threats and the enemy within which closely resembles President Bouteflika's speeches about women. On International Women's Day in 2007, he declared:

> The Algerian woman has, across time, overcome many challenges. From Lalla Fatma N'Soumer to Hassiba Boulmerka [middle-distance runner who won gold for Algeria in the 1992 Olympics in Barcelona, and who was threatened by Islamists for her 'unMuslim' sporting attire], via the courageous *mujahidat* and the women martyrs of the national tragedy [the 1990s], the Algerian woman has forced respect by her courage, her resistance and her heroism.[54]

On the one hand, compared to the alternative, the old regime seemed the best of a bad choice for urban, educated, politically committed *mujahidat*. On the other hand, as Algeria began to emerge from the 1990s, co-opting elements of this feminist–nationalist narrative was a politically astute move for Bouteflika to attract international support after a decade of highly mediatised civil violence.

From the vantage point of the 2010s, there is evidence that the narrative of the nation associated with 'the *mujahidat*' has diverged once again from the official line. In 2009, Annie Steiner wrote to *El Watan* to declare her support for the War of Independence veteran Mohamed Gharbi, condemned to death for shooting a terrorist earlier that year.[55] Gharbi's case was seen by many as a symbol of the failure of Bouteflika's controversial 2005 Charter for Peace and National Reconciliation, presented as a key measure to restore civil peace to Algeria through granting immunity to members of the armed forces and amnesties for Islamist guerrillas. Despite supposedly being approved by a massive majority of Algerians in a referendum, this charter is the subject of widespread popular resentment.[56] Notably, it is commonly argued that so-called *repentis*, those terrorists who repented and were thus pardoned, have received special treatment such as housing and business grants, over and above that which 'ordinary' Algerians, including victims of terrorism, are entitled to.

In April 2011, Louisette Ighilahriz was involved in a very public spat with the wartime leader of the FLN–ALN's ZAA, Yacef Saadi. At a screening of a new documentary about women in the

Algiers bomb network, *Fidaiyett* (produced by Lamia Gacemi), Saadi accused Ighilahriz of inventing her wartime role.[57] With the support of Annie Steiner and Fettouma Ouzegane, Ighilahriz called a press conference and retorted that Saadi himself was a traitor. She dared him to 'be a man' and give up his parliamentary immunity as a presidentially selected senator to come and face her, as a citizen, in court to dispute the facts. Saadi did not take up the challenge and said that his comments had been misinterpreted.[58] Ighilahriz emerged from the confrontation as the vindicated underdog who had forced Saadi to back down despite his greater political power.

Finally, in summer 2011, 'the *mujahidat*' brought their support to a mediatised campaign led by the inhabitants of a housing estate in Algiers, the Cité des Bois des Pins, against the destruction of an adjoining forest, which was being cleared to make way for a multi-storey car park and shopping centre. This development was bitterly opposed through both legal challenges and direct action. Large numbers of police surrounded the site, seeking to enable the works to continue whilst residents, including many women and children, tried to physically halt the deforestation. Violent clashes occurred, with the police accused of brutality and harassment. In an open letter, the *mujahidat* Djamila Bouhired, Fettouma Ouzegane, Zoulikha Bekaddour, Louisette Ighilahriz and Louisa Oudarène argued that the authorities' claims that they were simply protecting property reproduced the same kinds of justifications as those used by General Massu and the paratroopers of the 1957 'Battle of Algiers'.[59] Other critics made unfavourable comparisons between Boumediene's reforestation drive and Bouteflika's deforestation,[60] compared the destruction of the Bois des Pins to the environmental damage wrought by the Banu Hilal confederation of tribes which marched from Egypt into North Africa in the eleventh century and expressed suspicions that those who would benefit from the new shops would be *repentis*.[61] In a filmed exchange between Djamila Bouhired and an elderly female resident of the housing estate uploaded on to YouTube, Bouhired described those responsible for the car park as '*harkis*' and 'thieves' 'with no religion, no belonging, no origins and no nationalism', reassuring her interlocutor, 'I don't know you, but your children are my children'.[62]

The Gharbi, Ighilahriz–Saadi and Cité des Bois des Pins examples highlight that since the 2010s 'the *mujahidat*', a group of women who are in many ways a social elite, have begun to be recast in the media not just as the conscience of the nation, but more broadly as representatives of 'ordinary' citizens against illegitimate and arbitrary power. Their public interventions have become part of a wider critique of social injustice, political oppression and *la hogra* (contempt of the powerful for the 'ordinary' Algerian). This is a distinct development from the 1980s image of 'the *mujahidat*' as respected insiders with privileged access to influence the system on specific issues, or indeed the alliance of necessity between 'the *mujahidat*' and the state in the 'eradicator' camp during the civil violence of the 1990s.

By taking part in debates about *repentis*, parliamentary immunity and urban planning, 'the *mujahidat*' are participating in the creation of a language to talk about legitimacy and social justice which draws on a broad range of religious and political, national and transnational frames of reference, which both pre- and postdate the colonial period. A widely shared but also constantly evolving set of codes about true and false *mujahidin*, traitors and patriots, long-established residents and nouveau-riche opportunists, *repentis* and victims of terrorism enable us to jump from one mediatised controversy to the next and the frames of reference will be instantly familiar. The fluidity of this language is why it remains effective and relevant. The War of Independence is not the only reference, but it is a key benchmark. Yet the more the past is used as an unfavourable mirror to the present, the more that past – and specifically the War of Independence – becomes a rarefied object which cannot itself be critiqued.

Notes

1 Ministère de l'Information, *Les Femmes algériennes* (Algiers, n.d. [196–?]).
2 Interview with Salima Bouaziz (18 December 2005).
3 V.-B. Rosoux, 'Poids et usage du passé dans les relations franco-algériennes', *Annuaire français de relations internationales*, 2 (2001), 451–65, p. 457.
4 Interview with El Hora Kerkeb (1 June 2005).
5 Interview with Fadéla Mesli (20 December 2005).
6 M. Benrabah, *Language Conflict in Algeria: From Colonialism to Post-Independence* (Bristol: Multilingual Matters, 2013).

7 Interview with Habiba Chami (1 June 2005).

8 Interview with Mimi Maziz (18 December 2005).

9 Interview with Fettouma Ouzegane (6 June 2005).

10 Interview with Mimi Maziz (18 December 2005).

11 Interview with Jacqueline Guerroudj (15 and 18 December 2005).

12 Interview with Fadéla Mesli (20 December 2005).

13 Interview with Annie Steiner (22 June 2005).

14 In the 1970s, Mostefa Lacheraf proposed an alternative to the policy of rapid Arabisation through the adoption of classical Arabic (*fusha*) as sole official language. Instead, Lacheraf argued for a more gradual process, with Arabisation leading to the Algerianisation of language (an Arabic more closely based on Algerian *derja*). His views were rejected and he was forced to resign. Benrabah, *Language Conflict in Algeria*, p. 63.

15 Ameyar, *La Moudjahida Annie Fiorio-Steiner*, pp. 112–13.

16 Interview with Fadila Attia (19 June 2005).

17 Interview with Jacqueline Guerroudj (15 and 18 December 2005).

18 For example, a former member of the Communist Party might empha-sise his or her anti-fascist – rather than pro-Soviet – sympathies, whilst an interviewee from the non-communist left might be reluctant to dwell upon his or her experiences of Soviet oppression for fear of substantiat-ing post-1989 right-wing nationalist versions of the communist past. Mark, *The Unfinished Revolution*, p. 164.

19 Interview with Fadila Attia (19 June 2005).

20 Interview with Fatima Benmohand Berci (17 June 2005).

21 *Le Soir d'Algérie* (24 July 2006).

22 Interview with Akila Ouared (13 June 2005).

23 S. Boym, *The Future of Nostalgia* (New York: Basic Books, 2001), p. 58. Ed McAllister is currently working on a PhD at the University of Oxford about nostalgia for the Boumediene period. See his text 'Algeria's Belle Epoque (1): Postcards and Nostalgia: images of Algeria in the 1970s', *Textures du temps* (5 December 2012), http:// texturesdutemps.hypotheses.org/414 (accessed 19 May 2014).

24 Interview with Saliha Djeffal (21 June 2005).

25 Interview with Lucette Hadj Ali (18 December 2005).

26 Interview with Zhor Zerari (21 December 2005).

27 Ameyar, *La Moudjahida Annie Fiorio-Steiner*, pp. 111–12.

28 Zhor Zerari's attacks on the way in which *autogestion* is managed continued in *Algérie actualité* in the weekly editions 10–16 December, 17–23 December 1967 and 17 March 1968.

29 Interview with Zhor Zerari (21 December 2005).

30 *Algérie actualité* (8–14 October 1967). The title 'Messieurs les ronds de cuir' is a reference to a play from 1893 by the French author Georges Courteline on a similar theme.

31 *Algérie actualité* (22–8 October 1967).
32 *Algérie actualité* (26 March 1967).
33 'Hommage à Baya Hocine', Conference at the Centre National d'Etudes et de la Recherche sur le Mouvement National et la Révolution du Premier Novembre, 17 June 2000 [video recording].
34 Association des femmes de Boumerdes, *Voix de femmes*, 1 (1 November 1989).
35 *El Moudjahid* (20 June 1984).
36 There is a significant literature on the Family Code in Algeria, see for example Pruvost, *Femmes d'Algérie*, and Charrad, *States and Women's Rights*, as well as a wide range of journal articles.
37 *Le Monde* (22–3 November 1981), *Libération* (28 December 1981).
38 Hanoune, *Une autre voix pour l'Algérie*, p. 66.
39 K. Messaoudi with E. Schemla, *Une Algérienne débout* (Paris: Flammarion, 1995), p. 83.
40 Interview with Zhor Zerari (21 December 2005).
41 *L'Humanité* (18 June 2004).
42 Interview with Fadéla Mesli (20 December 2005).
43 B. Stora, *Histoire de l'Algérie depuis l'indépendance* (Paris: La Découverte, 1994), p. 95.
44 Motivations for joining the FIS were varied, for some it was ideological belief in the need for an Islamic state, for others a protest vote, for others still it was the opportunity to jump on the bandwagon. 'Algérie, 30 ans: les enfants de l'indépendance', *Autrement*, 60 (1992), p. 157. See also L. Bucaille, 'L'Engagement islamiste des femmes en Algérie', *Maghreb Machrek*, 144 (1994), 105–18.
45 Letter reproduced in *Le Matin*, *El Watan* and *Liberté* (24 March 1994).
46 Interview with Fadéla M'Rabet (1 November 2005).
47 Interview with Zhor Zerari (21 December 2005).
48 Interview with Lucette Hadj Ali (18 December 2005).
49 Interview with Mimi Maziz (18 December 2005).
50 Interview with Salima Bouaziz (18 December 2005).
51 Lavalette, *Juste algérienne*, pp. 139–40.
52 H. Roberts, 'Moral economy or moral polity? The political anthropology of Algerian riots', Crisis States Programme Development Research Centre, Working paper 17 (2002), http://eprints.lse.ac.uk/28292/1/WP17HRoberts.pdf (accessed 19 May 2014), pp. 12–13.
53 Interview with Akila Ouared (13 June 2005).
54 *El Moudjahid* (8 March 2007).
55 *El Watan* (18 June 2009), Reproduced in Ameyar, *La Moudjahida Annie Fioro-Steiner*, pp. 171–3.
56 A massive majority supposedly approved the charter, with a turnout of nearly eighty per cent: both these official claims are hotly disputed.

H. Zerrouky, 'L'Algérie après la Charte pour la paix et la réconciliation nationale', *Recherches internationales*, 75:1 (2006), 25–40.

57 *Liberté* (9 May 2011); *Ennahar* (5 May 2011).

58 *Le Jeune Indépendant* (5 May 2011); *Tout sur l'Algérie* (4 May 2011).

59 *Le Soir d'Algérie* (24 August 2011).

60 K. Daoud, 'Du barrage vert de Houari au déboisement de Abdelaziz', *Le Quotidien d'Oran* (10 August 2011).

61 A. Belkaïd, 'Alger: la bataille du Bois des pins', *Slate Afrique* (15 August 2011).

62 'Hydra: Djamila Bouhired au Bois des pins', youtube.com/watch?v=zYHwtKXs2fM (accessed 19 May 2014). Translation W. Benkhaled / N. Vince.

6

Being remembered and forgotten

The past as a nation-building narrative: From glorification to victimhood

On my first visit to the Museum of the Mujahid in Algiers in 2005, one of its employees insisted on showing me around, an act of both generosity and surveillance. Since I had mentioned to him the subject of my research, he immediately led me to the corner of the museum with ten or so objects and photographs relating to the participation of women during the war, introducing it as 'shamefully' small.

There is an academic, a popular and, as this example shows, a semi-official argument that Algerian women have been forgotten in the writing of Algerian history. Yet 'the Algerian woman' and 'the Algerian female combatant' have been part of the national narrative since 1962. Women have been represented in selective, stereotypical and reductive ways. But, by their very nature, national narratives compress complicated and diverse histories into simplistic useful pasts, and there is very little Algerian innovation on its favoured tropes: women are wombs of the nation, guardians of national essence or courageous teenage fighters. Undoubtedly Algerian women have been pushed into a secondary role in the war story, but their presence, however marginal, has none the less been a constituent part of the epic narrative of resistance. It is the ultimate symbol, after all, of a struggle 'by the people, for the people'.

Representations of women in the War of Independence, both as victims and fighters, began to be spun into a national narrative before the conflict was finished and independence won. Gendered stereotypes sought to rally Algerians to the nationalist cause to defend 'their women' by fighting 'like men' and win over international sympathy through demonstrating the commitment of

Figure 5 Women in Algiers walk past a poster celebrating the independence struggle, 1982

everyone (read: women) and exposing the horrific treatment meted out to civilians (read: women and children). The first monuments commemorating the martyrs of the war appeared in FLN–ALN bases in Morocco and Tunisia whilst the conflict was still raging and Hassiba Ben Bouali had a children's home for Algerian refugees in Morocco named after her in 1960.

Under the presidencies of Ben Bella and Boumediene, texts produced in the state-owned media dedicated to women in the liberation struggle followed similar themes to those dating from the war years. Newspaper articles on the national days of 1 November and 5 July were either anonymous accounts of stoic resistance in the face of violence and destitution or glorious tales of action and audacity by women in the Algiers bomb network. There were very few portraits of well-known figures, or at least any who were alive. Djamila Bouhired was presented as a 'national heroine' when her ambassadorial travels in the immediate post-independence years were described, but it was her current, rather than historical, role which was the focus of attention.[1] Zhor Zerari was something of a star reporter – her articles, unlike most journalists' copy at the time, were credited – but she was described as a 'special correspondent', not as a *mujahida*.[2] The historical legitimacy of Djamila Boupacha, Djamila Bouhired and Zohra Drif was key in justifying their selection as representatives of the new Algerian nation, but they were presented as symbols of a forward-looking Algeria, rather than being 'commemorated'. Indeed, in the 1960s and 1970s, there was a dividing line between celebrating the participation of women in the war in abstract, anonymous terms, and referring to female veterans as specific individuals. For the state, the celebration of living individuals, male or female, was at odds with the leitmotif 'one sole hero, the people'. As Chapter 5 demonstrates, for many female veterans there was a reluctance to be presented as *mujahidat* until the 1980s, when they felt obliged to contribute to the creation of this identity for strategic reasons.

Instead, the commemorative style of the first two decades of independence is encapsulated by an article which appeared in *El Moudjahid* in 1966 under the title 'The Algerian women in the revolution: despite suffering, serving the Ideal'. This anonymous account was presented as the true story of a rural woman, with the emphasis on the rurality of the struggle considered a mark of its authenticity. The article depicted the lack of a male head of household as a threat, exposing women to the 'multiple dangers which menace both the family and the motherland' – a thinly veiled reference to rape. In a classic nationalist gendered division of labour, the text described men going off to 'liberate the birth land' whilst women 'preserved the unity of family life'.[3] In another genre, a 1969 article about heroic, armed *mujahidat* brought these women into a broader narrative about national construction. In 'Combatants of yesterday and today: Algerian women have never capitulated', an anonymous third-person narrator revealed women's roles as nurses in the *maquis*, planting bombs in Algiers, replacing male members of their family and helping the *mujahidin* in the countryside. Seven years after independence, the article informed us, these women had put aside military weapons in order to liberate Algeria from economic dependency – that is to say, participate in socialist development.[4] One exception to these generalising accounts was an article about women in the urban guerrilla movement published in *El Moudjahid* in 1976. An early example of an officially endorsed nationalist–feminist narrative, the text unusually included a first-person interview with an identified interviewee. Fella Hadj Mahfoud, former member of the Algiers bomb network, talked about her anger against the colonial system but also her subversion of paternal authority, albeit framed in the language of brothers and sisters in combat: 'my father didn't know what I was doing for the Brothers'.[5]

Commemorative practices in the 1960s and 1970s sought to construct Algeria's international image as well as reinforce the national narrative. Boumediene's 1 November celebrations were elaborate military displays: tanks, Katyusha rocket launchers and MiG 21 fighter jets imported from the Soviet Union accompanied parades of army units, war veterans and activists in the FLN, JFLN, UNEA, UNFA and UGTA. Photographs of the 1 November 1967 parade – which took place five months after Israel's defeat of the Arab states in the Six Day War – included armed young women carrying submachine guns, described as 'students mobilised for paramilitary training', and other female students marching in military uniforms.[6] Such displays of women's military and sporting prowess were not to the taste of all. In a Friday prayer transmitted on the radio in 1965, Shaykh Abdellatif Soltani, a member of the conservative religious organisation Al Qiyam, condemned the display of 'girls wearing little clothing' on 1 November, denouncing the event as contrary to the Muslim religion and mores.[7] One wonders what he would have made of the 1974 celebrations, which featured attractive young women, wearing cheerleader-style outfits, including a big '20' on their tight white tops, marching down the street and across the pages of *El Moudjahid*, which added the caption 'They are the age of the revolution'.[8]

Whilst self-consciously seeking to demonstrate socialist and pan-Arab modernity, commemoration was also about integrating the War of Independence into a longer narrative of permanent Algerian resistance against French colonial aggression. The Emir Abdelkader in the 1830s and 1840s, Fatma N'Soumer in the 1850s and El Mokrani in 1871 make up the triptych of nineteenth-century heroes of Algerian resistance. In May 1963, Djamila Boupacha and Nasser made an official visit to the newly opened Fatma N'Soumer Centre for Daughters of Shuhada in Algiers. This positioned the *mujahidat* of 1954–62 as the direct descendants of the anti-colonial struggle which had begun in the nineteenth century and pitched the young girls in the orphanage as representing the future of the struggle for freedom, equality and pan-Arab unity. It was a neat narrative of who we are, where we come from and where we are going.

Inaugurated in 1982, the concrete palms of Maqam al-Shahid are often described as Chadli's symbolic break with the Boumediene years and socialist rigour – the monument was built by Canadians and was located by a new shopping precinct and cultural centre, Riad el Feth.[9] When women participated in commemoration ceremonies in the 1980s there were fewer guns and gymnastics displays. A 5 July youth event in 1982 featured young women wearing distinctly looser garments than in the previous two decades.[10] At the same time, in keeping with the more individualist tone of the 1980s, eyewitness accounts began to be an increasingly popular feature of newspaper special editions. Moreover, rather than only focusing on women in the Algiers bomb network, journalists began interviewing women described as previously forgotten, which included rural women and *maquisardes*.[11]

What is most striking about 1980s accounts of women at war is that the violence that they were subjected to, in particular gender-specific brutality, became increasingly foregrounded, although victims of rape remained anonymous or dead. An article on 'Algerian women in combat' on 5 July 1982 talked about the 'anonymous majority' of women who endured 'vexations, humiliations

Figure 6 A couple outside the Riad el Feth shopping precinct, at the foot of Maqam al-Shahid (the Monument to the Martyr) in Algiers, 1999

and sacrifices, with no regrets, but instead with dignity, abnegation and courage' and who were 'raped, beaten and deliberately
humiliated', paying the price for their patriotism 'in their flesh
and their honour'.[12] Or, even more graphically, an International
Women's Day event in Tizi Ouzou in 1982 honoured 'the example
of Tassadit', the pregnant wife of a *maquisard* who was interrogated in her village by *harkis*. The article describes how even under
torture she said nothing about her husband's whereabouts. The
soldiers bet on the sex of the child, her stomach was ripped open
and the baby thrown to the commander's dog. Tassadit died. The
UNFA named a workshop in Draa Ben Khedda in her memory.[13]
The increasingly explicit violence in accounts began to fill the gap
left by ebbing self-confidence in a glorifying national narrative
about the onward march of progress.

Putting the war on a pedestal and criticism within safe boundaries

The official end of the single-party state and the emergence of a free
press in 1989, the arrival of many veterans at retirement age and
the transnational explosion of memory production led to a plethora
of new memoirs and press articles about the War of Independence.
More often than not, the latter took the form of interviews with
historical actors. With the development of new media, it has
become even more difficult for the state to keep under surveillance,
let alone control, the circulation of information. Whereas previously state television, state newspapers and state radio dominated
public memory, there are now Facebook pages about the war and
self-published online eyewitness accounts. Today, Fatma N'Soumer
has a Facebook page celebrating her life and Djamila Bouhired a
YouTube tribute, created after she went to the press in 2009 to
criticise the failure of the Algerian state to provide her with ade-
quate healthcare. The latter consists of a four-minute video entitled
'Yassef [*sic*] Saadi, why have you forgotten Djamila Bouhired?' It
blends archive images and clips of Bouhired found on the Internet
with more recent screen shots of newspaper articles about her. The
soundtrack is provided by Ben Badis's set-to-music patriotic poem,
'The Algerian people is Muslim and belongs to Arabity'.[14]
    Yet the end of the state monopoly on memory has had an impact
on the quantity of information available about the war rather than
provoking a major qualitative shift in the language and frames of

reference used to discuss it. There remains a strong emphasis on victimhood. For example, in August 2000, the independent daily newspaper *Le Matin*, founded by former members of the PAGS in 1991 (and effectively banned in 2004), interviewed Ouerdia Hadj Mahfoud. This *mujahida* had been interviewed by the state organ *El Moudjahid* in 1976 under her *nom de guerre* 'Fella'. This 2000 interview needs to be placed in the particular context of the debate over the French army's use of torture during the war which erupted in France from June 2000 onwards, and it is to be expected that Fella/Ouerdia talks in far more detail about the physical abuse she endured in this later interview. Violence reduced in the 1976 article to generalising phrases such as '[Fella] passed through many centres of torture where she met other women activists who were in the FLN bomb network'[15] in the 2000 text become references to blood, excrement and sexual violence: '[General] Bigeard knows me. Between the tortures of the bathtub and electricity, he ordered the paras to bring me naked into his office ...'[16] The photograph of a smiling young woman in a wartime prison which accompanied the 1976 text is replaced by that of a tired and anxious Ouerdia in her sixties in the 2000 article. In 2000, it was no longer possible for Fella/Ouerdia to argue, as she had done in 1976, that 'Today Algerians have everything they need to live happily',[17] because this was patently not true after a decade of civil violence. The increased violence in published accounts from the 1980s onwards, which at times verges on the positively gory, is not just a consequence of violence becoming more banal in Algerian society in the 1990s or the specific context of the reopening of the torture debates in 2000. It also reflects developments in Algerian and transnational historiography in this period, when being a victim became less problematic than being a hero.

Furthermore, although today there are more voices talking about the War of Independence, and some previously occulted figures such as Messali Hadj now have a place in public memory, these plural memories have many points of connectedness. These points of connectedness include the justness of the revolution and the collective participation of the people (although what they fought *for* is contested) and the steadfast commitment of the 'real' combatants of the struggle (although *who* these true fighters are is debated). Again, this highlights the need to distinguish between 'official' and 'dominant' historical narratives: in contemporary Algeria the official version is also the dominant version, diffused through the state-owned media, the education system and state-sponsored processes of memorialisation. At the same time, elements of this dominant version can also be found in other (oppositional) versions of the war. In short, certain elements of the official version are dominant not only because they are officially promoted but also because they are widely held to be true throughout society, including by those who consider themselves to be 'anti-system'. Indeed, the more the post-1962 period becomes, or is perceived as, a cruel reality, the more the war period metamorphoses into an idealised, rarefied object, a lost paradise of hope, solidarity and purity of purpose. In the words of Khadjidja Belguembour, a former nurse in the *maquis* and passionate critic of post-independence Algeria: 'What I experienced was so beautiful and clean that it needs to be conserved jealously. It mustn't be touched.'[18]

The flip side of this is that many elements of 'oppositional' versions of the past have been so often repeated that they too have become part of the dominant narrative. Amongst these oppositional perspectives, which we might more accurately categorise as acceptable, or consensual, criticism, is the idea that independence was a bit disappointing. In 1991, it was state organ *El Moudjahid*, not one of the new independent newspapers, which featured an interview with Khadjidja Belguembour, introducing the *mujahida* with the lines 'the dreams she had when she was a little girl have not been realised and the promises made during the liberation struggle have evaporated'.[19] Another consensual criticism is the idea that the war generation needs to step aside, enabling demographically dominant younger generations to take their place in politics, state infrastructure, the economy and society more generally.[20] In the words of Fadila Attia:

> That's enough now, they're old, they should have rest. Let the young people take over. I'm not saying Bouteflika is old, he's still young [Bouteflika was sixty-eight at the time of the interview in 2005], but there are old people who have been in post since '62 and who should step back. There are people who are fifty who haven't got a job. Doctors without a job. Here it is always the same networks going round. And it's not just me saying that, it's the newspapers that say it. That's why young people leave. And the pathetic ones stay.[21]

Although this might seem like a resounding criticism, albeit with some careful qualifications, of a stagnant political system and society reliant on systems of patronage, this is not only an oppositional discourse. On the contrary, it is also a leitmotif of the revolutionary family as it continues to hold on to power. As Fadila Attia puts it: 'Even the president said, fifty years, that's enough. We are veterans, we got our due, we got our part, *barakat* [enough]!' In fact, Bouteflika has been saying for a number of years that it is time for younger generations to take over[22] – while at the same time amending the constitution to allow himself to run for a third term in 2009, and running for a fourth term in 2014 despite serious health problems.

Finally, one of the most common critiques relates to the problem of false *mujahidin*, butt of jokes and considered source of all evil in independent Algeria. This is a favoured subject of cartoonists such as Ali Dilem and Slim and a key theme in cult films such as *Le Clandestin / Taxi al-Makhfi* (Benamar Bakhti, 1991). Deeply rooted in popular culture is the idea that real *mujahidin* do not have an officially attributed *mujahid* card and do not talk about the war expansively to anyone who will listen. A true *mujahid* is discreet, and most probably destitute. Everyone has a darkly funny story to tell about a fake. Malika Koriche describes the day she was arrested in August 1957. She was waiting at the beach for Malika Ighilahriz, sister of Louisette and fellow member of the Algiers bomb network, to come and take her to a safe house. As she swam and sunbathed, a young man at the beach struck up conversation with her. As time passed and still Malika Ighilahriz did not arrive, Malika Koriche realised that her underground cell was potentially in trouble. She packed up her things and was leaving the beach when she was stopped by two French paratroopers:

> They asked me my name. I said 'Fatima', my middle name. 'You are Koriche,' they said – but they hadn't said the name Malika at that point. Then suddenly, the man on the beach shouted 'Malika, you've forgotten your towel!' And the paratroopers took me. They also took the man, I tried to explain that he had done nothing, but they weren't listening. After independence, I bumped into him once, and he told me that he did a year and a half in prison, and that he had been given veteran papers. I said to him, 'Good for you!'[23]

There is a consensus that there is a problem of false *mujahidin*: the size of the problem and who is false is much more controversial. Khadjidja Belguembour describes being confronted by frustrated younger members of her own family when she goes to weddings:

'They ask me "What have you done? Why did you make France leave? These are thieves [in power]."'[24] This is emphatically not a form of colonial nostalgia, but deliberately provocative shorthand for underlining just how bad those who rule are perceived to be. Khadjidja says that her stock response is that the real *mujahidin*, those who forced France out, are not those in power. Because attacking false *mujahidin* is about calling into question individual legitimacy based on wartime credentials or lack thereof, it does not call into question the legitimacy of the *mujahidin* as a symbol of the nation.

Disappointment with post-independence Algeria, the idea that younger generations need to take over from veterans and the issue of false *mujahidin* are instantly recognisable codes: they provide a space, albeit a space with shifting and contested limits, within which political criticism of the present can be aired using the past, without undermining the fundamental role of the War of Independence as a social glue, the building block of Algerian society. These politicised public narratives resonate across urban and rural interviews – women in the village of Agraradj also blame post-independence woes on *harkis* taking positions of power after 1962 and express their sympathies with excluded younger generations.

Whose duty to remember what, and for whom?

It is in this context of seeking to make a political critique of the present without undermining the nation-building capacities of the past that we need to locate historical works about Algerian women during the War of Independence. Djamila Amrane's *Les Femmes algériennes pendant la guerre* (Algerian women during the war, 1991) pioneered the study of women during the War of Independence. It is written by a former combatant and historian (who subsequently became a professor at the University of Toulouse) who interviewed eighty-eight women and had access to the Ministry of Mujahidin's archives of 10,949 officially registered female militants. Her aim was to right a wrong: 'It seemed to me a profound injustice that the history of these seven years of war was written ignoring half of the Algerian people: women. It is this half, forgotten by historians and eyewitnesses, historical actors and writers, that I will try to bring back to life.'[25] Djamila Amrane's work is a major contribution to knowledge about the conflict, but it writes women back into the national narrative rather than challenging the structuring frameworks and idioms that characterise the dominant discourse. The war continues to exist in a bubble of courage, audacity, abnegation and equality, disconnected from what followed. Amrane concludes by arguing that for women:

> The War of National Liberation provoked a spontaneous drive towards a simple and clear goal, which was independence. In the exceptional context of war, this effort translated into exceptional attitudes, but it was sustained neither by a political education nor by personal ambitions which could have allowed it to endure after the war.[26]

The exceptionality – indeed exemplarity – of the war is also a key theme in the work of academics belonging to the first postwar generation who have written about the *mujahidat*. Malika El Korso, who runs a research group on women's participation in the War of Independence at the state-funded Centre National d'Etudes et de la Recherche sur le Mouvement National et la Révolution du Premier Novembre (National Centre for Study and Research on the National Movement and the Revolution of 1 November) in Algiers, sees the war as the high point in the history of Algerian women, on a downwards spiral ever since.[27] Khaoula Taleb Ibrahimi is a linguist and women's rights activist, as well as the granddaughter of 'ulama Shaykh Bachir al-Ibrahimi and niece of Ahmed Taleb al-Ibrahimi, the minister for education who under Boumediene drove the Arabisation agenda. She was a child during the War of Independence. When Khaoula Taleb Ibrahimi was approached to write a chapter in a volume edited by two of the leading historians of Algeria, Benjamin Stora and Mohamed Harbi,[28] on the role of the *mujahidat*, she was initially apprehensive as it is not her specialism. However, as she started researching the topic, she describes becoming more and more interested in the way in which it spoke to her personal trajectory as an Algerian woman:

> It allowed me to ask myself a certain number of questions about myself, because I am a woman: what is the future of women in our country, in history, what happened, how were these women – and this is an idea I really liked – how were they in rupture with their society? [...] In the first place, I'm not a historian, if I [wrote the chapter] it was essentially from the point of view of a citizen. That is

to say, me, the generation after independence, what relationship do I have to these women, what have they given me, what can they bring the country, and what can I bring them? And how I could be the link between these women and young people today who know nothing about them? [...] I would like the women of my generation, and young people, to pay more attention to keeping this memory alive, so we can conserve some traces of these women and so they can be a motivation to continue.[29]

For these academics, writing history is also an act of citizenship. In different ways, they all insist that celebrating Algerian women's role in the war is a duty, a *devoir de mémoire*, because it will create a more positive image of Algerian women in the present. It is seen as necessary to insist that women fought alongside men, that they were considered their equals and that if they are not their equals today it is because they have been forgotten.

Using women's role in the national past to promote women in the present is fraught with potential pitfalls, as Cynthia Enloe explains:

In Quebec, the Philippines and Afro-America nationalist women have become wary of nationalist spokespeople who glorify the pre-colonial past. They have become uncomfortable when women warriors and queens are offered as proof that women had genuine influence over land and sexuality in the past. And yet they have to conduct these historical explorations carefully, knowing that outsiders might use their findings to discredit the nationalism they want to reform.[30]

On the one hand, there is the risk of complicity in the glorified, sanitised national narrative, which brushes under the carpet ongoing political and social resistance to changes in women's roles. On the other hand, foregrounding political and social resistance to women playing an active role in nationalist struggles in the past – as for example, Gilbert Meynier does in his *Histoire intérieure du FLN* when he argues that 'The ALN replaced the father in the management of the fairer sex'[31] – is open to manipulation. It could be used as evidence that there were never any 'authentically Algerian' examples of gender equality, and, by implication, that there never can be. This tension is the subtext to many historical works about women during the war – including, to a certain extent, this book – revealing that this is not just an issue for historians who are employees of a state which continues to guard closely the production of historical knowledge.[32] This tension is at its most visible when talking to educated, politically engaged *mujahidat* about the writing of their history.

In June 2005, Fettouma Ouzegane began the process of forming an association, the Mouvement National de Solidarité et de Soutien à la Lutte des Femmes (National Movement of Solidarity and Support for the Women's Struggle), in opposition to the government and to fight discrimination against women. Point number one, in the aims of the association, declared that: '[It is necessary] to associate ourselves with the writing of the history of the national liberation struggle so that we, *mujahidat*, re-appropriate our past, the memory of Algerian women'.[33] When I asked Fettouma why this was the number one task, she responded: 'Listen, after all, restoring an objective and true history is about putting the women's struggle back in its rightful place.' When I asked her what was missing in the current history, she replied: 'Everything is missing in the history: women's combat in the town, women's fight in the *maquis*, women's fight in health services, in training, in liaison activities, their struggle was very wide ranging.'[34]

Yet Fettouma Ouzegane's categorisation reproduces exactly the same typologies of women's roles as those which can be found in the Museum of the Mujahid and the Museum of the Army. Here we see in action the hegemonic power of the dominant discourse: even someone who wants to re-engage with the past as a way of rewriting the present follows the established framework of existing public history. Fettouma continues to insist that, if the full extent of women's wartime engagement were better known, Algeria would be a better place. In her view, historical research is not just an academic endeavour conducted with methodological and ethical rigour, it also provides the direct means for citizens to effect change in the present.

Such a claim is debatable: the ambiguities, grey areas and nuances of historical research do not easily fit into black-and-white moral judgements.[35] Archives rarely serve up 'smoking guns', which memory activists often insist must exist, somewhere, and which would provide a definitive version of what happened, who was innocent and who was guilty.[36] Nevertheless, the view that remembering the 'true' past can 'save' the present is one expressed in the published memoirs of *mujahidat*. The few women who have written autobiographies have done so in the past decade, and all seem to have been motivated by their anxieties about the society around them self-destructing because it has forgotten its past, or, more precisely, the values which that past is seen to embody. In the final chapters of Louisette Ighilahriz's memoirs, *Algérienne*, her incomprehension of the 1990s, her inability to grasp how Algerians could kill each other, or why some claimed Algeria needed to be 'Islamised' when they were already Muslim, features extensively: 'When we fought for our independence, we fought sincerely for ideals that I still defend today'.[37] When Louisette Ighilahriz talks about her increasingly visible role in public history in Algeria, she describes having a 'duty to remember': 'So that future generations are aware of the problems, [so] that [they know] resistance is not easy, Algerian independence was not given, we had to seize this independence, this liberty'.[38]

For educated interviewees who have access to published history, 'being forgotten' is not only about *who* is forgotten but also about what symbolic message these absent figures are seen to carry about a present and future Algeria. This in part explains why, when urban, educated *mujahidat* are asked to comment on public history, they both critique it and reinforce its central message of one sole hero, the people, solidarity and unity of purpose. The documentary *Barberousse, mes soeurs* (Barberousse, my sisters, 1985), directed by Hassan Bouabdellah and produced by Algerian state television, is a case in point. The documentary is about women who were imprisoned in the infamous Barberousse prison during the War of Independence. It was pitched as an opportunity for women to 'answer back' to a made-for-television film directed by Hadj Rahim in 1982. *Serkadji* (Barberousse's post-independence name) tells the story of FLN militants who were imprisoned and executed, but ignores the presence and activism of the women who were incarcerated behind the same prison walls.

One of the participants in the documentary is Annie Steiner. Annie told me – as did many interviewees – that she was, in general, reluctant to give many interviews, as she did not want to give the impression that what she did during the war was more important than the role of anyone else. When she did give interviews, she explained that she preferred to privilege Algerian interviewers and Arabophone publications, in order to reach an Algerian public which was not necessarily Francophone – i.e. including large parts of the younger population.[39] The first time that Annie Steiner spoke publicly about her wartime experiences was in the mid-1980s for *Barberousse, mes soeurs*. She says that she chose to participate because it appealed for witnesses in what she describes as a 'democratic' way: there were advertisements in the newspapers and on television. The women she had been imprisoned alongside called each other, encouraging each other to participate.[40] Bouabdellah's set up was straightforward: he screened *Serkadji* and filmed women's reactions. His spectators proved to be sharp critics. They were quick to underline what they felt was unrealistic about the film and what was different in the women's quarters compared to those of the men. The final lines of *Barberousse, mes soeurs* are spoken by Annie Steiner:

> The sisters, they were young. Baya [Hocine] was only sixteen and she was condemned to death. They were young and, it needs to be said, they were beautiful. Perhaps it was the beauty of youth; perhaps it was the interior beauty of an ideal, of an exceptional situation. It was an exceptional beauty, that I will never forget.[41]

Annie Steiner's reaction to the opportunity that *Barberousse, mes soeurs* offered to tell 'her', or rather 'women's', story is telling. It shows that even when women are invited to 'answer back' – albeit within the boundaries of a state-controlled framework, and 1985 was still the period of the single-party state – they often produce a very similar message to official history: the details might vary, different individuals might need to be brought into the story, but there is 'one sole hero, the people' and the War of Independence is idealised as an intense moment of moral purity and unity of purpose. It is perhaps no coincidence that at around the same time as Annie Steiner singled out the teenage Baya Hocine as radiating the 'interior beauty of an ideal', an older Baya Hocine was resigning from the National Assembly in disgust, under the insults of those critical of her opposition to the Family Code.

Annie Steiner's emphasis on Algerians telling their story – in Arabic as well as in French – also underlines the importance she attaches to the role of the past in nation-building. The idea that Algerians should write their own history was a leitmotif of the 1960s and 1970s, when Algerian historians were called upon by the state to 'decolonise' history. This is a theme which has returned to prominence in official circles since 2000, following increased interest from international scholars in Algerian history. In April 2012, Zohra Drif supported a manifesto entitled 'Against colonialism by other means', to defend an Algerian writing of history against foreign attempts at revisionism. She particularly denounced 'the fact that the new generation likes talking about our problems with those who previously colonised us'.[42] Others would disagree. In the village of Agraradj, Fatima Berci insists that the outside world needs to know that 'a sachet of coffee costs 10,000 dinars [100 'new' dinars or €1]. I want foreign countries to know that so that there are reactions!'[43] Fadéla M'Rabet has little patience for claims that a nation's dirty linen should be washed in private: 'Many people think that you must not criticise your country because the foreigner will capitalise on it. It's immature. The intellectual must be an uncompromising observer.'[44] However, as Fadéla M'Rabet points out herself, many would disagree with her, and both M'Rabet and Berci, at these points in their respective interviews, were criticising the present, not the past.

In a group interview, I asked three former nurses in the *wilaya* V (Oran), El Hora Kerkeb (who became a police social worker), Habiba Chami (who became a senior member of the UNFA) and Yamina Salem (who became a pharmacist) if they felt that there were things missing from the public history of the War of Independence:

> HC: There are eyewitness accounts that are missing, there are battles that are missing [*the women start talking about a major battle they participated in*] [...] We should do some pilgrimages too.
> EK: Yes, I said that to you once, we we'll visit the locations of battles.

Later in the interview, the women come back to the theme of what is missing from their own history:

> YS: Let me explain to you. Women are often very keen to tell you their stories. Because often we are [lost] in the mass, the men are always in the front –
> HC [*interrupts*]: [We are] in the margins of the men.
> YS [*continues*]: So women fight more to put themselves forward, so they are not forgotten, so that people do not forget the role they played during the revolution.
> EK: All the same, we weren't forgotten.
> YS: No. At the start, you only saw the men, after the women came forward little by little on to the front of the scene.
> EK: All the same, we didn't let ourselves be pushed aside.
> YS: We fought to continue, to be recognised, so that our role in the revolution was not forgotten. And we also showed that we were the

equals of men. Even if we are better than them at many things. [*The women laugh and then start talking about their children, before returning to discuss history*]
YS: It's history, the history of Algeria. It needs to be written. We perhaps need to wait for one more generation, the actors will no longer be of this world and the truth can be told. Because there are things that can't be said because we are still alive.
EK: I think that the education system hasn't really –
HC [*interrupts*]: We need to write down eyewitness accounts.
YS: But the truths are often deformed.[45]

Each woman presents a different perspective – and some voices are more critical than others, noticeably on the question of the place of women within public history. Yet all three women share key arguments: the wish to multiply the number of voices talking about the war in the public sphere, the desire to tell a positive, socially useful story and the need to exercise some control over the narrative – either by ensuring that one's voice is heard, by insisting that one's voice has been heard or by accepting that certain things need to be silenced while the wartime generation is still alive.

Many *mujahidat* recognise that for many young people they might seem ancient history, disconnected from day-to-day life, even though these same women argue that the message which they have to transmit is more relevant than ever. This is why interviewees such as El Hora Kerkeb, Djamila Boupacha and Fadila Attia accept invitations to go into schools, albeit with varying results. El Hora Kerkeb and Djamila Boupacha talk about the children being interested in their war stories and the message of civic responsibility they seek to convey. Fadila Attia, however, despairingly describes how a group of high-school students in an affluent part of Algiers whom she was trying, in her words, to 'motivate', half-jokingly asked her whether the Governor Robert Lacoste, whose cabinet she worked in during the war as an FLN spy, was related to the expensive Lacoste clothing brand.[46] The responsibility which these women place on the citizen-forming capacities of the teaching of the past is huge, and is widely shared across Algerian society, despite the fact that history as a discipline has a relatively low status. In 2007, the Minister of Education, Boubekeur Benbouzid, announced that he was once again going to re-examine school textbooks, in particular in History and Islamic Education, and introduce more civic education. Benbouzid explicitly stated that the failure of teaching in schools to impregnate children with 'the love of the motherland' was part of the explanation for the 'black decade' in the 1990s.[47]

When I spoke to urban women about what they felt was 'missing' from their history, their most common response was the stories of rural women. For Saliha Djeffal: 'It should particularly not be forgotten that the national liberation struggle was led by peasants. Rural women helped the revolution 200 per cent, and we don't see them. And unfortunately they were not recognised after independence. And yet they certainly gave more than we could give.'[48] On the one hand, this is very much within the boundaries of the dominant version of the war, which emphasises the rural *maquis* as a mark of the deep-rooted authenticity of the struggle. On the other hand, Saliha expresses a sentiment that many well-known, or merely better-known-than-rural women veterans express, regardless of their political allegiances: they are uncomfortable with urban, educated women being foregrounded.

For Fadila Attia, 'We have forgotten a lot of women, the poor things. They gave so much, especially rural women in the countryside.' Fadila herself felt somewhat excluded from the circle of women in the bomb network who were imprisoned together:

> All these women from Barberousse, I didn't know them. I met them well after. I worked in anonymity, in secret. I was arrested but I was never put on trial, so I was unknown until 1984. It wasn't in '62 that I was recognised, it was in '84. Yacef Saadi said, 'There's one that's still missing, who was in the bomb network, who you don't know'. And it's like that for all the unknown women.[49]

This foregrounding of the same, well-known urban women is not something which these women themselves necessarily feel comfortable with. When I ask Djamila Boupacha what it is like to be one of the best-known historical actors of the War of Independence, frequently cited as a heroine, she tells me: 'I have always been [*she hesitates*] I don't like it. There are many other women who suffered more than we did and we don't know them. [On social occasions] I always want to be presented under my husband's name.'[50] Louisette Ighilahriz states that 'when there were actions [in the *maquis*], we fled. And the army, who did they find in the *douars*? Women, children, the elderly – they raped them, they beat them, they imprisoned them. They battered them and we fled. They were the guardians of the temple who bore the brunt of everything.'[51] The slogan 'one sole hero, the people' continues to resonate not just because it is promoted by the state but also because these women feel at ease within it.

These well-known women are much more comfortable with local recognition and respect from their neighbours. When giving me directions to her home on the telephone, Boupacha told me roughly how to get to her neighbourhood and then said to ask in the street 'for Djamila Boupacha'. Annie Steiner describes how people honked their horns at her in the street after the screening of *Barberousse, mes soeurs*.[52] El Hora Kerkeb talks about the television interviews she has given and how afterwards her neighbours knocked at her door: '"Mrs Kerkeb", they said "We didn't know that you were a *mujahida*".'[53] Fadila Attia states:

> I did my duty, I participated in the revolution neither to make money nor to write a book. I've done loads of interviews, which are well known, people know me, that's enough. You go right to the start [*she points in the direction of the beginning of her very large, working-class housing estate*] and you ask for 'the blonde *mujahida*' and they know where I live, even in the market there, and that is the real populace.[54]

This respect from 'ordinary people' is for many *mujahidat* the most valued form of recognition – it is seen as more genuine, more legitimate and with no obvious political or economic interest behind it. It is the ideal combination of anonymity and recognition.

This local recognition is also a reflection of how a reputation of 'being a *mujahida*' builds upon wider networks of social hierarchies and sociability. Djamila Bouazza explains that all her neighbours know her as a *mujahida*, she has lived in her house since independence. In fact, she adds, her roots in her neighbourhood in Algiers go back to the period before independence – her family, she explains, is from the area.[55] Her historical status fuses with the respect and status conferred on her as an older woman, a member of a well-known local family and a long-standing inhabitant. This underlines the importance of not limiting our understanding of commemoration to what is public and state-organised. We also need to explore how remembering the role of individuals interacts with pre-existing forms of social organisation and marks of respect.

The social occasions of memory

The way in which Djamila Bouazza relates to the public representation of her history exemplifies the importance of the social role
of the past. Mathaf al-Jaysh, the Museum of the Army, opened
in Algiers in June 1985. Upon entering the museum, if you turn
left and walk past the bronze statue of the Emir Abdelkader,
towards the section of the museum displaying the personal effects
of Boumediene – his car, items of clothing, gifts from other
statesmen – a glance upwards will reveal a striking stained glass
window. It depicts Algerians fighting for independence, including
soldiers and civilian demonstrators, and is dominated by the figure
of a woman who looks remarkably like Djamila Bouhired in her
youth. In the display cabinets below are enlarged versions of the
mug shots taken of Djamila Bouazza upon her arrest in 1957, full-
face and then in profile. The placard she was made to hold provides
the only explanatory caption: 'Djamila Bouazza: 92409 11.5.57.'
    Djamila Bouazza's life after independence was hard. Her
husband, Abboud Boussouf, also a veteran, opposed Boumediene's
coup d'état. He was arrested, tortured and imprisoned between
1966 and 1971, accused of plotting against the state. In the late
1970s and early 1980s, Boussouf travelled to the United Kingdom
to meet with Labour Members of Parliament as part of a Free Ben
Bella campaign – the former president was still under house arrest
in M'Sila, a town bordering the desert three hundred kilometres
south of Algiers.[56] Boussouf continued to be arrested, imprisoned
and then released only to be re-arrested throughout the 1980s.
    In 1967, Djamila Bouazza delivered by hand a letter to
Boumediene from her husband, seeking his release.[57] She describes
Boumediene politely receiving her, only to inform her 'That's not
how we do politics' – although this ambiguous phrase could have
been a reference to her husband's political opposition, rather than
her personal petitioning leaning on wartime ties. Boumediene did,
however, pay for the former combatant to be sent to a private clinic
in France for six months when, under the strain of secret police
raids on her home, government threats to expropriate her house
and the financial pressure of bringing up three children alone,
Djamila Bouazza's weight plummeted to a life-threatening forty
kilos. She says that she has destroyed all photographs of herself
from this period in order to forget.[58]

Abboud Boussouf also tried to employ his wife's revolutionary status in campaigning. In an eighteen-page pamphlet entitled *Une Caste au service de l'ancien colonisateur* (A caste in the service of the former coloniser), published on the symbolic date of 5 July 1987, Boussouf sought to draw on his wife's revolutionary credentials in a scathing critique of the political manipulation of the War of Independence by the state. Djamila Bouazza featured in a full-page photograph, which dated from the war, and was described as 'the first young woman condemned to death by the French military tribunals in Algeria after having made the *colons* [wealthy settlers] tremble by blowing up their palaces with explosives'. The pamphlet denounced the fact that she had subsequently been 'exiled in Europe by the former auxiliaries of the colonial army, who have become the masters of Algeria'.[59]

All of this is indicative of the ways in which Djamila Bouazza's image has been strategically used by herself and her husband since 1962, in oppositional activities against the political system. Therefore, when I interviewed her in 2005, I was interested in how she felt about her image being used in official commemorative practices. Djamila Bouazza told me that recently two men from the army had visited her, to ask for a photograph in order to make a portrait of her for the Museum of the Army. These kinds of oil paintings can be found dotted around the museum: many of them are of women, including women who died during the war such as Hassiba Ben Bouali, Ourida Meddad and Fadila Saadane, and some who survived, such as Djamila Boupacha, Djoher Akrour and Djamila Bouhired. The portraits are all painted from photographs taken around the time of the anti-colonial conflict.

I asked Djamila Bouazza why, given that her family had evidently suffered at the hands of 'the system', she had acquiesced in their request for a photograph. For Djamila Bouazza, the gesture of giving her photograph did not seem important. She hinted that she handed it over so she would be left in peace. Later in the interview, we returned to the question of official commemoration. Djamila said that she attended official commemorations. She showed me two medals which she had received, one given to her by Chadli, the other by Bouteflika in 2000. They were inscribed in classical Arabic, a language which Djamila doesn't read (she reads and writes French and speaks dialectical Arabic) – she explained that her attempts to learn *fusha* in prison were thwarted by prison guards destroying her papers. Again, when I tried to understand why Bouazza participated in award ceremonies, she suggested she was unwell and anxious about what might happen if she did not participate: 'They have hurt my family enough, they are hypocrites', 'I don't want to get involved', 'I'm not in good health'. She is still scared that 'they could take me away' and she has a dependent daughter to take care of.

Yet Djamila Bouazza's decision to participate in official ceremonies and commemorations does not straightforwardly seem to be one based on anxiety about the potential political consequences of not participating. Although her medals were not ostentatiously on display, she spontaneously showed them to me. When I presented to her an article from the official organ *El Moudjahid* describing *mujahidat* gathering every 1 November, she enthusiastically recognised it. She said that she gave the photograph to the journalist and pointed herself out to me in the picture. 'Like real sisters', she said: 'We don't forget each other'. She was pleased when I mentioned that in a previous interview three women who had been part of the *maquis* in the *wilaya* V had cited the 'three Djamilas' as their heroines, adding, 'I really like the girls [i.e. veterans] from Oran'.[60] She explained that, when she was in prison in France, she had met a number of women from Oran. Then, remembering both her time in prison and this western Algerian city prompted Djamila Bouazza to explain how, in the post-independence period when her husband was imprisoned, she had decided to leave Algiers for Oran without telling anyone, not even her parents. She found a group of former *mujahidat* all living in the same apartment block and she spent a peaceful few days with them. When I asked Djamila Bouazza whether she had been on any pilgrimages to wartime *lieux de mémoire*, she said that she had been back to Barberousse – to visit her incarcerated husband in the post-independence period.

In Djamila Bouazza's memories, places – cities and prisons – intertwine wartime and post-independence histories into a longer narrative of repression against her and her family. Her image as a war veteran was used, not always successfully, as a political weapon in opposition to the state after 1962. Yet, in contrast to these stories weaving back and forth across the colonial and post-colonial periods, the way in which she relates to her public memory is characterised by a series of compartmentalisations. The fact that the state is capable of selectively incorporating 'problematic' figures is hardly exceptional; the way in which Djamila Bouhired's defence team stigmatised Djamila Bouazza when both women were on trial in 1957 can be glossed over and her husband's post-independence oppositional activities can be forgotten. Djamila's engagement with public processes of commemoration is perhaps more surprising. Yet, whilst commemoration ceremonies are designed to be a forum for the legitimisation of the political system in place, Djamila Bouazza does not necessarily consider these ceremonies in such terms. Instead, she puts the emphasis on the social aspect – it is an opportunity to meet friends and also to have her social status as a *mujahida* valorised. In short, Djamila Bouazza makes a clear distinction between the political implications of such participation and the social aspect (in terms of sociability and social capital) that such reunions provide.

Of twenty-two interviewees who responded to the question 'Do you attend official ceremonies?', eleven said that they quite regularly went to such commemorations, two replied that they occasionally took up invitations, two responded that they were invited but chose not to go and seven said that they were never or only exceptionally invited. The seven women who were never invited included four out of five of rural interviewees, their war veteran status either not recognised or their role too anonymous to benefit from an official invitation. Most urban interviewees who received invitations for commemoration ceremonies did attend, although they were often very selective about the aspects of these ceremonies with which they chose to engage. Louisette Ighilahriz, who on the one hand might be considered a critical voice of the political system, on the other hand talks about her medals in the following terms: 'It warms my heart, yes, it makes me happy. I very much like receiving them.'[61] When I asked Fadila Attia if she attended many commemoration ceremonies, her reply was: 'Oh yes. Sometimes I have ten a month, other times I have one a week. Sometimes I can't go because I'm ill, and then I choose, I go to art exhibition previews, conferences, shows and receptions. It's a pleasant moment, and if it wasn't pleasant I wouldn't go. It keeps my mind active, it does me good.'[62]

Many interviewees appreciate being recognised even though they are not necessarily in agreement with the political system, enjoying the social aspect of such occasions whilst appearing to turn a deaf ear to the language of political legitimisation which surrounds them. Instead, these women integrate commemorative ceremonies into a longer-established calendar of social events and rites of passage – marriages, baccalaureate successes for younger family members, circumcisions – where they can meet up with women whom they fought with, or whom they were imprisoned alongside, drink tea, eat cake and reminisce.

The past as a socio-economic demand

Although none of the rural women I interviewed had ever attended a state commemoration ceremony, their wartime roles have not been forgotten in their families or in their local communities. Fatima Berci was presented to me by her neighbours in Agraradj as 'the leader of the *mujahidat*'. Ferroudja Amarouche's daughter and husband both sat in on the interview and contributed to her story. They added stories about women from the villages in and around the family home in Bouzeguene, even though her husband Tahar was not present at the time (he was in the *maquis* and then in prison) and their daughter was a tiny baby, thus indicating that they have told the stories amongst themselves many times before. Chérifa Akache's granddaughter persuaded her initially reluctant grandmother not to tell her story anonymously and instead use her real name. The poems that rural women spontaneously recited about the war during interviews clearly point to the construction and transmission of a historical narrative.[63] Among the poems women recited to me, the death and absence of sons and fathers after the war are central themes, as well as the role of mothers in explaining these absences to younger generations:

> The terrible war that was cruel
> That killed too many *mujahidin*
> A tomb without walls
> He says: 'Oh my beloved mother'
> I give myself to the grace of the Saints.

> It is said:[64] 'The daughter of the *mujahid* cries and doesn't want to eat her dinner'.
> She asks her mother: 'Oh mother, where is my father?'
> Her mother replies: 'Oh my daughter, your father died a *shahid*, only the Eternal remains'.
> It is said: 'The daughter of the *mujahid* cries and doesn't want to drink her coffee'.

She asks her mother: 'Oh mother, where is my father?'
She says to her: 'Oh my daughter, your father died a *shahid* but he
brought us freedom'.[65]

War memorials and cemeteries in the area surrounding the village
of Agraradj include the graves of women and men, with signs
inscribed in Arabic, Tamazight (written in Tifinagh script) and
French. The local secondary school, educating children from the
villages of Agraradj and Tamassit, is named after Omar Yermeche,
a relative of Fatma Yermeche who was killed during the war.
The memory of these interviewees then, is very much alive, and
it is also transmitted. Certainly, it is a fact that these women have
little place in the national narrative as individuals. Whereas the
most famous women from the urban guerrilla network have their
portraits in the Museum of the Mujahid or the Museum of the
Army, rural women – as well as 'non-famous' urban women – are
represented through a few black-and-white photographs with terse
captions, such as 'the participation of women in the 11 December
1960 demonstrations' or 'refugees'. Yet when these rural women
talk about being 'forgotten', as Chapters 1 and 3 began to explore,
they are not talking about being 'forgotten' from the national narrative of the past. Instead, what these women mean by being 'forgotten' is that their suffering and sacrifices in the struggle for Algerian
independence have not been recognised either through the specific
provision of a sufficient pension or through the general creation of
wealth and a welfare state. 'They give 15,000 dinars per trimester
(about €150), it's nothing', highlights Fatma Yermeche.[66]
    The need to be looked after and the failure of the state to fulfil
this need are powerfully expressed in the way rural interviewees
talk about their physical, and sometimes psychological, ailments.
Chérifa Akache states that since she was tortured with electricity she
cannot change a light bulb.[67] Ferroudja Amarouche describes trying
to escape the suffocating heat generated by all the cooking that she
did in secret for the *mujahidin* by taking snatched breaks outside in
the cold: 'That was when I started repeatedly having bronchitis, I
became asthmatic. I made couscous, doughnuts … and I had to do
it almost in the dark, I just used the light of the fire so that no one
could see me.'[68] Fatima Benmohand Berci talks about being given
a model of an Algerian flag to sew copies just before independence.
She puts the rheumatism she suffers from today down to sewing so

many.[69] One of the most powerful symbols of the Algerian nation – the flag – is still giving Fatima her aches and pains.

These *mujahidat*'s demands on the state go beyond individual pensions: they are also arguing for the sacrifice of communities to be recognised through benefits for the community ('by the people, for the people'). The perceived failure of the state to do this heightens the importance of the war story as a symbol of betrayal. Towards the end of my interview with Fatima Berci, I asked her if she had any regrets. Her response was an emphatic no, insisting, in French, '*jamais* [never]'. She then continued in Tamazight:

> But there are regrets because the action of Algeria was insufficient. We weren't expecting it to turn out like this. There are young people who have no work. When they want them to do the army [military service], they call upon young people, but there's no work afterwards. We need to wake up, we need to revolt against injustice even now. Our country is rich but the wealth is eaten up by those who are there [in power]. The cost of living is high. The man who has seven children and doesn't have a job what is he meant to do? Let them throw the people into the sea, and those who rule can stay.[70]

Khadjidja Belguembour has discovered the very concrete meaning of 'being forgotten' during regular visits which she has made since the mid-1960s to the remote villages in the Constantine region which she had passed through as a *maquisarde*:

> KB: Sometimes it doesn't go well, because [the villagers] say, 'Well, you lived with us, we sheltered you, we watched over you, we fed you, we gave you the blankets of our children and the food of our children, and after '62 we never saw you again. We are here in the same misery as during the war of national liberation.'
> NV: When they say, 'We never saw you again', who are they referring to?
> KB: They are talking in general, all the historic leaders, the organisers […] At the start it doesn't go well, but I always manage to bring them round in the end, I explain certain problems, that it's not the men that they knew, who they sheltered, who [today] run the country to give them their rights. And it's like that – sometimes it's hard to convince them.

During the civil violence of the 1990s, Khadjidja was forced to stop her trips. In 2002, she says that she 'took all the risks' to go back, despite police at roadblocks, concerned for her safety, pleading with her not to drive on. She describes finding people she knew, including a woman who worked for the *mujahidin*, whose husband had been killed. She met the *garde champêtre* (rural guard / forest ranger) and through their discussion they discovered that it was his mother who was one of the women who cooked for Khadjidja. Together, Khadjidja and the *garde champêtre* visited the different places in the village where she had hidden, looked for wood or fetched water:

> I hadn't forgotten anything, although I can't walk like I used to. Afterwards, other women came, the wives of *mujahidin*, they came around me with their children. I cried because I saw that they've never known independence: they have no roads, they don't have running water in their homes, they don't have gas, they have nothing for their children. That is what disappointed me the most. [*She pauses*] I had forgotten nothing, nothing, not the smallest detail.[71]

This is what Khadjidja, and these rural women, mean by being 'forgotten': it is not their absence from national days, monuments, museums or school textbooks. Instead, 'being forgotten' refers to the absence of the socio-economic improvement that independence was expected to bring, despite the promises of wartime discourse and the optimism of the 1960s and 1970s.

The past as a dangerous place

Yet some forgetting is necessary. Maintaining a sanitised, glorified image of the war is not just a way to make political or socioeconomic demands in the present, or a guarantee of national unity or a means to ensure that reminiscing remains an enjoyable social occasion. Forgetting can also be a form of defence against dangerous memories.

Many of the women whom I interviewed are surrounded by their own history. They live not far from places where they were tortured and incarcerated. They are exposed to increasing numbers of commemoration ceremonies, books, press articles, films and television documentaries. Louisette Ighilahriz says that she tries to avoid passing by Paradou-Hydra, the garrison where she was imprisoned and tortured.[72] For Khadjidja Belguembour, 'What does it for me, is when I see a documentary on television about the war. I sleep badly and I have nightmares.'[73] When I ask Chérifa Akache if she watches films or documentaries about the war, she replies: 'I watch them, and when I watch them I cry. When they take away her son in the film, it was exactly like that.'[74] Chérifa Akache is referring to Mohamed-Lakhdar Hamina's 1966 film *Le Vent des Aurès / Rih al-awaras*, the story of a rural woman desperately but determinedly visiting a series of French army camps in a search for her son, who has been arrested. The main part is played by the celebrated Algerian actress Keltoum (Aïcha Ajouri), who largely acts out the role through her body language and facial expressions rather than through spoken dialogue, and, for Berberophone Chérifa, this makes this Arabic-language film accessible.

Fatima Benmohand Berci says she avoid watching documentaries: 'I don't like to. I refuse to watch them because it hurts too much to remember bad times. It hasn't left my eyes, the images are still there, the terrible things that happened, what I saw.' And yet when I ask her if she talks about the war often she replies with a French '*bien sûr* [of course]'. She continues in Tamazight: 'We gather together like we're doing now, we talk about what France did. We also talk about the actions of the *mujahidin*, it's our pride.'[75] These interviewees suggest that there is a certain visual, public memory which is particularly painful for them to confront because it evokes memories which they cannot always control.

All topics in oral interviews have codes, meaning that they have to be talked about in certain ways. Relations between men and women in the independence struggle have to be talked about in a certain way, with the insistence on brothers and sisters; summer 1962 has to be talked about in a certain way, with the insistence on not profiteering from the disorder; Boumediene has to be talked about in a certain way, with the insistence on economic development rather than political oppression. The gendered violence to which women were subjected is so taboo, both socially and culturally, that it has to be talked about using a very specific set of codes.

The number of Algerian women raped following arrest or during raids on villages during the War of Independence is extremely difficult to quantify. The wartime diary of Mouloud Feraoun suggests that rape was commonplace in Kabylia, notably during the huge military operations launched in 1959 as part of the Plan Challe. The historian Raphaëlle Branche also argues that rape was widespread, if not systematic.[76] Outside of the context of war, victims of rape would have been considered by their communities to be as guilty as the perpetrators of the crime, and ostracised accordingly. However, when Feraoun wonders in his wartime diary what will happen to raped women in the Ouadhias (Kabylia), he says the men will not cut the throats of their 'dishonoured daughters' – there are, after all, simply far too many.[77] In a case study of villages in the commune of Iflissen in Kabylia in 1969, the ethnographer Camille Lacoste-Dujardin confirmed Feraoun's hypothesis: 'They have chosen to forget. Not only have husbands not divorced, and the young girls rapidly married, but they also tried to get the victims to abort, so that no child would be born of these rapes.'[78]

This direct vocabulary is not that which women employ themselves to speak about such subjects. The women in the village of Agraradj, however, do make it understood that the women who had 'suffered' were not rejected by the community. According to Fatima Berci: 'There were some young girls who had their honour [*esser*] taken'.[79] Fatima Benmohand Berci describes one particular incident in the village of Agraradj:

> I can remember what happened in this village, I don't know about other places. One time the village was bombed by France, they burned the whole village. My mother had sent me to get something. I came back with another woman, and when we got back, we started running in all directions so we wouldn't be taken by the French. In the end they didn't catch us. The other women were taken, and they took them into the ravine and they did a monstrosity to them.[80]

This 'monstrosity' is a euphemism for rape. Yet whilst rape is spoken of through euphemisms and anonymous stories that happened to other women, other forms of sexual humiliation are dealt with quite differently by the women of Agraradj. Fatma Yermeche and Fatima Berci together recount an incident in which the French army, having caught a group of women, including Fatma's sister, and one man bringing supplies for the *mujahidin* to a nearby forest, stripped all nine and forced them to walk back to the village naked. This punishment was particularly cruel given that the French soldiers would have been well aware of the modesty of women in the region – even making them take off the belt that they traditionally wear was humiliating. Yet when the two women tell this story, they do so laughing, inciting the hilarity of the other women listening. The account even has a punch line, when the male neighbour takes a branch from a tree and tells the women, 'My sisters, you can go in

front or you can follow on behind, we're not going back together'.[81]
Unlike rape, these kinds of humiliations are judged by those who
recount them as safe enough to talk about, as long as they are presented in the form of a comic sketch to a restricted, female-only
audience.

The euphemisms that women use and the silences they keep
are the same conventions that the raped women themselves were
expected to conform to by their families, local communities and
wider society, whether these women were rural or urban and
regardless of their social background. The rape of women was – and
is – part of the official narrative of colonial barbarity, but in this
narrative victims are always usually dead, or, more often, anonymous. Louisette Ighilahriz was able to talk about her brutal and
repeated rape at the hands of the French army only after the death
of her father and when her mother was no longer mentally able to
understand. She says she does not know whether her father knew
about what happened to her: 'Mum knew. Did she tell Dad? It's the
big question.'[82] This in part explains why when, in 2000, Louisette
chose to speak out publicly against the torture and rape she was
subjected to during the war, it was problematic both for her former
sisters-in-arms and for her family.

On 20 June 2000, just a few days after President Bouteflika had
made a historic state visit to France, an interview by the French
journalist Florence Beaugé with Louisette Ighilahriz made front-
page news in the French daily *Le Monde*. Her account of the pro-
longed and sadistic torture – and later, it emerged, rape – which
she had suffered at the hands of the French army during the 1957
'Battle of Algiers' created a media storm. Long-retired French army
generals nearing the end of their lives agreed to be interviewed.
Jacques Massu confessed to and regretted the use of torture under
his command, Paul Aussaresses admitted to and justified torture as
an interrogation technique, Marcel Bigeard and Maurice Schmitt
vigorously denied all accusations against them and the men under
their command.[83] Other Algerian victims of torture also spoke out
and were interviewed in the French and Algerian press. Zhor Zerari
and Malika Koriche also accused General Schmitt of brutal torture
in *Le Monde*.[84] In 2002, Louisette Ighilahriz instigated a court case
against General Schmitt after he denounced her autobiography as
'a web of fabrications and untruths' in a television programme.[85]
She was awarded a symbolic €1 in October 2003, which she lost

on appeal in November 2005 as Schmitt benefited from an earlier amnesty law. As a result of media interest in her story, in 2001 Ighilahriz published her memoirs, *Algérienne.*

Louisette Ighilahriz's story gave renewed impetus to a French *retour de mémoire* about a war which, as a nation, it had long sought to forget.[86] In Algeria, her story provoked a different set of reactions. The Algerian press participated in the debate, but the Algerian state was conspicuously non-committal. Despite usually seeking to capitalise on popular anti-colonialism, the Algerian army's own 'dirty war' against the Islamist challenge was all too recent. The story resonated differently for younger generations. A member of Rassemblement Actions Jeunesse (Rally for Youth Action, RAJ), created in 1993, told me that after the publication of Louisette Ighilahriz's account, when he used to see her in the street – they live in the same area of Algiers – he would go up to her and wordlessly kiss her hand, out of respect, for having the courage to tell such a difficult story. The 1988 generation, to which the founders of RAJ belong, had also been subject to brutal repression by the Algerian state and forms of sexual torture which are socially and culturally taboo and against which they had few, if any, forms of legal redress.

Yet not all of Louisette Ighilahriz's fellow *mujahidat* appreciated her sudden public prominence. Amongst female veterans, some seemed to resent the foregrounding of her personal story in what had largely been an anonymous collective history. She was perceived by some to have broken the taboo 'one sole hero, the people'. When I interviewed her in 2005, Fettouma Ouzegane went as far as claiming that Louisette Ighilahriz's limp and walking stick were the result of a car crash, not an injury sustained in the *maquis,*[87] although in 2011 Fettouma Ouzegane was at the forefront of the campaign to defend Louisette from claims by Yacef Saadi that she had invented her involvement in the Algiers bomb network.

In addition to this resentment of her newfound – albeit undesired – fame, Louisette Ighilahriz says that many women found it hard to accept that she had publicly spoken about being raped. Ighilahriz says her husband encouraged her to speak out, but other members of her family had greater difficulty accepting her stance, including her children. When Ighilahriz was invited in 2002 to participate in a French documentary on torture and rape during the war,[88] she says that a number of other female veterans initially agreed to join their testimony with hers. Ighilahriz then describes these women as backing out, because, she says, they were put under pressure from their disapproving families: 'I found myself alone. They let me drop. It was very hard. They let me be taken for a liar.'[89]

It seemed intrusive to ask Louisette Ighilahriz who these other women were, so their reasons for dropping out of the documentary cannot be cross-referenced. However, the desire to keep rape and extreme violence silenced is revealed in a telling exchange which I had with Djamila Bouazza. Djamila is friends with Louisette Ighilahriz. She says that she knew little about her war story until she read *Algérienne*, as they were not together in prison. 'I didn't know that all that happened to her', Djamila Bouazza told me. I asked her if reading Louisette Ighilahriz's autobiography was a shock. She said that it was, and that she had telephoned Louisette immediately after finishing the book. I waited, expectantly, thinking that Djamila was going to tell me that she had not known about the violence Louisette had been subjected to, or that reading about it on paper had been a shock. But instead she simply stated that she had not known that her friend had been sent to Corsica under house arrest after her release from prison in metropolitan France.[90]

During my group interview in Algiers with Habiba Chami, El Hora Kerkeb and Yamina Salem, Habiba Chami passed around a photo of the three women in the *maquis*. They laughed loudly, even though, as Habiba then explained, they had been crying that day, hungry and miserable. For Yamina Salem, there is a clear demarcation between what can be talked about and what is too painful to evoke: 'I don't talk much about the war to my children, I don't know why I'm talking so much today. [*She laughs*] Generally, I don't talk [about the war]. I don't know where to start, and there is a part of it which has remained rooted inside me, the hardest, biggest bits and at the same time, I think about that part all the time.'[91] The really painful part of women's memories is a lonely place: others may sympathise but no one wants to share. This is not about refusing to address a hidden trauma – these women know exactly what their most painful memories are. Instead, it is about individuals setting up boundaries, and seeking to maintain them as far as possible, in order to avoid what could be personally and socially dangerous for them to unpack in front of an audience, be that in public, amongst their former sisters-in-arms or within their families.

Conclusion

The participation of Algerian women in the War of Independence has generated stories which have been remembered, celebrated, politicised or pointedly forgotten at many different levels of society – within families, communities, regions and at state level. Rather than seeing the production of a national narrative on women at war as a top-down process, we need to examine how female veterans and other members of society participate in practices of remembering the past. By foregrounding the economic, social and personal as well as political consequences of remembering and forgetting, we gain a much richer understanding of what is commonly termed memory politics.

For many interviewees, their status as a *mujahida* fuses with other marks of social standing which they may have acquired before the war, as members of locally well-known, or long-established, families, or subsequently, as they became mothers and grandmothers. When these women get together to talk about the war with other villagers, former cellmates or fellow *maquisardes*, mostly in the home, but sometimes over the tea and cake provided at an academic roundtable or at an official commemoration ceremony, these women's stories are the basis of real – as well as imagined – communities. These communities have unwritten codes about what can be said, how it should be said and what needs to be left unsaid in order for women to maintain their composure both as individuals and as group members.

At state level, 'women in the war' has been a marginalised and rarefied but nevertheless constituent element of the Algerian national narrative since 1962. The language used to describe women in public, state-sponsored discourse has shifted, as the 1960s narrative of 'women in socialist construction as the logical continuation of the anti-colonial struggle' became, in the context of civil violence in Algeria and a dominant international lexicon of victimhood and reparation in the 1990s, a story of 'martyrised women as the ultimate symbol of French and Islamist barbarity'.

Beyond a specifically gendered perspective and these not always subtle shifts in attributed official meanings, the War of Independence has proved a consistently reliable source of metaphors about solidarity, unity and fairness. These metaphors have been also used, ever since the crisis of summer 1962, to formulate political criticisms of independent Algeria. The War of Independence is celebrated as a moment of fraternity and equality, an unflattering mirror held up to present. Yet at the same time, adhesion to these metaphors creates a shared space. Statements and references made in contemporary Algeria about the war might be oppositional in intent, but they have been so widely repeated that they have become part of the lexicon of dominant history, a kind of conformist counter-history. In a nation built on the myth of one and a half million martyrs, historical 'controversies' and new or shocking 'revelations' allow political debate to take place within socially safe boundaries, a reassuringly familiar common framework.

When campaigning against the state as 'the *mujahidat*', urban, educated veterans are sometimes described as employing a double-edged sword. On the one hand, by underlining their historical role in fighting for liberation they increase their chances of being listened to. On the other hand, they risk suggesting that rights are earned, rather than inalienable, and they remain constrained by this symbolic language.[92] But we can also look at this use of the past in contemporary political debate in another way: 'the *mujahidat*' are not just forced to evoke the war as a last-ditch attempt to make themselves heard. They also evoke the war because this allows them to make a series of critiques of the current political system, which presents itself as the legitimate heir of 1954–62, without undermining the social importance of 1954–62 as the foundation block of Algerian society.

Official slogans such as 'one sole hero, the people' and 'by the people, for the people' may attract little attention in official speeches, emblazoned on public buildings or on the masthead of the daily newspaper *El Moudjahid*. Yet these slogans are profoundly engrained in the way in which interviewees of all backgrounds talk about the war and postwar: they are reflected in suspicion of the (too) publicly visible *mujahid*, the emphasis on collective above individual action, the perception that the majority who fought have been forgotten by the few who benefited, or the insistence on the need to tell the war story as a socially useful lesson for younger generations. These are powerful narrative frames, inexorably entwined with interviewees' own personal histories. In the headquarters of the FLN in the wealthy Algiers district of Hydra, Saliha Djeffal underlines the impossibility, for her, of breaking from certain frames, however imperfect the readings of the past they might give:

NV: Do you have any heroines from the war period?
SD: You know, the slogan of the Algerian revolution, was 'One sole hero, the people.' But for me, I have to say, that when I was young, when I was in France, we learnt of the arrest of Djamila Bouhired. Djamila Bouhired remains for me a symbol. Not a heroine, a symbol.
NV: So for you, 'one sole hero, the people' remains –
SD [*interrupting*]: Yes, for me that's something I believed in when I was fifteen years old. To call that into question is to call into question a whole trajectory. And I don't want to do that.[93]

Notes

1 *Alger républicain* (19 March 1963).
2 For example, Zhor Zerari's series of special reports on oil exploitation in the Sahara, published in *Le Peuple* (17–18, 20–2, 24–9 and 2 March 1964).
3 *El Moudjahid* (1 November 1966).
4 *El Moudjahid* (31 October 1969).
5 *El Moudjahid* (2 November 1976).
6 *El Moudjahid* (2 November 1967).
7 Harbi, *L'Islamisme dans tous ses états*, p. 136.
8 *El Moudjahid* (1 November 1974).
9 N. Driss, 'L'Irruption de Makkam Ech-Chahid dans le paysage algérois, monument et vulnérabilité des representations', *L'Homme et la société*, 146 (2002), 61–76; C. Chaulet-Achour, 'Un espace nouveau dans la cité: réalisation et inscription littéraire de Riad el Feth à Alger', *Francofonía*, 8 (1999), 157–71.
10 *El Moudjahid* (5 July 1982).
11 For example, see *El Moudjahid* on 1 November 1984 for the stories of women living of in the villages of Ighzer Amokrane in Kabylia, and *El Moudjahid* on 20 August 1987 and 1 November 1987 respectively for the eyewitness accounts of *maquisardes* Meriem Mokhtari and Baya Elkehla (Toumia Laribi).
12 *El Moudjahid* (5 July 1982).
13 *El Moudjahid* (8 March 1982).
14 'Yassef Saadi, pourquoi vous avez oublié Djamila Bouhired?', www.youtube.com/watch?v=8oy-12P2tTY. Uploaded on 15 December 2009 by the user carinalina2001; by June 2014, the video had more than 52,000 views (accessed 20 June 2014).
15 *El Moudjahid* (2 November 1976).
16 *Le Matin* (11–12 August 2000).
17 *El Moudjahid* (2 November 1976).
18 Interview with Khadjidja Belguembour (14 June 2005).

19 *El Moudjahid* (1 November 1991).
20 In 2010, 47.9 per cent of the Algerian population was under the age of 24 and only 4.7 per cent over the age of 65 – that is to say, of an age where they could have credibly played a role in the War of Independence. United Nations, *World Population Prospects 2010: The 2012 Revision, Volume II: Demographic Profiles*, http://esa.un.org/unpd/wpp/Demographic-Profiles/pdfs/12.pdf (accessed 6 May 2014).
21 Interview with Fadila Attia (19 June 2005).
22 For example, on 8 May 2012, Bouteflika made a speech in Sétif in which he repeatedly stated that his generation was finished (*djili tab djnanou*) and that after fifty years in power young people needed to take over from the war generation. *L'Expression* (9 May 2012).
23 Interview with Malika Koriche (18, 21 and 22 December 2005).
24 Interview with Khadjidja Belguembour (14 June 2005).
25 Amrane, *Les Femmes algériennes dans la guerre*, p. 14.
26 *Ibid.*, p. 272.
27 El Korso, 'Une double realité pour un même vécu', pp. 100–1.
28 Taleb Ibrahimi, 'Les Algériennes et la guerre de libération nationale', p. 314.
29 Interview with Khaoula Taleb Ibrahimi (5 March 2007).
30 Enloe, *Bananas, Beaches and Bases*, p. 61.
31 Meynier, *Histoire intérieure du FLN*, p. 227.
32 By the mid-1970s, the Centre National d'Etudes Historiques (National Centre for Historical Studies, CNEH) had the oversight and approval of all historical research. See Stora, *La Gangrène et l'oubli*, p. 229. Control over historical production has continued even with the introduction of pluralism and the free press. For example, the Centre National d'Etudes et de la Recherche sur le Mouvement National et la Révolution du Premier Novembre, founded in 1994, is under the aegis of the Ministry of Mujahidin. Officials from the Ministries of Research, Culture, Education and Defence all sit on its board. See Branche, 'The martyr's torch', p. 434.
33 Mouvement National de Solidarité et de Soutien à la Lutte des Femmes, 'Objectifs' (c. 2005) (documentation provided by Fettouma Ouzegane).
34 Interview with Fettouma Ouzegane (6 June 2005).
35 The tension between historical methods and approaches and contemporary political, legal and media demands for clear-cut judgements was demonstrated in France in 1997, when the French resistance heroes Lucie and Raymond Aubrac tried to rally historians to defend them from accusations that they had betrayed Jean Moulin to the Gestapo in 1943. The Aubracs sought to clear their names by organising a panel of historians at the office of French daily newspaper *Libération*. The meeting was unsatisfactory for all concerned, as the historians struggled

to scientifically interrogate and cross-reference the memories of the two resisters. See H. Rousso, 'Peut-on faire l'histoire du temps présent?', *L'Histoire*, 384 (2013), p. 8.

36 House and Macmaster, *Paris 1961*, p. 11.

37 Ighilahriz, *Algérienne*, p. 248.

38 Interview with Louisette Ighilahriz (8 June 2005).

39 Fortunately for my research, what interviewees said about whom they preferred to speak to and what they thought they should say was not always the same as whom they spoke to and what they spoke about in practice.

40 Interview with Annie Steiner (22 June 2005).

41 *Barberousse, mes soeurs* (Hassan Bouabdellah, 1985).

42 *L'Expression* (18 April 2012).

43 Interview with Fatima Berci (16 June 2005).

44 Interview with Fadéla M'Rabet (1 November 2005).

45 Interview with El Hora Kerkeb, Habiba Chami and Yamina Salem (1 June 2005).

46 Interview with Fadila Attia (19 June 2005).

47 *El Watan* (18 March 2007).

48 Interview with Saliha Djeffal (21 June 2005).

49 Interview with Fadila Attia (19 June 2005).

50 Interview with Djamila Boupacha (11 June 2005).

51 Interview with Louisette Ighilahriz (8 June 2005).

52 Interview with Annie Steiner (22 June 2005).

53 Interview with El Hora Kerkeb (1 June 2005).

54 Interview with Fadila Attia (19 June 2005).

55 Interview with Djamila Bouazza (3 and 9 June 2005).

56 A report of Boussouf's visit to the UK was published in *The Times* (12 June 1980), alongside a photograph of Boussouf and Ben Bella.

57 Letter to President Boumediene (15 February 1967) (Private papers Abboud Boussouf).

58 Interview with Djamila Bouazza (3 and 9 June 2005).

59 *Une caste au service de l'ancien colonisateur* [pamphlet] (5 July 1987) (Private papers Abboud Boussouf).

60 Interview with Djamila Bouazza (3 and 9 June 2005).

61 Interview with Louisette Ighilahriz (8 June 2005).

62 Interview with Fadila Attia (19 June 2005).

63 There is a very long tradition of oral poetry in the region of Kabylia which has been studied by linguists, anthropologists and literature experts, and not least by the celebrated novelist and intellectual Mouloud Mammeri. Whilst some poets became well-known authors, Salem Chaker underlines that the large-scale poetic production which characterised the War of Independence was largely feminine and

anonymous. Each village would have its own creators, and traditional forms would be adapted into rhyming verse, epic poems, songs and satirical skits, which have subsequently been transmitted through repeated recitals. See S. Chaker, 'Une tradition de résistance et de lutte: la poésie berbère kabyle, un parcours poétique', *Revue du monde musulman de la Méditerrannée*, 51 (1989), 11–31.

64 This is a form of poem in Kabylia which begins each line with a phrase which is broadly equivalent to 'he said / she said', translated here as 'it is said'. This structure calls upon the audience to listen by indicating that a poem will follow.

65 With thanks to Lydia Aït Saadi-Bouras for her translations of these two poems.

66 Interview with Fatma Yermeche (16 June 2005).

67 Interview with Chérifa Akache (21 June 2005).

68 Interview with Ferroudja Amarouche (10 December 2005).

69 Interview with Fatima Benmohand Berci (17 June 2005).

70 Interview with Fatima Berci (16 June 2005).

71 Interview with Khadjidja Belguembour (14 June 2005).

72 Interview with Louisette Ighilahriz (8 June 2005).

73 Interview with Khadjidja Belguembour (14 June 2005).

74 Interview with Chérifa Akache (21 June 2005).

75 Interview with Fatima Benmohand Berci (17 June 2005).

76 R. Branche, 'Des viols pendant la guerre d'Algérie', *Vingtième siècle*, 75 (2002), 123–32.

77 Feraoun, *Journal 1955–1962*, p. 185.

78 Lacoste-Dujardin, *Opération Oiseau bleu*, p. 158.

79 'Honour' is used here to translate the term '*esser*'. Pierre Bourdieu describes *esser* as 'the secret, the prestige, the radiance, the "glory", the "presence"' in 'The sentiment of honour in Kabyle Society', in J. G. Peristiany (ed.), *Honour and Shame: The Values of Mediterranean Society* (Chicago: Chicago University Press, 1966), p. 217.

80 Interview with Fatima Berci (16 June 2005).

81 Interviews with Fatma Yermeche and Fatima Berci (16 June 2005). This is a theme developed in N. Vince, 'Transgressing boundaries: gender, race, religion and "Françaises musulmanes" during the Algerian War of Independence', *French Historical Studies*, 33:3 (2010), 445–74.

82 Interview with Louisette Ighilahriz (8 June 2005).

83 Massu and Bigeard interviewed in *Le Monde* (22 June 2000); Aussaresses and Massu interviewed in *Le Monde* (23 November 2000); Massu interviewed in *Le Figaro* (15 June 2001). See also P. Aussaresses, *Services spéciaux, Algérie 1955–1957: mon témoignage sur la torture* (Paris: Perrin, 2001).

84 *Le Monde* (15 June 2001 and 19 March 2005). Malika Koriche was also interviewed for *Pièces à conviction* (France 3, 27 June 2001).

85 *Culture et dépendances* (France 3, 6 March 2002).

86 The reopening of the torture debates, and Louisette Ighilahriz's role in this, have received significant academic attention, in addition to the public debate which they provoked. The journalist who initially interviewed Louisette, Florence Beaugé, has published a comprehensive account of the media debate and political reaction in *Algérie: une guerre sans gloire: histoire d'une enquête* (Paris: Calmann-Lévy, 2005).

87 Interview with Fettouma Ouzegane (6 June 2005).

88 The documentary was screened as 'Viol, le dernier tabou de la guerre d'Algérie', by V. Gaget and P. Jasselin, *Envoyé Spécial* (France 2, 7 February 2002).

89 Interview with Louisette Ighilahriz (8 June 2005).

90 Interview with Djamila Bouazza (3 and 9 June 2005).

91 Interview with Yamina Salem (1 June 2005).

92 Gadant argues: 'The status of women finds itself hostage to, on the one hand, a religious, conservative and unequal representation, and, on the other hand, the conception that merit is linked to rights, putting these women under the constant obligation to prove their patriotism and their refusal of Westernisation'. M. Gadant, 'Nationalité et citoyenneté, les femmes algériennes et leurs droits', *Peuples méditerranéens*, 44–5 (1988), 293–337, p. 307.

93 Interview with Saliha Djeffal (21 June 2005).

Conclusion

This book has sought to interweave a history of what happened to women who participated in the War of Independence after 1962 with an examination of how these female veterans have constructed, mobilised or marginalised their memories of the anti-colonial conflict at different points across the same period. The study of both post-independence history and the place of memory within this history has in turn provided insights into how these women participated in or related to the language and practical tasks of state- and nation-building. Exploring the intersections between discourses about women and interviewees' lived experiences, and between 'official' and 'vernacular' memory, this book has aimed to go beyond a vision of Algerian women after 1962 being 'sent back into the kitchen' and forgotten from history. Instead, what emerges is a story of the contradictions and compromises of state- and nation-building after decolonisation and an account of how nationalist narratives can be deconstructed, fragmented and reconstructed in new forms without necessarily losing their symbolic power.

This story of post-colonial contradictions and compromises demands that we pay closer attention to how Algerian history has been periodised, not only in terms of the chronological division of time but also in terms of the moral judgements brought to bear on each period. Discussions of post-independence Algerian history have often been articulated in a language of 'when did it all go wrong?' The year 1962 is the most common response to this question, although 1965, 1979, 1984 or 1992 are also often put forward. Closer examination of women's war stories reveals 1962 to be a deceptive chronological marker. Firstly, the war stories of many interviewees ended not with formal Algerian independence but with the end of their active engagement. For the rural women

I interviewed, this was 1959–60 after the Jumelles operation. For many urban women in the bomb network, this was 1957–8, when they were captured, tried and imprisoned. Some women might talk about prison, but the latest chronological point which they will spontaneously advance to is often long before March 1962, when they were released from prison as a result of the Evian Accords. Secondly, whilst independence in 1962 presented significant opportunities as well as new challenges for some interviewees, there were also important continuities which had a determining effect on women's postwar lives. In short, if you had an education, the possibilities for social advancement were far greater than if you did not. The year 1962 nevertheless marked a major shift in how interviewees of all social backgrounds saw their relationship to the state: they had moved from a colonial state to which they owed nothing and of which they expected nothing to a post-colonial state to which everything was owed, and of which much was expected.

In the 1960s and 1970s, the Algerian state, as many other African and Middle Eastern countries at this time, tried to reimagine the boundaries of the nation through the image, rights and roles of women. A repressive, patriarchal state which has sought to instrumentalise women, and a socially conservative society, have both undeniably characterised post-independence Algeria. Yet we also need to bring some light and shade to this assessment. In this period, there was not a straightforward confrontation between 'tradition' and 'modernity'. Indeed, conservative religious visions and Marxist revolutionary zeal could find common ground: this would be a 'serious' revolution. Educated women sought to appropriate this language, as well as insisting on gender-neutral citizenship, to try to jump over the gender gap. Like many men of their generation, these educated women also shared in the enthusiasm of rebuilding Algeria as a model for the Third World.

This again raises the question of chronology. When was this 'lost'? Not after Boumediene's coup in 1965, perhaps not even after Chadli came to power in 1979. The Family Code in 1984 marked an important symbolic rupture with the state and gender-neutral citizenship. At this point, a group of urban, educated female veterans became 'the *mujahidat*', fashioning themselves as a symbol against state repression and reactionary, patriarchal politics. As these women realigned their life stories to a new political era, a feminist version of the nationalist genealogy was born. At the same time, the rupture with the state's nationalist narrative was never complete. Listening to these interviewees talk, there is not one clear moment when working to construct the nation-state metamorphosed into fighting the state in the name of an excluded nation. For rural interviewees, 'those that rule' always remain distant and remote, but they still make demands of the state: evidence, however tenuous, of a form of social contract.

The fact that women's oral histories reveal the messy situations of both war and post-colonial state- and nation-building is what makes it so significant that, at the same time, interviewees also reproduce homogenising myths. Interviewees can both recount their complicated lived experiences and decontextualise the past to extract its symbolic value. The War of Independence remains a key metaphor of unity, equality and solidarity, a benchmark against which all subsequent events are measured, and thus a powerful political tool. It provides the basis upon which repose many of the binaries that structure contemporary political language: during the war / after the war; interior army / exterior army; true/false *mujahidin*; patriot/*harki*; authentic/foreign.

This is a language familiar not only to those who participated in the war but also to those who do not have direct experience of it. In 2007, I used a mixture of interviews and questionnaires to survey ninety-five trainee teachers in their early twenties at the Ecole Normale Supérieure (teacher training college, ENS) in Bouzaréah, Algiers, exploring how they understood different representations of the *mujahidat* during and after the war which they had – or had not – been exposed to through school textbooks, state discourse, the media and family stories.[1] The study revealed a number of similarities in how this younger generation and veteran interviewees frame the War of Independence.

Firstly, across generations, informants can be both believers and sceptics. They can reproduce abstract, idealised images about women's respected and valued wartime roles, whilst simultaneously casting doubt on the veracity of these myths through accounts of their own experiences or the experiences of women they know. Secondly, students simultaneously promoted the need for a more objective ('historical') history and a more patriotic ('citizen-forming') history. They shared with older generations the desire to maintain a glorified image of 'the war' as a noble, collective endeavour, whilst at the same time demanding to discover a 'true' version of the past. Across generations, the desire to be inclusive co-exists alongside the belief that being able to definitively identify 'real' and 'false' patriots, and exclude the latter, would strengthen the unity and wellbeing of the nation.

There were also some key differences between the way in which these students saw the *mujahidat* and the way in which interviewees see themselves, or, indeed, the way in which the first post-independence generation of Algerian female academics write about the *mujahidat*. In an era of resurgent religious forms of identification and social conservatism in Algeria and beyond, whilst some students adopted the feminist version of the *mujahida* as warrior woman, many other students had a much more conservative image of female veterans, which they used as a tool of moral and social control to condemn the supposed Westernisation of younger generations of Algerian women. Women who participated in the anti-colonial struggle were not only sanctified as national heroines by these students, they were also reimagined as saintly ancestors in a much more literal, religious sense, and relocated in an abstract and atemporal framework of ideas about licit and illicit social organisation, religious sacrifice and cultural authenticity. Students' image of the *mujahidat* thus encapsulates James Fentress and Chris Wickham's argument that 'the way memories of the past are generated and understood by given social groups is a direct guide to how they understand their position in the present'.[2] These students participate in the dominant societal discourse – on the importance and glory of the war in the nation's narrative of itself – and at the same time transform aspects of this narrative to fit with the changed context of their own time.

The endurance of the War of Independence as a structuring metaphor owes much to its flexibility. It remains relevant and meaningful not because of fifty-year-old 'unhealed wounds' but because it is constantly evolving, incorporating transnational and new national references into its basic framework and language of sovereignty versus foreign interference; the people versus the power; morality versus immorality (or the licit versus the illicit); 'real' versus 'false' problems. A political language of dichotomies should not distract us from the fact that these oppositions work because they are part of the same whole. The war is of course not the only frame of reference in contemporary Algeria, even less so a guarantee of social stability. But emphasising the way in which it creates a shared language, shared for the very reason that it can mean different things to different individuals and groups, is an important counterpoint to claims that Algeria is locked in an endless crisis of self-discovery and self-destruction, or a stereotypical depiction of an omnipresent Algerian national past promoted by a self-serving elite disconnected from the uninterested, dispossessed masses. This shared language is what makes the War of Independence both a location of political contestation and a form of social glue. Ferocious debates might take place about the winners and losers of independence, its rightful heirs and usurping imposters, but this is within a collectively appropriated framework which does not question the role of the war as the founding block of post-independence society. This framework allows people to contest the established order, without taking it apart.

The language of the war no longer guarantees loyalty to the political system which has sought to capitalise on it for the past fifty years, but it still links citizens to each other. This might seem an unconvincing claim in a society dominated demographically, if not politically, by young people who are often described as uninterested in the war and disillusioned with politics. But the real test of the power of a dominant societal discourse is when individuals reproduce it even when it contradicts with their lived experiences, even when they profess that they do not believe in it, or even when they think that they do not know about it.

Notes

1 For the full findings of this survey, see N. Vince, 'Saintly grandmothers: youth reception and reinterpretation of the national past in contemporary Algeria', *Journal of North African Studies*, 18:1 (2013), 32–52.
2 J. Fentress and C. Wickham, *Social Memory* (Oxford: Blackwell, 1992), p. 117, quoted in House and Macmaster, *Paris 1961*, p. 190.

Appendix: Brief biographies of interviewees

Akache, Chérifa: born in the village of Aït Abderrahmane (Ouacifs, Kabylia). Married with two children when the war began, she provided logistical support for rural guerrillas in the ALN. A war widow, after independence she migrated to Algiers where she worked from home, weaving.

Amarouche, Ferroudja: born in the village of Bouzeguene (Azazga, Kabylia). Married with three children when the war began, she provided logistical support for rural guerrillas in the ALN. After independence, she migrated to Algiers with her husband, and had a further six children.

Attia, Fadila: born in the town of Bougie (today Béjaïa). She moved to Algiers as a young woman and worked in the offices of the colonial administration as a spy for the FLN. After independence she was a secretary in various government ministries.

Belguembour, Khadjidja: born in a small village (*douar* Ben Yeftah) in the Aurès mountains. She joined the *wilaya* II (Constantine region) as a teenager, learning nursing skills on the job. Married and divorced after independence, she moved to Algiers and worked as a nurse.

Ben Ali, Bahia: born in the town of Blida. Married with one child when the war began, she joined the *maquis* in the *wilaya* IV (Algiers region). After independence, she moved to Algiers where she opened a furniture business with her husband.

Benmohand Berci, Fatima: born in Tunisia, but as a child moved back to her family's village of origin, Agraradj (Azazga, Kabylia). Married when the war began, she provided logistical support for rural guerrillas in the ALN. She remained in Agraradj after independence.

Berci, Fatima: born in Agraradj (Azazga, Kabylia). Married with two children when the war began, she provided logistical support for rural guerrillas in the ALN. She briefly moved Algiers two years before the end of the war, but moved back to Agraradj after independence.

Bouaziz [Sahraoui], **Salima**: born in Blida. She was a prize-winning athlete as a teenager and moved to Algiers to continue her studies. As a result of wartime repression, she left for France, where she joined the FF–FLN. Here she met her future husband Rabah Bouzaiz, a member of the FLN Federal Committee. She moved back to Algiers after independence and worked as a doctor.

Bouazza, Djamila: a high-school student in Algiers when the war began, from a family of small business owners. Member of the Algiers bomb network, she was arrested and condemned to death. She married Abboud Boussouf in prison at the end of the war and they had three children. She worked for the state press agency after her husband was imprisoned for his political activities under Boumediene.

Boupacha, Djamila: a trainee nurse in Algiers when the war began, she became a member of the Algiers bomb network. Her arrest and torture were the subject of a book by Gisèle Halimi and Simone de Beauvoir. After independence she married and had children, working for a state employment agency before concentrating on raising her family.

Chami, Habiba: from a comfortably off background, she joined the *maquis* in the *wilaya* V (Oran region) as a nurse. After independence, she held a senior role within the UNFA and married and had six children.

Djeffal [Sassi], **Saliha**: born in Sétif, she was studying in France when she became an activist in the FF–FLN. After independence, she moved back to Algeria, married, had children and joined the JFLN. In 2005, she was a senior member of the party of the FLN.

Drif [Bitat], **Zohra**: born in the town of Tiaret, daughter of a *qadi* (judge of 'indigenous affairs' in colonial Algeria). She was a law student in Algiers when she joined the bomb network and was captured alongside ZAA leader Yacef Saadi. After independence, she married the founding member of the FLN Rabah Bitat, had three children and worked as a lawyer. In 2005, she was a presidentially appointed senator.

Guerroudj, Jacqueline: born in France, she moved to Algeria in

1948. Before the war she was a teacher, member of the PCA and married with five children. She joined the Algiers bomb network, was captured, imprisoned and sentenced to death. After independence she worked as a secretary in the National Assembly and in the library of the UGTA.

Hadj Ali [Larribère], **Lucette:** Born in the city of Oran, of European origin. Before the war she was a journalist, a member of the PCA and married with two children. She joined the independence struggle in Algiers. After independence she divorced her first husband and married fellow PCA member Bachir Hadj Ali. She worked as a teacher and was a member of the PAGS.

Ighilahriz, Louisette: Born in Oujda in Morocco, where her father was a gendarme, although her parents were originally from Kabylia. She was a high-school student when she joined the Algiers bomb network. After independence she was a member of the UNFA, married and had two children. In 2000, she played a key role in reopening debates in France about the use of torture during the War of Independence.

Kerkeb, El Hora: from a comfortably off background, she joined the *maquis* in the *wilaya* V (Oran region) as a nurse. After independence, she married, had children and worked as social worker for the police.

Koriche, Malika: born in Algiers, she was briefly married and divorced aged fifteen. She joined the Algiers bomb network and was arrested and imprisoned. After independence, she remarried and divorced, worked as a telephonist and joined the party of the FLN.

Maziz, Mimi: born in Algiers, as a student she transported materials for the FLN. She then moved to France and worked for the FF–FLN. She returned to Algiers after independence and worked as a journalist for *Révolution africaine*.

Mesli, Fadéla: born in Oujda, Morocco, into a middle-class family originally from Tlemcen. She was a student nurse when the war began, and was one of the first women to join the *maquis,* in the *wilaya* IV (Algiers region). After independence, she was a deputy in the 1962 Constituent Assembly and in the National Assembly 1977–82, as well as working as an anesthetist. She married and had two children.

M'Rabet, Fadéla: born in the city of Philippeville (today Skikda). She was a student in Strasbourg and an activist in the FF–FLN. After independence, she returned to Algeria and presented a radio show dealing with social problems with her husband Maurice Tarik Maschino. She wrote two critiques of the position of women in independent Algeria, *La Femme algérienne* (1964) and *Les Algériennes* (1967). She went into exile in 1971 and in 2005 she lived in France.

Ouared [Abdelmoumène], **Akila**: born in the city of Constantine into a family of trade unionists, she was a student activist in the FF–FLN. After independence, she moved back to Algeria, married and had children. She worked as a doctor and was a member of the UNFA until 1982. In 2005, she was president of the association Défense et Promotion des Droits des Femmes.

Ouzegane, Fettouma: married with five children at the outbreak of the war, she worked as a liaison agent in the Algiers bomb network. After independence, she engaged in clandestine political activity against the single-party state. In 2005, she was president of numerous associations campaigning on women's rights issues.

Salem, Yamina: from a comfortably off background, she joined the *maquis* in the *wilaya* V (Oran region) as a nurse. After independence, she married, had children and worked as a pharmacist.

Steiner [Fiorio], **Annie**: born in Marengo (today Hadjout) in the region of Tipaza, of European origin. She was married with two children at the start of the war, and joined the FLN in part as a result of her work in the Centres sociaux. Arrested and imprisoned, after independence she divorced and worked as a judicial adviser to the Algerian government.

Yermeche, Fatma: from the village of Agraradj (Azazga, Kabylia), she was married when the war broke out. She provided logistical support for rural guerrillas in the ALN. She remained in Agraradj after independence.

Zerari, Zhor: a high-school student when the war broke out, she joined the Algiers bomb network. Arrested and imprisoned, after independence she worked as a journalist, notably for *Le Peuple* and *Algérie actualité*. She married and divorced and had two children.

Select bibliography

Archive sources

Algerian National Archives (ANA), Algiers
Fonds Du Gouvernement Provisoire De La République Algérienne (GPRA);
Ministère des Affaires Etrangères (MAE): boxes 8; 53; 78; 96; 136; 181;
251; 252; 312

Archives Nationales d'Outre Mer (ANOM), previously Centre des Archives
d'Outre-Mer (CAOM), Aix en Provence
5/SAS/5: Aghribs; 5/SAS/18: Bouzeguene

Bibliothèque Nationale de France (BNF), Paris
Consulted for access to the Algerian press, notably:
Alger ce soir (daily), October 1964–September 1965
Algérie actualité (weekly), October 1965–December 1974
Alger républicain (daily), October 1962–December 1964
Al Chaab (daily), October 1962–March 1963 (becomes *Le Peuple*)
Femmes d'Algérie (monthly), September 1944–April 1946
El Moudjahid (daily), throughout war period to present
Le Peuple (daily), May 1963–June 1965
Révolution africaine (weekly), 2 February 1963–2/8 December 1966

National Archives (NA), London
FO371/119356,   FO371/125915;   FO371/125922;   FO371/125926;
   FO317/131654;   FO371/131697;   FO371/131698;   FO371/138620;
   FO371/147244;   FO371/147340;   FO371/147341;   FO371/147388;
   FO1110/1480; JR1015/247; JR1015/248.
Service Historique de la Défense (SHD), formerly Service Historique de
   l'Armée de Terre (SHAT), Paris
Archives marked with * required special permission (*dérogation*) to consult
   them at the time of my research.
1H1241*;   1H1246*;   1H1254*;   1H1436*;   1H1446*;   1H1513*;

1H1532*; 1H1564*; 1H1582*; 1H1585*; 1H1619*; 1H1623*; 1H1631*; 1H1636*; 1H1643*; 1H1644*; 1H1646*; 1H1670*; 1H1699*; 1H2589; 1H2757*; 1H2878*; 1H2879; 1H3120*; 1H4443*

Selected published works and theses

Abu-Lughod, L. (ed.), *Remaking Women: Feminism and Modernity in the Middle East* (Princeton: Princeton University Press, 1998)

Ageron, C.-R., *La Guerre d'Algérie et les Algériens, 1954–1962* (Paris: Armand Colin, 1997)

Aïth Mansour Amrouche, F., *Histoire de ma vie* (Paris: Maspero, 1968)

Amer, A. M., 'La Crise du Front de libération nationale de l'été 1962: indépendance et enjeux de pouvoirs' (PhD dissertation, Université Paris Diderot (Paris 7), 2010)

Ameyar, H., *La Moudjahida Annie Fiorio-Steiner, une vie pour l'Algérie* (Algiers: Association les amis de Abdelhamid Benzine, 2011)

Amin, S., *Chauri Chaura, Event, Metaphor, Memory* (Berkeley: University of California Press, 1995)

Amrane, D., *Des Femmes algériennes dans la guerre d'Algérie* (Paris: Karthala, 1994)

Amrane, D., *Les Femmes algériennes dans la guerre* (Paris: Plon, 1991)

Arnaud, G. and Vergès, J., *Pour Djamila Bouhired* (Paris: Editions de minuit, 1957)

Beaugé, F., *Algérie: une guerre sans gloire: histoire d'une enquête* (Paris: Calmann-Lévy, 2005)

Benyahia, M., *La Conjuration au pouvoir: récit d'un maquisard de l'ALN* (Algiers: ENAP Editions, 1999)

Bessis, S., 'Femmes et socialisme, le cas algérien', *Les Cahiers d'histoire sociale*, 19 (2002), 25–32

Bouatta, C., 'Feminine militancy: moudjahidates during and after the Algerian War', in V. Moghadam (ed.), *Gender and National Identity: Women and Politics in Muslim Societies* (London: Zed Books, 1994)

Boym, S., *The Future of Nostalgia* (New York: Basic Books, 2001)

Brac de la Perrière, C., *Derrière les héros ... les employés de maison musulmanes en service chez les Européens à Alger pendant la guerre d'Algérie (1954–1962)* (Paris: L'Harmattan, 1987)

Branche, R., 'The martyr's torch: memory and power in Algeria', *Journal of North African Studies*, 16:3 (2011), 431–43

Branche, R., *La Guerre d'Algérie: une histoire apaisée?* (Paris: Seuil, 2005)

Branche, R., 'Des viols pendant la guerre d'Algérie', *Vingtième siècle*, 75 (2002), 123–32

Branche, R., *La Torture et l'armée pendant la guerre d'Algérie, 1954–1962* (Paris: Gallimard, 2001)

Carlier, O., 'Le Moudjahid, mort ou vif', in A. Dayan Rosenman and L. Valensi (eds), *La Guerre d'Algérie dans la mémoire et l'imaginaire* (Paris: Bouchène, 2004)

Carlier, O., *Entre nation et jihad: histoire sociale des radicalismes algériens* (Paris: Presses de Sciences Po, 1995)

Chaliand, G. and Minces, J., *L'Algérie indépendante: bilan d'une révolution nationale* (Paris: Maspero, 1972)

Charrad, M., *States and Women's Rights: The Making of Post-Colonial Tunisia, Algeria and Morocco* (Berkeley: University of California Press, 2001)

Clancy-Smith, J., 'Islam, gender and identities in the making of French Algeria, 1830–1962', in J. Clancy-Smith and F. Gouda (eds), *Domesticating the Empire: Race, Gender and Family Life in French and Dutch Colonialisms* (Charlottesville: University Press of Virginia, 1998)

Dahmani, M., *Atlas économique et social de la Grande Kabylie* (Algiers: Office des publications universitaires, 1990)

Djebar, A., *Les Alouettes naïves* (Paris: Juillard, 1967)

Dore-Audibert, A., *Des Françaises d'Algérie dans la guerre de libération* (Paris: Karthala, 1995)

Drif, Z., *La Mort de mes frères* (Paris: François Maspero, 1961)

El Korso, M. 'Une double réalité pour un même vécu', *Confluences Méditerranée*, 17 (1996), 99–108

Enloe, C., *Bananas, Beaches and Bases: Making Feminist Sense of International Politics* (Berkeley: University of California Press, 2000 [1989])

Esméralda, H. G., *Un été en enfer: Barbarie à la française. Témoignage sur la généralisation de la torture, Algérie, 1957* (Paris: Exils, 2004)

Evans, M., *Algeria: France's Undeclared War* (Oxford: Oxford University Press: 2012)

Evans, M. and Phillips, J., *Algeria: Anger of the Dispossessed* (London: Yale University Press, 2007)

Fanon, F., *Sociologie d'une révolution (l'An V de la révolution algérienne)* (Paris: Maspero, 1972 [1959])

Feraoun, M., *Journal, 1955–1962* (Paris: Editions du Seuil, 1962)

Fremeaux, J., 'Les SAS (Sections administratives spécialisées)', *Guerres mondiales et conflits contemporains*, 208 (2002), 55–68

Gadant, M., *Le Nationalisme algérien et les femmes* (Paris: L'Harmattan, 1995)

Gadant, M., 'Nationalité et citoyenneté, les femmes algériennes et leurs droits', *Peuples méditerranéens*, 44–5 (1988), 293–337

Garanger, M., *Femmes algériennes 1960* (Paris: Contrejour, 1989 [1982])

Godard, Y., *Les Trois Batailles d'Alger Tome I: les paras dans la ville* (Paris: Fayard, 1972)

Gordon, D., *Women of Algeria: An Essay in Change* (Cambridge, Mass.: Harvard Middle Eastern Monograph Series, 1968)

Guerroudj, J., *Des Douars et des prisons* (Algiers: Bouchène, 1991)

Haddab, Z., 'Les Femmes, la guerre de libération et la politique en Algérie', in iMed Institut Méditerranéen, *Les Algériennes, citoyennes en devenir* (Oran: MM Editions, 2000)

Hadj Ali, B., *Lettres à Lucette 1965–1966* (Algiers: Editions RSM, 2002)

Halimi, G. and de Beauvoir, S., *Djamila Boupacha* (Paris: Gallimard, 1962)

Hamilton, P. and Shopes, L., *Oral History and Public Memories* (Philadelphia: Temple University Press, 2008)

Hanoune, L. with Mouffok, G., *Une autre voix pour l'Algérie* (Paris: La Découverte, 1996)

Harbi, M., *L'Islamisme dans tous ses états* (Paris: Arcantère, 1991)

Harbi, M. 'Les Révoltes logiques', *Cahier du Centre de recherches sur les idéologies de la révolte*, 11 (1979–80), 78–93

Harbi, M., *FLN, mirage et réalité: des origines à la prise du pouvoir (1945–1962)* (Paris: Editions Jeune Afrique, 1980)

Helie-Lucas, M.-A., 'Women, nationalism and religion in the Algerian liberation struggle', in M. Badran and M. Cooke (eds), *Opening the Gates: An Anthology of Arab Feminist Writing* (Indianapolis: Indiana University Press, 2nd edn, 2004 [1990])

Hobsbawm, E., *Nations and Nationalism since 1780: Programme, Myth, Reality* (Cambridge: Cambridge University Press, 2nd edn, 1992 [1990])

Hodgkin, K. and Radstone, S. (eds), *Memory, History, Nation: Contested Pasts* (New Brunswick: Transaction, 2006)

House, J. and Macmaster, N. (2006) *Paris 1961: Algerians, State Terror and Memory* (Oxford: Oxford University Press, 2006)

Ighilahriz, L. with Nivat, A., *Algérienne* (Paris: Fayard and Calmann Lévy, 2001)

Jansen, W., *Women without Men: Gender and Marginality in an Algerian Town*, (Leiden: E. J. Brill, 1987)

Joseph, S. (ed.) *Gender and Citizenship in the Middle East* (New York: Syracuse University Press, 2000)

Kansteiner, W., 'Finding meaning in memory: a methodological critique of collective memory studies', *History and Theory*, 41 (2002), 179–97

Khanna, R., *Algeria Cuts: Women and Representation, 1830 to the Present* (Stanford: Stanford University Press, 2008)

Knauss, P., 'Algerian women since independence', in J. P. Entelis and P. C. Naylor (eds), *State and Society in Algeria* (Boulder: Westview Press, 1992)

Lacoste-Dujardin, C., *Opération Oiseau bleu: des kabyles, des ethnologues et la guerre d'Algérie* (Paris: La Découverte, 1997)

Lacoste-Dujardin, C., *Un Village algérien: structures et évolution récente* (Algiers: SNED, 1976)

Lavalette, E. S., *Juste algérienne: comme une tissure* (Algiers: Barzakh, 2013)

Lazreg, M., *Torture and the Twilight of Empire: From Algiers to Baghdad* (Princeton and Oxford: Princeton University Press, 2008)

Lazreg, M., *The Eloquence of Silence: Algerian Women in Question* (New York: Routledge, 1994)

Lévy, C., 'La Journée du 8 mars 1965 à Alger', *Clio: histoire, femmes et société*, 5 (1997), www.clio.revues.org/pdf/415 (accessed 19 May 2014)

Lippert, A., 'Algerian women's access to power: 1962–1985', in I. L. Markovitz (ed.), *Studies in Power and Class in Africa* (New York: Oxford University Press, 1987)

Macmaster, N., 'Des révolutionnaires invisibles: les femmes algériennes et l'organisation de la Section des femmes du FLN en France métropolitaine', *Revue d'Histoire moderne et contemporaine*, 59:4 (2012), 164–90

Macmaster, N., *Burning the Veil: The Algerian War and the 'Emancipation' of Muslim Women* (Manchester: Manchester University Press, 2009)

Mahé, A., *Histoire de la Grande Kabylie: anthropologie historique du lien social dans les communautés villageoises* (Paris: Bouchène, 2001)

Manceron, G. and Remaoun, H., *D'une rive à l'autre: la guerre d'Algérie de la mémoire à l'histoire* (Paris: Syros, 1993)

Mark, J. *The Unfinished Revolution: Making Sense of the Communist Past in Central-Eastern Europe* (New Haven: Yale University Press, 2010)

McDougall, J., 'Dream of exile, promise of home: language, education and arabism in Algeria', *International Journal of Middle East Studies*, 43 (2011), 251–70

McDougall, J., *History and Culture of Nationalism in Algeria* (Cambridge: Cambridge University Press, 2006)

McDougall, J., 'Savage wars? Codes of violence in Algeria, 1830s–1990s', *Third World Quarterly*, 26:1 (2005), 117–31.

Mechakra, Y., *La Grotte éclatée* (Algiers: SNED, 1979)

Merridale, C., *Night of Stone: Death and Memory in Twentieth-Century Russia* (New York: Viking Penguin, 2001)

Merolla, D., *Gender and Community in the Kabyle Literary Space: Cultural Strategies in the Oral and the Written* (Leiden: Research School CNWS, 1996)

Messaoudi, K. with Schemla, E., *Une Algérienne débout* (Paris: Flammarion, 1995)

Meynier, G., *Histoire intérieure du FLN 1954–1962* (Paris: Fayard, 2002)

Minces, J., *L'Algérie de la révolution (1963–1964)* (Paris: L'Harmattan, 1988)

Minces, J., *L'Algérie de Boumediene* (Paris: Presses de la cité, 1978)

M'Rabet, F., *La Femme algérienne, suivi de Les Algériennes* (Paris: Maspero, 1969)

Ottoway, D. and Ottaway, M., *Algeria: The Politics of a Socialist Revolution* (Berkeley: University of California Press, 1970)

Pruvost, L., *Femmes d'Algérie: société, famille et citoyenneté* (Algiers: Casbah Editions, 2002)

Radstone, S., 'What place is this? Transcultural memory and the locations of memory studies', *Parallax*, 17:4 (2011), 109–23

Rahal, M., 'Fused together and torn apart: stories and violence in contemporary Algeria', *History and Memory*, 24:1 (2012), 118–51

Redjala, R., *L'Opposition en Algérie depuis 1962: tome 1. Le PRS-CNDR-FFS* (Paris: L'Harmattan, 1988)

Roberts, H., *The Battlefield Algeria 1988–2002: Studies in a Broken Polity* (London: Verso, 2003)

Rothberg, M. *Multidirectional Memory: Remembering the Holocaust in the Age of Decolonization* (Stanford: Stanford University Press, 2009)

Saadia-et-Lakhdar [Rabah and Salima Bouaziz], *L'Aliénation colonialiste et la résistance de la famille algérienne* (Lausanne: La Cité, 1961)

Sadi, S., *Amirouche: Une vie, deux morts, un testament* (Paris: L'Harmattan, 2010)

Sai, F.-Z., *Mouvement national et question féminine: des origines à la veille de la Guerre de libération nationale* (Algiers: Editions Dar El Gharb, 2002)

Sai, F.-Z., *Les Algériennes dans les espaces politiques: entre la fin d'un millénaire et l'aube d'un autre* (Algiers: Editions Dar El Gharb, n.d.)

Sambron, D., *Femmes musulmanes, guerre d'Algérie 1954–1962* (Paris: Autrement, 2007)

Seferdjeli, R., 'Rethinking the history of the mujahidat during the Algerian War', *Interventions: International Journal of Postcolonial Studies*, 14:2 (2012), 238–55

Seferdjeli, R. '"Fight with us, women, and we will emancipate you": France, the FLN and the struggle over women in the Algerian war of national liberation, 1954–1962' (PhD dissertation, London School of Economics, 2004)

Simon, C. *Algérie, les années pieds-rouges: des rêves de l'indépendance au désenchantement (1962–1969)* (Paris: La Découverte, 2011)

Slyomovics, S., '"Hassiba Ben Bouali, if you could see our Algeria": women and public space in Algeria', *Middle East Report*, 192 (1995), 8–13

Stora, B., *Histoire de l'Algérie depuis l'indépendance* (Paris: La Découverte, 1994)

Stora, B., *La Gangrène et l'oubli: la mémoire de la guerre d'Algérie* (Paris: La Découverte, 1991)

Summerfield, P., *Reconstructing Women's Lives: Discourse and Subjectivity in Oral Histories of the Second World War* (Manchester: Manchester University Press, 1998)

Surkis, J. 'Ethics and violence: Simone de Beauvoir, Djamila Boupacha and the Algerian War', *French Politics, Culture & Society*, 28:2 (2010), 38–55

Tai, H.-T. H., *The Country of Memory: Remaking the Past in Late Socialist Vietnam* (Berkeley: University of California Press, 2001)

Taleb Ibrahimi, K., 'Les Algériennes et la guerre de libération nationale: l'émergence des femmes dans l'espace publique et politique au cours de la guerre et l'après guerre', in M. Harbi and B. Stora (eds), *La Guerre d'Algérie, 1954–2004: la fin de l'amnésie* (Paris: Hachette, 2004)

Thénault, S., *La Guerre d'indépendance algérienne* (Paris: Flammarion, 2005)

Vandevelde-Dallière, H., *Femmes algériennes: à travers la condition féminine dans le Constantinois depuis l'Indépendance* (Algiers: Office des publications universitaires, 1980)

Vince, N., 'Saintly grandmothers: youth reception and reinterpretation of the national past in contemporary Algeria', *Journal of North African Studies*, 18:1 (2013), 32–52

Vince, N., 'Transgressing boundaries: gender, race, religion and "Françaises musulmanes" during the Algerian War of Independence', *French Historical Studies*, 33:3 (2010), 445–74

Whitfield, L., 'The French military under female fire: the public opinion campaign and justice in the case of Djamila Boupacha, 1960–62', *Contemporary French Civilisation*, 20 (1996), 76–90

Yuval-Davis, N. and Anthias, F. (eds), *Woman, Nation, State* (Basingstoke: Macmillan, 1989)

Zerari, Z. *Poèmes de prison* (Algiers: Bouchène, 1988)

Zerdoumi, N., *Enfant d'hier: l'éducation de l'enfant en milieu traditionnel algérien* (Paris: Maspero, 1970)

Index

Note: page numbers in *italic* refer to illustrations

Lightning Source UK Ltd.
Milton Keynes UK
UKOW06n1318281115

263694UK00016B/198/P